Dear Future Exam Success Story

First of all, **THANK YOU** for purchasing Mometrix study materials!

Second, congratulations! You are one of the few determined test-takers who are committed to doing whatever it takes to excel on your exam. **You have come to the right place.** We developed these study materials with one goal in mind: to deliver you the information you need in a format that's concise and easy to use.

In addition to optimizing your guide for the content of the test, we've outlined our recommended steps for breaking down the preparation process into small, attainable goals so you can make sure you stay on track.

We've also analyzed the entire test-taking process, identifying the most common pitfalls and showing how you can overcome them and be ready for any curveball the test throws you.

Standardized testing is one of the biggest obstacles on your road to success, which only increases the importance of doing well in the high-pressure, high-stakes environment of test day. Your results on this test could have a significant impact on your future, and this guide provides the information and practical advice to help you achieve your full potential on test day.

Your success is our success

We would love to hear from you! If you would like to share the story of your exam success or if you have any questions or comments in regard to our products, please contact us at **800-673-8175** or **support@mometrix.com**.

Thanks again for your business and we wish you continued success!

Sincerely,
The Mometrix Test Preparation Team

I0894305

Need more help? Check out our flashcards at:
http://MometrixFlashcards.com/DSST

Written and edited by the Mometrix Exam Secrets Test Prep Team
Printed in the United States of America

Mometrix
TEST PREPARATION

DSST®

Business Mathematics Exam Secrets Study Guide

TABLE OF CONTENTS

Introduction

Thank you for purchasing this resource! You have made the choice to prepare yourself for a test that could have a huge impact on your future, and this guide is designed to help you be fully ready for test day. Obviously, it's important to have a solid understanding of the test material, but you also need to be prepared for the unique environment and stressors of the test, so that you can perform to the best of your abilities.

For this purpose, the first section that appears in this guide is the **Secret Keys**. We've devoted countless hours to meticulously researching what works and what doesn't, and we've boiled down our findings to the five most impactful steps you can take to improve your performance on the test. We start at the beginning with study planning and move through the preparation process, all the way to the testing strategies that will help you get the most out of what you know when you're finally sitting in front of the test.

We recommend that you start preparing for your test as far in advance as possible. However, if you've bought this guide as a last-minute study resource and only have a few days before your test, we recommend that you skip over the first two Secret Keys since they address a long-term study plan.

If you struggle with **test anxiety**, we strongly encourage you to check out our recommendations for how you can overcome it. Test anxiety is a formidable foe, but it can be beaten, and we want to make sure you have the tools you need to defeat it.

Secret Key #1 – Plan Big, Study Small

There's a lot riding on your performance. If you want to ace this test, you're going to need to keep your skills sharp and the material fresh in your mind. You need a plan that lets you review everything you need to know while still fitting in your schedule. We'll break this strategy down into three categories.

Information Organization

Start with the information you already have: the official test outline. From this, you can make a complete list of all the concepts you need to cover before the test. Organize these concepts into groups that can be studied together, and create a list of any related vocabulary you need to learn so you can brush up on any difficult terms. You'll want to keep this vocabulary list handy once you actually start studying since you may need to add to it along the way.

Time Management

Once you have your set of study concepts, decide how to spread them out over the time you have left before the test. Break your study plan into small, clear goals so you have a manageable task for each day and know exactly what you're doing. Then just focus on one small step at a time. When you manage your time this way, you don't need to spend hours at a time studying. Studying a small block of content for a short period each day helps you retain information better and avoid stressing over how much you have left to do. You can relax knowing that you have a plan to cover everything in time. In order for this strategy to be effective though, you have to start studying early and stick to your schedule. Avoid the exhaustion and futility that comes from last-minute cramming!

Study Environment

The environment you study in has a big impact on your learning. Studying in a coffee shop, while probably more enjoyable, is not likely to be as fruitful as studying in a quiet room. It's important to keep distractions to a minimum. You're only planning to study for a short block of time, so make the most of it. Don't pause to check your phone or get up to find a snack. It's also important to **avoid multitasking**. Research has consistently shown that multitasking will make your studying dramatically less effective. Your study area should also be comfortable and well-lit so you don't have the distraction of straining your eyes or sitting on an uncomfortable chair.

The time of day you study is also important. You want to be rested and alert. Don't wait until just before bedtime. Study when you'll be most likely to comprehend and remember. Even better, if you know what time of day your test will be, set that time aside for study. That way your brain will be used to working on that subject at that specific time and you'll have a better chance of recalling information.

Finally, it can be helpful to team up with others who are studying for the same test. Your actual studying should be done in as isolated an environment as possible, but the work of organizing the information and setting up the study plan can be divided up. In between study sessions, you can discuss with your teammates the concepts that you're all studying and quiz each other on the details. Just be sure that your teammates are as serious about the test as you are. If you find that your study time is being replaced with social time, you might need to find a new team.

Secret Key #2 – Make Your Studying Count

You're devoting a lot of time and effort to preparing for this test, so you want to be absolutely certain it will pay off. This means doing more than just reading the content and hoping you can remember it on test day. It's important to make every minute of study count. There are two main areas you can focus on to make your studying count.

Retention

It doesn't matter how much time you study if you can't remember the material. You need to make sure you are retaining the concepts. To check your retention of the information you're learning, try recalling it at later times with minimal prompting. Try carrying around flashcards and glance at one or two from time to time or ask a friend who's also studying for the test to quiz you.

To enhance your retention, look for ways to put the information into practice so that you can apply it rather than simply recalling it. If you're using the information in practical ways, it will be much easier to remember. Similarly, it helps to solidify a concept in your mind if you're not only reading it to yourself but also explaining it to someone else. Ask a friend to let you teach them about a concept you're a little shaky on (or speak aloud to an imaginary audience if necessary). As you try to summarize, define, give examples, and answer your friend's questions, you'll understand the concepts better and they will stay with you longer. Finally, step back for a big picture view and ask yourself how each piece of information fits with the whole subject. When you link the different concepts together and see them working together as a whole, it's easier to remember the individual components.

Finally, practice showing your work on any multi step problems, even if you're just studying. Writing out each step you take to solve a problem will help solidify the process in your mind, and you'll be more likely to remember it during the test.

Modality

Modality simply refers to the means or method by which you study. Choosing a study modality that fits your own individual learning style is crucial. No two people learn best in exactly the same way, so it's important to know your strengths and use them to your advantage.

For example, if you learn best by visualization, focus on visualizing a concept in your mind and draw an image or a diagram. Try color-coding your notes, illustrating them, or creating symbols that will trigger your mind to recall a learned concept. If you learn best by hearing or discussing information, find a study partner who learns the same way or read aloud to yourself. Think about how to put the information in your own words. Imagine that you are giving a lecture on the topic and record yourself so you can listen to it later.

For any learning style, flashcards can be helpful. Organize the information so you can take advantage of spare moments to review. Underline key words or phrases. Use different colors for different categories. Mnemonic devices (such as creating a short list in which every item starts with the same letter) can also help with retention. Find what works best for you and use it to store the information in your mind most effectively and easily.

Secret Key #3 – Practice the Right Way

Your success on test day depends not only on how many hours you put into preparing, but also on whether you prepared the right way. It's good to check along the way to see if your studying is paying off. One of the most effective ways to do this is by taking practice tests to evaluate your progress. Practice tests are useful because they show exactly where you need to improve. Every time you take a practice test, pay special attention to these three groups of questions:

- The questions you got wrong
- The questions you had to guess on, even if you guessed right
- The questions you found difficult or slow to work through

This will show you exactly what your weak areas are, and where you need to devote more study time. Ask yourself why each of these questions gave you trouble. Was it because you didn't understand the material? Was it because you didn't remember the vocabulary? Do you need more repetitions on this type of question to build speed and confidence? Dig into those questions and figure out how you can strengthen your weak areas as you go back to review the material.

Additionally, many practice tests have a section explaining the answer choices. It can be tempting to read the explanation and think that you now have a good understanding of the concept. However, an explanation likely only covers part of the question's broader context. Even if the explanation makes perfect sense, **go back and investigate** every concept related to the question until you're positive you have a thorough understanding.

As you go along, keep in mind that the practice test is just that: practice. Memorizing these questions and answers will not be very helpful on the actual test because it is unlikely to have any of the same exact questions. If you only know the right answers to the sample questions, you won't be prepared for the real thing. **Study the concepts** until you understand them fully, and then you'll be able to answer any question that shows up on the test.

It's important to wait on the practice tests until you're ready. If you take a test on your first day of study, you may be overwhelmed by the amount of material covered and how much you need to learn. Work up to it gradually.

On test day, you'll need to be prepared for answering questions, managing your time, and using the test-taking strategies you've learned. It's a lot to balance, like a mental marathon that will have a big impact on your future. Like training for a marathon, you'll need to start slowly and work your way up. When test day arrives, you'll be ready.

Start with the strategies you've read in the first two Secret Keys—plan your course and study in the way that works best for you. If you have time, consider using multiple study resources to get different approaches to the same concepts. It can be helpful to see difficult concepts from more than one angle. Then find a good source for practice tests. Many times, the test website will suggest potential study resources or provide sample tests.

Practice Test Strategy

If you're able to find at least three practice tests, we recommend this strategy:

UNTIMED AND OPEN-BOOK PRACTICE

Take the first test with no time constraints and with your notes and study guide handy. Take your time and focus on applying the strategies you've learned.

TIMED AND OPEN-BOOK PRACTICE

Take the second practice test open-book as well, but set a timer and practice pacing yourself to finish in time.

TIMED AND CLOSED-BOOK PRACTICE

Take any other practice tests as if it were test day. Set a timer and put away your study materials. Sit at a table or desk in a quiet room, imagine yourself at the testing center, and answer questions as quickly and accurately as possible.

Keep repeating timed and closed-book tests on a regular basis until you run out of practice tests or it's time for the actual test. Your mind will be ready for the schedule and stress of test day, and you'll be able to focus on recalling the material you've learned.

Secret Key #4 – Pace Yourself

Once you're fully prepared for the material on the test, your biggest challenge on test day will be managing your time. Just knowing that the clock is ticking can make you panic even if you have plenty of time left. Work on pacing yourself so you can build confidence against the time constraints of the exam. Pacing is a difficult skill to master, especially in a high-pressure environment, so **practice is vital**.

Set time expectations for your pace based on how much time is available. For example, if a section has 60 questions and the time limit is 30 minutes, you know you have to average 30 seconds or less per question in order to answer them all. Although 30 seconds is the hard limit, set 25 seconds per question as your goal, so you reserve extra time to spend on harder questions. When you budget extra time for the harder questions, you no longer have any reason to stress when those questions take longer to answer.

Don't let this time expectation distract you from working through the test at a calm, steady pace, but keep it in mind so you don't spend too much time on any one question. Recognize that taking extra time on one question you don't understand may keep you from answering two that you do understand later in the test. If your time limit for a question is up and you're still not sure of the answer, mark it and move on, and come back to it later if the time and the test format allow. If the testing format doesn't allow you to return to earlier questions, just make an educated guess; then put it out of your mind and move on.

On the easier questions, be careful not to rush. It may seem wise to hurry through them so you have more time for the challenging ones, but it's not worth missing one if you know the concept and just didn't take the time to read the question fully. Work efficiently but make sure you understand the question and have looked at all of the answer choices, since more than one may seem right at first.

Even if you're paying attention to the time, you may find yourself a little behind at some point. You should speed up to get back on track, but do so wisely. Don't panic; just take a few seconds less on each question until you're caught up. Don't guess without thinking, but do look through the answer choices and eliminate any you know are wrong. If you can get down to two choices, it is often worthwhile to guess from those. Once you've chosen an answer, move on and don't dwell on any that you skipped or had to hurry through. If a question was taking too long, chances are it was one of the harder ones, so you weren't as likely to get it right anyway.

On the other hand, if you find yourself getting ahead of schedule, it may be beneficial to slow down a little. The more quickly you work, the more likely you are to make a careless mistake that will affect your score. You've budgeted time for each question, so don't be afraid to spend that time. Practice an efficient but careful pace to get the most out of the time you have.

Secret Key #5 – Have a Plan for Guessing

When you're taking the test, you may find yourself stuck on a question. Some of the answer choices seem better than others, but you don't see the one answer choice that is obviously correct. What do you do?

The scenario described above is very common, yet most test takers have not effectively prepared for it. Developing and practicing a plan for guessing may be one of the single most effective uses of your time as you get ready for the exam.

In developing your plan for guessing, there are three questions to address:

- When should you start the guessing process?
- How should you narrow down the choices?
- Which answer should you choose?

When to Start the Guessing Process

Unless your plan for guessing is to select C every time (which, despite its merits, is not what we recommend), you need to leave yourself enough time to apply your answer elimination strategies. Since you have a limited amount of time for each question, that means that if you're going to give yourself the best shot at guessing correctly, you have to decide quickly whether or not you will guess.

Of course, the best-case scenario is that you don't have to guess at all, so first, see if you can answer the question based on your knowledge of the subject and basic reasoning skills. Focus on the key words in the question and try to jog your memory of related topics. Give yourself a chance to bring the knowledge to mind, but once you realize that you don't have (or you can't access) the knowledge you need to answer the question, it's time to start the guessing process.

It's almost always better to start the guessing process too early than too late. It only takes a few seconds to remember something and answer the question from knowledge. Carefully eliminating wrong answer choices takes longer. Plus, going through the process of eliminating answer choices can actually help jog your memory.

Summary: Start the guessing process as soon as you decide that you can't answer the question based on your knowledge.

How to Narrow Down the Choices

The next chapter in this book (**Test-Taking Strategies**) includes a wide range of strategies for how to approach questions and how to look for answer choices to eliminate. You will definitely want to read those carefully, practice them, and figure out which ones work best for you. Here though, we're going to address a mindset rather than a particular strategy.

Your odds of guessing an answer correctly depend on how many options you are choosing from.

Number of options left	5	4	3	2	1
Odds of guessing correctly	20%	25%	33%	50%	100%

You can see from this chart just how valuable it is to be able to eliminate incorrect answers and make an educated guess, but there are two things that many test takers do that cause them to miss out on the benefits of guessing:

- Accidentally eliminating the correct answer
- Selecting an answer based on an impression

We'll look at the first one here, and the second one in the next section.

To avoid accidentally eliminating the correct answer, we recommend a thought exercise called **the $5 challenge**. In this challenge, you only eliminate an answer choice from contention if you are willing to bet $5 on it being wrong. Why $5? Five dollars is a small but not insignificant amount of money. It's an amount you could afford to lose but wouldn't want to throw away. And while losing $5 once might not hurt too much, doing it twenty times will set you back $100. In the same way, each small decision you make—eliminating a choice here, guessing on a question there—won't by itself impact your score very much, but when you put them all together, they can make a big difference. By holding each answer choice elimination decision to a higher standard, you can reduce the risk of accidentally eliminating the correct answer.

The $5 challenge can also be applied in a positive sense: If you are willing to bet $5 that an answer choice *is* correct, go ahead and mark it as correct.

Summary: Only eliminate an answer choice if you are willing to bet $5 that it is wrong.

Which Answer to Choose

You're taking the test. You've run into a hard question and decided you'll have to guess. You've eliminated all the answer choices you're willing to bet $5 on. Now you have to pick an answer. Why do we even need to talk about this? Why can't you just pick whichever one you feel like when the time comes?

The answer to these questions is that if you don't come into the test with a plan, you'll rely on your impression to select an answer choice, and if you do that, you risk falling into a trap. The test writers know that everyone who takes their test will be guessing on some of the questions, so they intentionally write wrong answer choices to seem plausible. You still have to pick an answer though, and if the wrong answer choices are designed to look right, how can you ever be sure that you're not falling for their trap? The best solution we've found to this dilemma is to take the decision out of your hands entirely. Here is the process we recommend:

Once you've eliminated any choices that you are confident (willing to bet $5) are wrong, select the first remaining choice as your answer.

Whether you choose to select the first remaining choice, the second, or the last, the important thing is that you use some preselected standard. Using this approach guarantees that you will not be enticed into selecting an answer choice that looks right, because you are not basing your decision on how the answer choices look.

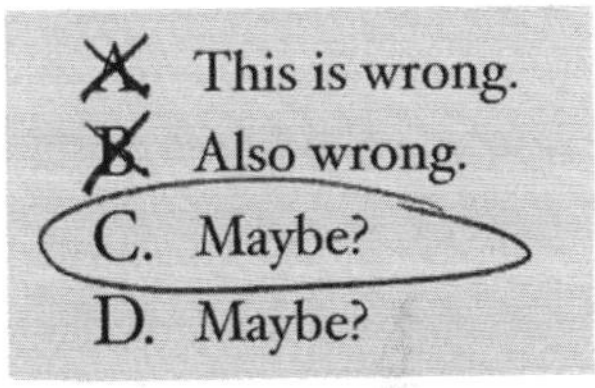

This is not meant to make you question your knowledge. Instead, it is to help you recognize the difference between your knowledge and your impressions. There's a huge difference between thinking an answer is right because of what you know, and thinking an answer is right because it looks or sounds like it should be right.

Summary: To ensure that your selection is appropriately random, make a predetermined selection from among all answer choices you have not eliminated.

Test-Taking Strategies

This section contains a list of test-taking strategies that you may find helpful as you work through the test. By taking what you know and applying logical thought, you can maximize your chances of answering any question correctly!

It is very important to realize that every question is different and every person is different: no single strategy will work on every question, and no single strategy will work for every person. That's why we've included all of them here, so you can try them out and determine which ones work best for different types of questions and which ones work best for you.

Question Strategies

☑ Read Carefully

Read the question and the answer choices carefully. Don't miss the question because you misread the terms. You have plenty of time to read each question thoroughly and make sure you understand what is being asked. Yet a happy medium must be attained, so don't waste too much time. You must read carefully and efficiently.

☑ Contextual Clues

Look for contextual clues. If the question includes a word you are not familiar with, look at the immediate context for some indication of what the word might mean. Contextual clues can often give you all the information you need to decipher the meaning of an unfamiliar word. Even if you can't determine the meaning, you may be able to narrow down the possibilities enough to make a solid guess at the answer to the question.

☑ Prefixes

If you're having trouble with a word in the question or answer choices, try dissecting it. Take advantage of every clue that the word might include. Prefixes can be a huge help. Usually, they allow you to determine a basic meaning. *Pre-* means before, *post-* means after, *pro-* is positive, *de-* is negative. From prefixes, you can get an idea of the general meaning of the word and try to put it into context.

☑ Hedge Words

Watch out for critical hedge words, such as *likely, may, can, often, almost, mostly, usually, generally, rarely,* and *sometimes.* Question writers insert these hedge phrases to cover every possibility. Often an answer choice will be wrong simply because it leaves no room for exception. Be on guard for answer choices that have definitive words such as *exactly* and *always.*

☑ Switchback Words

Stay alert for *switchbacks.* These are the words and phrases frequently used to alert you to shifts in thought. The most common switchback words are *but, although,* and *however.* Others include *nevertheless, on the other hand, even though, while, in spite of, despite,* and *regardless of.* Switchback words are important to catch because they can change the direction of the question or an answer choice.

✅ FACE VALUE

When in doubt, use common sense. Accept the situation in the problem at face value. Don't read too much into it. These problems will not require you to make wild assumptions. If you have to go beyond creativity and warp time or space in order to have an answer choice fit the question, then you should move on and consider the other answer choices. These are normal problems rooted in reality. The applicable relationship or explanation may not be readily apparent, but it is there for you to figure out. Use your common sense to interpret anything that isn't clear.

Answer Choice Strategies

✅ ANSWER SELECTION

The most thorough way to pick an answer choice is to identify and eliminate wrong answers until only one is left, then confirm it is the correct answer. Sometimes an answer choice may immediately seem right, but be careful. The test writers will usually put more than one reasonable answer choice on each question, so take a second to read all of them and make sure that the other choices are not equally obvious. As long as you have time left, it is better to read every answer choice than to pick the first one that looks right without checking the others.

✅ ANSWER CHOICE FAMILIES

An answer choice family consists of two (in rare cases, three) answer choices that are very similar in construction and cannot all be true at the same time. If you see two answer choices that are direct opposites or parallels, one of them is usually the correct answer. For instance, if one answer choice says that quantity *x* increases and another either says that quantity *x* decreases (opposite) or says that quantity *y* increases (parallel), then those answer choices would fall into the same family. An answer choice that doesn't match the construction of the answer choice family is more likely to be incorrect. Most questions will not have answer choice families, but when they do appear, you should be prepared to recognize them.

✅ ELIMINATE ANSWERS

Eliminate answer choices as soon as you realize they are wrong, but make sure you consider all possibilities. If you are eliminating answer choices and realize that the last one you are left with is also wrong, don't panic. Start over and consider each choice again. There may be something you missed the first time that you will realize on the second pass.

✅ AVOID FACT TRAPS

Don't be distracted by an answer choice that is factually true but doesn't answer the question. You are looking for the choice that answers the question. Stay focused on what the question is asking for so you don't accidentally pick an answer that is true but incorrect. Always go back to the question and make sure the answer choice you've selected actually answers the question and is not merely a true statement.

✅ EXTREME STATEMENTS

In general, you should avoid answers that put forth extreme actions as standard practice or proclaim controversial ideas as established fact. An answer choice that states the "process should be used in certain situations, if…" is much more likely to be correct than one that states the "process should be discontinued completely." The first is a calm rational statement and doesn't even make a definitive, uncompromising stance, using a hedge word *if* to provide wiggle room, whereas the second choice is far more extreme.

☑ BENCHMARK

As you read through the answer choices and you come across one that seems to answer the question well, mentally select that answer choice. This is not your final answer, but it's the one that will help you evaluate the other answer choices. The one that you selected is your benchmark or standard for judging each of the other answer choices. Every other answer choice must be compared to your benchmark. That choice is correct until proven otherwise by another answer choice beating it. If you find a better answer, then that one becomes your new benchmark. Once you've decided that no other choice answers the question as well as your benchmark, you have your final answer.

☑ PREDICT THE ANSWER

Before you even start looking at the answer choices, it is often best to try to predict the answer. When you come up with the answer on your own, it is easier to avoid distractions and traps because you will know exactly what to look for. The right answer choice is unlikely to be word-for-word what you came up with, but it should be a close match. Even if you are confident that you have the right answer, you should still take the time to read each option before moving on.

General Strategies

☑ TOUGH QUESTIONS

If you are stumped on a problem or it appears too hard or too difficult, don't waste time. Move on! Remember though, if you can quickly check for obviously incorrect answer choices, your chances of guessing correctly are greatly improved. Before you completely give up, at least try to knock out a couple of possible answers. Eliminate what you can and then guess at the remaining answer choices before moving on.

☑ CHECK YOUR WORK

Since you will probably not know every term listed and the answer to every question, it is important that you get credit for the ones that you do know. Don't miss any questions through careless mistakes. If at all possible, try to take a second to look back over your answer selection and make sure you've selected the correct answer choice and haven't made a costly careless mistake (such as marking an answer choice that you didn't mean to mark). This quick double check should more than pay for itself in caught mistakes for the time it costs.

☑ PACE YOURSELF

It's easy to be overwhelmed when you're looking at a page full of questions; your mind is confused and full of random thoughts, and the clock is ticking down faster than you would like. Calm down and maintain the pace that you have set for yourself. Especially as you get down to the last few minutes of the test, don't let the small numbers on the clock make you panic. As long as you are on track by monitoring your pace, you are guaranteed to have time for each question.

☑ DON'T RUSH

It is very easy to make errors when you are in a hurry. Maintaining a fast pace in answering questions is pointless if it makes you miss questions that you would have gotten right otherwise. Test writers like to include distracting information and wrong answers that seem right. Taking a little extra time to avoid careless mistakes can make all the difference in your test score. Find a pace that allows you to be confident in the answers that you select.

⊘ KEEP MOVING

Panicking will not help you pass the test, so do your best to stay calm and keep moving. Taking deep breaths and going through the answer elimination steps you practiced can help to break through a stress barrier and keep your pace.

Final Notes

The combination of a solid foundation of content knowledge and the confidence that comes from practicing your plan for applying that knowledge is the key to maximizing your performance on test day. As your foundation of content knowledge is built up and strengthened, you'll find that the strategies included in this chapter become more and more effective in helping you quickly sift through the distractions and traps of the test to isolate the correct answer.

Now that you're preparing to move forward into the test content chapters of this book, be sure to keep your goal in mind. As you read, think about how you will be able to apply this information on the test. If you've already seen sample questions for the test and you have an idea of the question format and style, try to come up with questions of your own that you can answer based on what you're reading. This will give you valuable practice applying your knowledge in the same ways you can expect to on test day.

Good luck and good studying!

Number Sense

Whole Number, Integer, Rational Number, Irrational Number, and Real Number

1. A *whole number* can be any positive counting number, including zero.
2. An *integer* can be a positive or negative counting number, including zero. An integer is not a decimal.
3. A *rational number* includes all integers plus values that can be written as a fraction of two integers.
4. An *irrational number* cannot be written as a fraction. These numbers are in decimal form and do not terminate or repeat. A common example of an irrational number is π.
5. A *real number* encompasses all numbers described above.

Therefore, whole numbers are integers and rational numbers. Integers are rational numbers but not necessarily whole numbers. All whole numbers, integers, rational numbers, and irrational numbers are real numbers.

Adding and Subtracting Signed Numbers

Addition

If the signs of two numbers are the same (both positive or both negative), add the absolute value of the numbers and apply the original sign to the sum. If the signs are different (one positive and one negative), calculate the absolute value of the numbers, and subtract the smaller value from the larger value. Apply the original sign of the number with the greater absolute value to the difference.

Subtraction

Change the subtraction sign to addition, while changing the sign of the number after that subtraction sign to the opposite of its original symbol. Then, follow the rules for addition.

Example: $x = 4 - 7$. Changing signs yields $x = 4 + (-7)$. Follow the rules for adding numbers with two different signs gives a solution of $x = -3$. If 7 had been negative originally, we would have changed its sign to an addition symbol ($x = 4 - (-7)$ is equal to $x = 4 + 7$).

Multiplying and Dividing Signed Numbers

Multiplication

If two numbers have the same sign (both positive or both negative), the product is positive. If two numbers have opposite signs (one positive and one negative), the product is negative. When more than two factors are multiplied together, count the number of negative factors. If there are an odd number of negative factors, the product is negative. If there is an even number of negative factors, the product is positive. If zero is a factor, the solution is zero.

Division

If the dividend and divisor have the same sign, the quotient is positive. If the dividend and divisor have opposite signs, the quotient is negative. If the dividend is zero, the answer is zero, unless the divisor is also zero. Anytime the divisor is zero, the quotient is undefined.

Exponent, Radical, and Absolute Value

An exponent is the power of a number and shows how many times the base value will be multiplied together. Example: In the expression x^4, the exponent, 4, tells us that the base, *x*, will be multiplied to itself 4 times, or $x^4 = x \cdot x \cdot x \cdot x$.

A radical is another word for the "root" of a number or mathematical expression. The most common radical is the square root. The solution of a square root is the value that, when multiplied by itself, produces the number inside the square root. Example: $\sqrt{16} = 4$. The square root of 16 is 4 because 4, when multiplied to itself, equals 16.

The absolute value of a number or mathematical expression represents its distance from zero on the number line and is, therefore, always positive. The absolute value sign is shown as two vertical bars. Example: $| -7 | = 7$. The absolute value of a negative seven equals seven because negative seven's distance from zero is seven.

Solving Equations That Include Radicals

Begin by isolating the radical term on one side of the equation, and move all other terms to the other side. Look at the index of the radical. Remember, if no number is given, the index is 2, meaning square root. Raise both sides of the equation to the power equal to the index of the radical. Solve the resulting equation as you would a normal polynomial equation. When you have found the roots, you MUST check them in the original problem to eliminate extraneous roots.

Working with Exponents

A positive integer exponent indicates the number of times the base is multiplied by itself. Anything raised to the zero power is equal to 1. A negative integer exponent means you must take the reciprocal of the result of the corresponding positive integer exponent. A fractional exponent signifies a root. The following formulas all apply to exponents:

$$x^0 = 1$$

$$x^{-n} = \frac{1}{x^n}$$

$$\left(\frac{a}{b}\right)^{-1} = \frac{b}{a}$$

$$(x^a)^b = x^{ab}$$

$$(xy)^n = x^n y^n$$

$$\left(\frac{x}{y}\right)^n = \frac{x^n}{y^n}$$

$$0^0 \textit{ is undefined}$$

Percent and Percentage

The term, percent, literally means "per hundred." A percentage is a ratio or proportion that can be expressed as a fraction with a denominator of 100. For example, the meaning of 25% is 25 portions of 100, or $^{25}/_{100}$. Many business measures are calculated in percentage terms, such as the interest rate, tax rate, market share, and discounts. In addition, percentage change is often used to define increases in profits, decreases in defects, or budget variances.

Fraction, Numerator, and Denominator

A fraction is a rational number that represents a portion of a whole value. For example, $^4/_5$ is a fraction. The top number, 4, is called the numerator. The bottom number, 5, is the denominator. The whole value would be $^5/_5$, which is equivalent to 1. However, the numerator in our example is

4, meaning 4 portions of 5. If a pizza were cut into 5 pieces, this fraction represents 4 of those pieces. A fraction also represents a quotient of the numerator divided by the denominator – in our example 4 divided by 5.

DECIMAL

A decimal is the portion of a number that is less than one. It is the result of the quotient of a fraction (its numerator divided by the denominator). For example, the decimal 0.5 represents the fraction $^1/_2$. Dividing 1 by 2 gives the decimal 0.5. A decimal has three forms: (1) terminating, (2) non-terminating, or (3) repeating.

A terminating decimal is one that has a definite end. You are able to write out all numerals of the decimal. Example: $\frac{1}{8} = 0.125$. This decimal ends at three positions after the decimal point.

A non-terminating decimal is one that does not have an end but continues indefinitely. When a non-terminating decimal is obtained as a solution, it is rounded to a certain number of digits, since all numerals cannot be written.

A repeating decimal is a type of non-terminating decimal. It also goes on indefinitely; however, the numerals have a pattern that recurs, over and over. Example: $\frac{1}{3} = 0.333333 \ldots$ One third written as a decimal is a repeating decimal because the "3" repeats indefinitely (often noted as $.\overline{33}$, where a bar is drawn over the sequence of numbers that repeat.)

CALCULATING THE REMAINING TWO MEASURES

GIVEN A PERCENTAGE

To obtain a fraction from a percentage, place the percentage number over one hundred and reduce the fraction. For example, let's use 46%. Place 46 over 100 and reduce: $^{46}/_{100} = {}^{23}/_{50}$. To obtain the decimal value from a percentage, first obtain the fraction, and then divide the numerator by the denominator. Dividing 46 by 100 yields the decimal value of 0.46.

GIVEN A FRACTION

To obtain a decimal from a fraction, divide the numerator by the denominator (*as shown above*). To obtain a percentage, calculate the decimal value and multiply the decimal by one hundred percent. If the fraction is $^{46}/_{100}$, the decimal is 0.46. Multiplying by 100% gives a percentage of 46% $(0.46 \times 100\% = 46\%)$.

GIVEN A DECIMAL

To calculate a percentage from a given decimal value, multiply by 100% (*as shown above*). To obtain a fraction from a decimal, place the whole value of the decimal over one hundred and reduce the fraction. If the decimal is 0.46, place the whole number 46 over 100 and reduce: $^{46}/_{100} = {}^{23}/_{50}$.

FINDING THE APPLIED TAX RATE

1. First you need to write what you know and what you are trying to find.
    a. Item Price without tax = $7.99
    b. Item Price with tax = $8.59
    c. Tax Rate = ? (let's call the tax rate, *t*)
2. Now, write an equation for what you want to find, in this case, the tax rate, *t*.

   a. Price with tax – Price without tax = t (Price without tax)
3. Since you have an equation with only one variable that is unknown, you can now solve.
   a. $\$8.59 - \$7.99 = t\ (\$7.99)$
   b. $t = 0.075$
4. The answer you calculate will be in decimal form, so multiply by 100% to get your tax rate.
   a. $t = 0.075 \times 100\% = 7.5\%$

ADDING AND SUBTRACTING FRACTIONS USING THE LEAST COMMON MULTIPLE

When adding or subtracting two fractions that do not have a common denominator (i.e. denominators that are multiples of each other), we must find the least common multiple (LCM).

ADDING FRACTIONS

Example: $^1/_2 + ^1/_3$. The smallest number into which 2 and 3 will divide is 6, so 6 is the least common multiple. Now that we know the LCM, we can rewrite the equation. To get the LCM of 6, we had to multiply the denominator by 3; therefore, we also have to multiply the numerator by 3 to keep the value of the fraction the same, which gives us $1 \times 3 = 3$. So, the first term, written in LCM form, is $^3/_6$. Applying the same logic to the second term, gives $^2/_6$. Rewriting the equation with common denominators yields $^3/_6 + ^2/_6$. From here, add the two numerators and place over the common denominator: $^5/_6$.

SUBTRACTING FRACTIONS

Subtracting fractions uses the same process as addition. Example: $^1/_2 - ^1/_3$. Find the least common multiple of 6. Rewrite the equation with the common denominator and solve: $^3/_6 - ^2/_6 = ^1/_6$.

MULTIPLYING AND DIVIDING FRACTIONS

MULTIPLYING FRACTIONS

To multiply two fractions, simply (1) multiply the numerators, (2) multiply the denominators, and (3) reduce the resulting fraction. Example: $^1/_2 \times ^2/_5 = ^2/_{10} = ^1/_5$.

DIVIDING FRACTIONS

To divide two fractions, (1) keep the first fraction the same, (2) take the inverse of the second fraction, and (3) multiply. Example: $^1/_2 \div ^2/_5 = ^1/_2 \times ^5/_2 = ^5/_4$.

Algebraic Concepts

Equation, Variable, and Unknown

Let's use the following mathematical statement to explain these three definitions: $x + 4 = 10$.

An equation is a mathematical condition where the value of two expressions is equal. In our example, $x + 4$ equals 10; therefore, $x + 4 = 10$ is called the equation.

A variable is a symbol, typically a letter, representing a number value. The variable in our example equation is x, which represents the number that will make the statement true.

An "unknown" is a variable in a mathematics equation or problem for which you must solve to obtain the value. In the example equation, x is the unknown because we must solve the equation to find the value x represents.

Solving a Mathematical Application Problem (i.e. "Word" Problem)

Determine the unknown in the problem and the variable you will use to represent it (e.g. x).

Write other variables or constants in terms of your unknown.

Draw a picture! A picture is worth a thousand words. You may be tempted to skip this step; however, seeing a picture tends to help the most when problem solving. You don't have to be an artist. A simple sketch, labeled with all known and unknown information will do.

From all the information you have, look for data that must equal each other, and write your equation.

Solve the equation by isolating the unknown variable onto one side of the equation and the answer on the other side.

Don't forget to check your solution in the original problem!

Mathematical Property That Can Be Used to Solve Equations

Paraphrased, the key property can be stated - What you do to one side of the equation, you must do to the other. This means that a number may be added, subtracted, multiplied, or divided on each side of the equation without changing its equality.

For example, consider the equation: $2x + 4 = x$. Subtract the number 4 from both sides of the equation: $2x + 4 - 4 = x - 4$. The equation was equal before we performed the subtraction operation, and now we have decreased each side of the equation by the <u>same</u> value. Therefore, the equation must still be equal.

Order of Operations to Follow When Solving Mathematical Expressions

If the expression is in fraction form, complete the order of operations separately for the numerator and then the denominator before reducing the fraction. Complete all expressions within parentheses first, using the listed order. Within each step below, solve left to right in order of occurrence.

- Then, move to the next operation.
- Exponents and Roots

- Multiplication and Division
- Addition and Subtraction
- At this point, if the expression was in fraction form, reduce if possible.

INEQUALITY, ENDPOINTS, AND INTERVAL NOTATION

An inequality is a mathematical expression that is greater than or less than another expression or quantity. For example, $-1 < x < 2$ and $\frac{2}{5} \leq x \leq 4$ are linear inequalities.

The endpoints of an inequality are the values on the number line between which lie the solution to the mathematical expression. In the first example above, -1 and 2 are the endpoints of the inequality. In the second example, $\frac{2}{5}$ and 4 are the endpoints.

Interval notation is often used to express the solution set of a linear inequality. This notation uses parentheses or brackets, depending on if the endpoints are included in the solution. Parentheses are used to indicate the endpoint is not part of the solution, while brackets indicate the endpoint is part of the solution. Notation for the first example above is (-1,2), while the second example is $[\frac{2}{5},4]$

EXPLAIN WHEN THE GRAPH OF A LINEAR INEQUALITY INCLUDES ENDPOINTS AND WHEN IT DOES NOT

The endpoint is included in the graph of an inequality when the endpoint value is part of the solution of the expression. For instance, when the solution reads "greater than *or equal to*" or "less than or *equal to*" the endpoint is part of the solution and the graph. When the solution reads "greater than" or "less than," the endpoint is not part of the solution or the graph.

Example Inequalities: (1) $-1 < x < 2$ and (2) $\frac{2}{5} \leq x \leq 4$.

The solution set of example (1) reads "x is greater than -1 and less than 2." This means neither endpoint is included in its solution and would not be part of the graph. The solution set for example (2) reads "x is greater than *or equal to* $\frac{2}{5}$ and less than *or equal to* 4." Both endpoints in this example are included in the solution and in the graph. When graphing the solution set of an inequality, typical notation is to use open circles at the endpoints that are not included in the solution and closed circles when the endpoints are included. However, another notation is to use parentheses and brackets on the number line, just as in interval notation.

SOLUTION OF A LINEAR INEQUALITY, AND ITS GRAPH, WHEN INFINITY OR NEGATIVE INFINITY IS PART OF THE SOLUTION SET

Let's say we have solved an inequality and obtained the solution set of $x \geq 4$. The interval notation is, then, $[4, \infty)$. A *bracket* on the left shows that 4 is part of the solution (since x is greater than *or equal to* 4.) We use a *parenthesis* on the right because infinity is never a true point we can reach. When infinity is graphed on the number line, an arrow is used to show that the solution set of the inequality keeps going. The graph of $x \geq 4$ is a closed circle at 4, with a line and an arrow pointing toward positive infinity. This example was given using positive infinity; however, the theory and rules are the same for negative infinity.

CHANGING THE DIRECTION OF THE INEQUALITY SYMBOL

As you solve an inequality, the symbol changes direction each time the expression is multiplied or divided through by a negative number. Adding and subtracting a negative number does not change the direction of the inequality symbol. To solve $-2x > 6$, we would divide by -2. However, since we are dividing by a negative number, we must reverse the sign. Solving, we obtain $x < -3$. This property of inequalities is easier to see when first considering a known true equation, such as $2 < 5$. It is a true statement to say that "2 is less than 5." Now, let's multiply both sides by -3 to obtain $-6 < -15$. After multiplying both sides by the same negative number, this statement is no longer true. However, the expression becomes true when we reverse the sign, yielding $-6 > -15$.

Solving the following inequality: $-2 < 4-\frac{1}{2}x \leq 6$

First, perform any addition or subtraction to isolate the term that contains the unknown variable. In this case, we'll subtract 4 from all three portions of the inequality to get: $-6 < -\frac{1}{2}x \leq 2$. The inequality symbols were not reversed because we were not multiply or dividing by a negative number.

Next, we need to multiply through by -2 to isolate x: $12 > x \geq -4$. Notice the inequality symbols changed direction because we multiplied by a negative value.

Don't forget to check your answer! Our solution says that x is greater than or equal to -4 but less than 12. Let's choose a number in our solution set to place into the original expression. Zero is typically the easiest, if it is part of the solution set. Placing zero into the original expression gives -2 < 4 ≤ 6, which is a true statement and validates this solution.

Now that we have verified our answer, let's rewrite the solution in interval notation: (-4, 12).

ABSOLUTE VALUE AFFECTS THE METHOD OF SOLVING A LINEAR INEQUALITY

When an absolute value appears in an inequality, you now must solve two separate problems since absolute value represents a distance from zero – which could be in either direction (positive or negative.)

First, isolate the absolute value on one side of the expression, with the remaining values and variables on the other side.

Then, remove the absolute value signs, and solve the problem as a typical inequality. This is the first part of the answer.

Now, go back to the point in the problem when the absolute value was isolated on one side.

For the side without the absolute value, multiply through by -1, *and* reverse the inequality sign.

Remove the absolute value signs, and solve the problem as an inequality problem. This is the second part of the answer.

The two inequalities you obtain for your answer are the solution set to the problem.

Solving the following inequality with an absolute value $|\,2x-4\,| - 4 > 1$

$$|\,2x-4\,| - 4 > 1$$

Isolate the absolute value: $|\,2x-4\,| > 5$

Remove absolute value and solve: $2x-4 > 5$; $2x > 9$; $x > \frac{9}{2}$ (first part of the answer)

Multiply right side by -1 and reverse sign: $|2x - 4| < -5$

Remove absolute value and solve: $2x - 4 < -5$; $2x < -1$; $x < -\frac{1}{2}$ (second part of the answer)

Solution: $x < -\frac{1}{2}$ **or** $x > \frac{9}{2}$

Solving a System of Two Linear Equations, with Variables *X* and *Y*, Using the Substitution Method

Let's use the following system of equations to explain the process: (1) $y - 2x = 3$ and (2) $4y + 3x = 2$.

First, choose the easier of the two equations to solve for one of the variables. In this case, *y* does not have a coefficient in equation (1) and would be simple to isolate. Solving equation (1) for *y* gives $y = 2x + 3$. We have isolated one variable in one of the equations. Now, we can substitute the right side of our new equation into equation (2) in place of the *y* variable. Substituting gives: $4(2x + 3) + 3x = 2$. We now have one equation with one unknown. Solving this equation gives us the value for *x*, which is $x = -\frac{10}{11}$. Use this value to substitute into either original equation to get the value of *y*, $y = 2\left(-\frac{10}{11}\right) + 3$ which gives $y = 1\frac{2}{11}$. Check your answer by substituting *x* into the other equation to ensure the value of *y* is the same.

Solving a System of Two Linear Equations, with Two Variables, Using the Elimination Method

Put both equations into standard form: $Ax + By = C$. When these two equations are added together, do they eliminate one variable? If the answer is no, choose a value that, when multiplied through both sides of one of the equations, eliminates a variable when added to the other equation. Adding the two equations gives one equation with one unknown. Solve for the remaining variable, and substitute this value into one of the equations to obtain the value of the second variable. Check your answers by using one of the values in the other equation. The answer should be the same regardless of the equation you use.

Solving the Following System of Equations Using the Elimination Method

(a) $\mathbf{2x + y = 5}$

(b) $\mathbf{-x + 3y = 8}$

27b

(a) $\mathbf{2x + y = 5}$

(b) $\mathbf{-x + 3y = 8}$

Determine if, when added, the equations eliminate one variable. This is not the case with these equations so we must move to the next step and eliminate a variable.

The easiest variable to eliminate in this system of equations is *x*. Let's multiply equation (b) by 2 to get $-2x + 6y = 16$.

Now, add equation (a) and the new form of equation (b) to obtain $7y = 21$ (*x* has been eliminated).

Solving gives: $y = 3$

To obtain x, substitute the solution for y into one of the equations and solve. Using equation (a) we get: $2x + (3) = 5$, or $x = 1$.

Check both equations to make sure these values for x and y are valid.

Quadratic Equation

A Quadratic Equation always has a degree of 2 (i.e. the variable is squared). The following are examples of quadratic equations: (1) $2x^2 + 5x + 3 = 0$, (2) $x^2 - 4x = -4$, and (3) $x^2 = 9$. Equation (1) is the standard form of the quadratic equation, where all terms are arranged on one side of the equation and set equal to zero. Techniques used to find the solutions of a quadratic equation include factoring, completing the square, or using the quadratic formula. Before factoring or using the quadratic formula, rearranging the equation into its standard form is typically required.

Zero-Factor Property

To use the Zero-Factor Property, first start by rearranging the quadratic equation into its standard form. Now, if you are able to factor the non-zero side of the equation, you can set each factor equal to zero and solve for the unknown variables. This technique is allowable because, if one of the two factors is equal to zero, the entire equation will be equal to zero. Note that there are two factors, which means you must solve for two solutions. However, the solutions to both factors could be the same. Check your answers by placing them into the original quadratic equation.

Complete the Square

To explain this concept, let's use the following quadratic equation: $2x^2 - 12x + 5 = 0$.

To use this technique, do not arrange the equation into standard form, as with other methods. Instead, rearrange the equation where all variables are on one side of the equation, and the constant is on the other: $2x^2 - 12x = -5$.

Now, divide both sides of the equation by the x^2 coefficient, 2, so that the leading coefficient becomes 1: $x^2 - 6x = -\frac{5}{2}$.

Next, divide the x coefficient by 2 and square it: 9. This value "completes the square."

Add this value to both sides of the equation: $x^2 - 6x + 9 = -\frac{5}{2} + 9$.

This easily factors as: $(x - 3)(x - 3) = \frac{13}{2}$ or $(x - 3)^2 = \frac{13}{2}$.

Finally, solve the equation: $x = 3 + \sqrt{\frac{13}{2}}$.

Quadratic Formula

The Quadratic Formula is: $x = \frac{-b \pm \sqrt{b^2 - 4ac}}{2a}$. The quadratic formula can be used to solve a quadratic equation when factoring the equation is not simple. First, the quadratic equation must be rearranged to its standard form: $ax^2 + bx + c = 0$. In standard form, it is easy to see the coefficients (a, b, c) that must be substituted into the equation. Solving the quadratic equation yields the two solutions of the original quadratic equation. Check both solutions in the original equation to find if they are valid solutions for x.

QUADRATIC FUNCTION

A quadratic function follows the equation pattern: $y = ax^2 + by^2 + c$, or $f(x) = ax^2 + by^2 + c$, where a, b, and c are real numbers and $a \neq 0$. The domain of a quadratic function is the set of all real numbers. The range is also real numbers but only those in the subset of the domain that satisfy the equation. To determine the number of roots of a quadratic equation, evaluate the expression $b^2 - 4ac$. If this value is positive, there are two unique, real roots. If this value equals zero, there is one root, which is a double root. If this value is less than zero, there are no real roots. To find the roots of a quadratic equation, solve the equation: $ax^2 + by^2 + c = 0$. In a quadratic function, the rate of change varies throughout, but a maximum or a minimum value for the amount of change does exist. Quadratic functions are useful in determining the solutions to situations such as how price changes of an item will affect its sales and profit margin.

GRAPHS OF A QUADRATIC FUNCTION

A quadratic function will always be a parabola when it is graphed. In the equation $f(x) = ax^2 + by^2 + c$, if a is positive, the parabola will open upward. If a is negative, the parabola will open downward. The axis of symmetry is a vertical line that passes through the vertex. To discover whether a parabola will intersect the x-axis, determine the number of real roots. An equation with two real roots will cross the x-axis twice. An equation with one real root will have its vertex on the x-axis. An equation with no real roots will not contact the x-axis.

EXTRAPOLATION AND INTERPOLATION

Extrapolation is the analysis of data points to forecast values outside the original data range. Extrapolation is often used by businesses to forecast future trends of expenses or revenue.

Interpolation is the analysis of data points to approximate values within the original data range.

REGRESSION ANALYSIS

Regression analysis, along with its coefficient of determination, can be used to study the relationship between two or more variables. Regression analysis is used to study the nature of the relationship, while the coefficient of determination measures the strength of that relationship. Linear regression is used to analyze the relationship between two variables, and multiple regression is used to analyze the relationship between more than two variables.

INTERPOLATE DATA

To interpolate data within a given range, first generate a scatter plot with the available data. Then, create the best-fit line. You can calculate the regression line using the least squares method or by using a data analysis package, such as Excel, to compute the equation of the line for you.

REGRESSION ANALYSIS IN EXTRAPOLATION

Using regression analysis in extrapolation means you are using a range of data to predict values outside that range. The regression line is the most accurate for the original data set. We cannot know how the data will behave outside of that range. For instance, data that appear linear over a short time period may be exponential or even seasonal over a longer time frame. Data extrapolation will be more accurate the more data history you can place in your analysis.

CARTESIAN COORDINATE PLANE

The Cartesian coordinate plane consists of two number lines placed perpendicular to each other and intersecting at the zero point, also known as the origin. The horizontal number line is known as the x-axis, with positive values to the right of the origin and negative values to the left. The vertical number line is known as the y-axis, with positive values above the origin and negative values below the origin. Any point on the plane can be identified by an ordered pair in the form (x,y), called coordinates. The x-value of the coordinate is called the abscissa, and the y-value of the coordinate is called the ordinate. The two number lines divide the plane into four quadrants: I, II, III, and IV.

Review Video: Cartesian Coordinate Plane and Graphing
Visit mometrix.com/academy and enter code: 115173

COORDINATE, ORIGIN, SLOPE, AND INTERCEPT

A coordinate is a point on a graph, where the first number is the x-value and the second number is the y-value. For example, (4, 2) is a coordinate in a real number graph, where 4 is the x-coordinate and 2 is the y-coordinate.

The origin is the point on a graph represented by the coordinates (0,0).

The slope of a line is the value of the change in the y-coordinate divided by the change in the x-coordinate: $\frac{\Delta y}{\Delta x}$. The slope of a line is often termed "rise over run."

An intercept is where a graph of a line crosses the x-axis or y-axis. A line crosses the x-axis at the x-intercept and the y-axis and the y-intercept.

SLOPE-INTERCEPT FORM VS. STANDARD FORM OF AN EQUATION

The slope-intercept form of a linear equation is solved for the dependent variable (typically designated as y) in terms of the independent variable (x): $y = mx + b$, where m = slope and b = y-intercept. The standard form of an equation can be obtained by rearranging the slope-intercept equation to a form of $Ax + By = C$, where A, B, and C are integers (i.e. not fractions). At times, you may also see the standard equation set equal to zero: $Ax + By + C = 0$. The standard form equation can easily be transformed back to the slope-intercept form by solving for y.

Difference between the slope and intercepts of lines $x = c$ and $y = c$, where c is a constant

$x = c$ is a vertical line with an undefined slope and an x-intercept of c

$y = c$ is a horizontal line with a slope equal to zero and a y-intercept of c

Except in the case when $c = 0$, the vertical line will not have a y-intercept, and the horizontal line will not have an x-intercept.

SLOPES OF PARALLEL AND PERPENDICULAR LINES

PARALLEL

Two parallel lines will have the same slope. For example, two lines have the following equations: (1) $y = 2x + 4$ and (2) $y = 2x - 9$. Equation (1) and (2) have a slope of 2. Since the slope is the same for both equations, these two lines are parallel.

PERPENDICULAR

A line that is perpendicular to another has a slope that is the negative inverse of the other line. For example, a line has the following equation: $y = \frac{4}{5}x + 9$. A line perpendicular to this line must have the negative inverse slope of $-\frac{5}{4}$.

Graphing a Two-Variable, Linear Inequality

When graphing a linear inequality that uses the symbol *greater than* (>) or *less than* (<) in the expression, use a dashed line to represent that the actual line is not part of the solution. If the inequality uses the symbol *greater than or equal to* (≥) or *less than or equal to* (≤), use a solid line, since any point on the line is a solution. All graphs of linear inequalities require that one side of the line is shaded. To determine which side to shade, select any point that is not on the line (the origin is an easy point to use if it is not on the line), and substitute the *x*- and *y*-values into the inequality. If the inequality is true, shade the side with that point. If the inequality is false, shade the other side of the line.

Function, Domain, Range, and the Vertical Line Test

A function is an equation that has exactly one value for *y* (the dependent variable) for each member of *x* (the independent variable).

The set of all values for *x* is the domain of the function.

The set of all corresponding values of *y* is the range of the function.

When looking at a graph of an equation, the easiest way to determine if the equation is a function is to conduct the vertical line test. If a vertical line drawn through any value of x crosses the graph in more than one place, the equation is not a function.

Argument, Domain of Definition, Graph, Zeros, and Intercepts

In functions with the notation, $f(x)$, the value substituted for *x* in the equation is called the argument.

The domain is the set of all values for x in a function. Unless otherwise given, assume the domain is the set of real numbers that will yield real numbers for the range. This is the domain of definition.

The graph of a function is the set of all ordered pairs (x, y) that satisfy the equation of the function.

The points that have zero as the value for *y* are called the zeros (or solutions) of the function.

These are also the *x*-intercepts, since this is the point at which the graph crosses the *x*-axis. The points that have zero as the value for *x* are the *y*-intercepts, since this is where the graph crosses the *y*-axis.

Constant Functions, Identity Functions, and the Zeros of Both

Constant functions are given by the equation $y = b$ or $f(x) = b$, where *b* is a real number. There is a single variable y in the equation, so there are no zeros unless $b = 0$, in which case every point is a zero. The graph of a constant function is a horizontal line of slope 0 that is positioned *b* units from the *x*-axis. If *b* is positive, the line is above the *x*-axis; if *b* is negative, the line is below the *x*-axis.

Identity functions are identified by the equation $y = x$ or $f(x) = x$, where every value of *y* is equal to its corresponding value of *x*. The only zero is the point (0,0). The graph is a diagonal line with slope 1.

Format, Domain, and Range of a Square Root Function

A square root function is one that contains a radical and is in the format $f(x) = \sqrt{ax + b}$. The domain is the set of all real numbers that yields a positive radicand or a radicand equal to zero. Because square root values are assumed to be positive unless otherwise identified, the range is all real numbers from zero to infinity. To find the zero of a square root function, set the radicand equal to zero and solve for x. The graph of a square root function is always to the right of the zero and always above the x-axis.

FORMAT, DOMAIN, AND RANGE OF AN ABSOLUTE VALUE FUNCTION

An absolute value function is in the format $f(x) = |ax + b|$. Like other functions, the domain is the set of all real numbers. However, because absolute value indicates positive value, the range is limited to positive real numbers. To find the zero of an absolute value function, set the portion inside the absolute value sign equal to zero and solve for x. An absolute value function is also known as a piecewise function because it must be solved in pieces – one for if the value inside the absolute value sign is positive and one for if the value is negative. The function can be expressed as

$$f(x) = \begin{cases} ax + b \, if \, ax + b \geq 0 \\ -(ax + b) if \, ax + b < 0 \end{cases}.$$

This will allow for an accurate statement of the range.

Statistics

Population vs. Sample

A population includes the entire data set you are interested in analyzing. Measures used to describe a population are called parameters.

A sample is a subset of data taken from the population. Any measure used to describe a sample is called a statistic. Often, populations of data are too large or difficult to analyze, so we analyze a sample of the population instead.

Central Tendency

Central Tendency is defined as a statistical value that gives a general propensity for the center of a data set. Its most common measures include the arithmetic mean, mode, and median. These statistics or parameters are used to summarize the data set and give information about its overall behavior.

Mean, Median, and Mode of a Data Set

The arithmetic mean, or simply called "the mean," is calculated by adding all values in the population or sample and dividing by the total number of data points that were summed. The mean is often called the *average*.

The median of a set of data is the value for which half of the population or sample are above and half are below. List the values of the data set in numerical order. If the number of data points is odd, the median will be middle number of the data set. If the number of data points is even, the median is calculated by averaging the two middle values of the data set.

The mode is the value in the data set that occurs most frequently. If all numbers in the population or sample are different (i.e. no repeated values), then a mode does not exist.

Possible Disadvantages of Using the Mean as a Measure of Central Tendency

While the mean is relatively easy to calculate and averages are understood by most people, the mean can be very misleading if it is used as the sole measure of central tendency. If the data set has outliers (data values that are unusually high or unusually low compared to the rest of the data values), the mean can be very distorted, especially if the data set has a small number of values. If unusually high values are countered with unusually low values, the mean is not affected as much. For example, if five of the twenty students in a class get a 100 on a test, but the other 15 students have an average of 60 on the same test, the class average would appear as 70. Whenever the mean is skewed by outliers, it is always a good idea to include the median as an alternate measure of central tendency.

Possible Disadvantages of Using the Median or the Mode as a Measure of Central Tendency

The big disadvantage of using the median as a measure of central tendency is that is relies solely on a value's relative size as compared to the other values in the set. When the individual values in a set of data are evenly dispersed, the median can be an accurate tool. However, if there is a group of rather large values or a group of rather small values that are not offset by a different group of values, the information that can be inferred from the median may not be accurate.

The main disadvantage of the mode is that the values of the other data in the set have no bearing on the mode. The mode may be the largest value, the smallest value, or a value anywhere in between in the set. The mode only tells which value or values, if any, occurred the most number of times. It does not give any suggestions about the remaining values in the set.

Dispersion

Dispersion is the degree of variation, or distribution, of the data around a particular measurement. When used together with the measures of central tendency, dispersion measures give a more accurate definition to a set of data. When values in a sample or population are all close to the mean, the data demonstrate less dispersion than when some values are much larger or smaller than the mean. The most common measures that express the amount of dispersion in a data set are the range, variance, and standard deviation.

How Range, Variance, and Standard Deviation of a Data Set Are Calculated

The range of a data set is calculated by subtracting the smallest value in the sample (or population) from the largest value.

The variance is calculated by taking the average of the squared deviations of the actual values in the data set from their mean. The variance measures the dispersion of the observed data from their expected value.

The standard deviation is the square root of the variance. The standard deviation is often considered the most useful dispersion measurement because it represents variability but is calculated in the same units as the original data.

Statistically Significant

Using the terminology "statistically significant" means that a relationship has been found among data. It means that we have some amount of certainty that this relationship did not happen by chance. However, a statistically significant relationship among data does not necessarily mean it is an important one. The relationship could be strong or weak. Therefore, after we have found a statistically significant relationship among data, we must use one of several tests (e.g. z-score, t-test, chi square test) to determine the strength of the relationship.

Null Hypothesis and Alternative Hypothesis

The first step in hypothesis testing is to state the Null and Alternative Hypotheses.

The Null Hypothesis is a statement that assumes there is no difference between observed and expected data and any relationship found occurred by chance. The null hypothesis is often given the symbol H_0.

The Alternative Hypothesis is a statement that represents the expected outcome. The alternative hypothesis is often given the symbol H_a or H_1.

Determining Statistical Significance Through Hypothesis Testing

Define the null and alternative hypotheses.

Choose the significance level you are willing to accept for error in your testing.

Determine the test statistic that is appropriate for your sample.

Select the test statistic and calculate its value.

Compare the calculated value of the test statistic to its critical value, which is based on the significance level chosen in step (3).

Make a decision to reject the null hypothesis and accept the alternative hypothesis or fail to reject the null hypothesis.

Type I and Type II Errors of Hypothesis Testing

A Type I error in hypothesis testing occurs when the decision is made to reject the null hypothesis, but the null hypothesis is true. A Type I error is often denoted by the symbol alpha, α.

A Type II error occurs when a decision is made to fail to reject the null hypothesis when the null hypothesis is actually false. A Type II error is denoted by the symbol beta, β.

There will always be some chance of error when making a decision through hypothesis testing. You can minimize the error through choosing a low significance level and increasing sample size.

Random Variable and Probability Distribution

In probability, the random variable is not really a variable, but rather a function that generates a variable with a real number value that is determined purely by chance and assigned to each possible outcome of a sample space. Once the values of the random variable have been determined, a probability distribution is set up. The probability distribution can be a chart, graph, formula, or table that gives the individual probabilities of all the values of the random variable. It described the range of possibilities for the random variable, and gives the probability of the random variable falling somewhere within that range.

Expected Value

Expected value is a method of determining expected outcome in a random situation. It is really a sum of the weighted probabilities of the possible outcomes. Multiply the probability of an event occurring by the weight assigned to that probability (such as the amount of money won or lost). A practical application of the expected value is to determine whether a game of chance is really fair. If the sum of the weighted probabilities is greater than or equal to zero, the game is generally considered fair because the player has a fair chance to win, or at least to break even. If the expected value is less than one, then players lose more than they win. For example, a lottery drawing allows the player to choose any three-digit number, 000-999. The probability of choosing the winning number is 1:1000. If it costs $1 to play, and a winning number receives $500, the expected value is:

$\left(-\$1 \cdot \frac{999}{1000}\right) + \left(\$500 \cdot \frac{1}{1000}\right) = -0.499 \cong -\$0.50$. You can expect to lose on average 50 cents for every dollar you spend.

Probability Distribution

A probability distribution is a function that shows all possible values a random variable (discrete or continuous) can have and the possibility that each will occur. Discrete probability distributions identify a finite set of outcomes and are often represented through bar charts. Common discrete probability distributions include the Poisson and Binomial distributions. Continuous distributions describe values that can occur over a continuous range and are represented by a curve. Continuous distributions include normal, exponential, and chi square distributions.

Normal Distribution

The Normal Distribution is the most important distribution in statistics. A normal distribution is symmetrical about its mean, and the mean, mode, and median are all equal. The mean of a normal distribution determines its center, while the standard deviation determines the shape of the curve. A normal distribution contains approximately 68% of its area under the curve at one standard deviation, 95% at two standard deviations, and 99.7% at three standard deviations.

Inferential Statistics and Sampling Distribution

Inferential statistics is the branch of statistics that uses samples to make predictions about an entire population. This type of statistics is often seen in political polls, where a sample of the population is questioned about a particular topic or politician to gain an understanding about the attitudes of the entire population of the country. Often, exit polls are conducted on election days using this method. Inferential statistics can have a large margin of error if you do not have a valid sample. The statistical values calculated from the various samples of the same size make up the sampling distribution. For example, if several samples of identical size are randomly selected from a large population and then the mean of each sample is calculated, the values of the means would be a sampling distribution.

Characteristics of the Sampling Distribution of the Mean

Represented by the symbol $\bar{x}$, the sampling distribution of the mean has three important characteristics. First, the mean of the sampling distribution of $\bar{x}$ equals the mean of the sampled population. The sampled population includes all of the samples in the distribution combined. Second, assuming the standard deviation is positive, the standard deviation of the sampling distribution of $\bar{x}$ equals the standard deviation of the sampled population divided by the square root of the sample size. Finally, as the sample size gets larger and closer to the actual population number, the sampling distribution of $\bar{x}$ gets closer to a normal distribution.

How a Weighted Average of a Sample Differs from an Arithmetic Average

In a weighted average, each data point is multiplied by value that represents its significance in that set of data. In this manner, more significant data is weighted more heavily in the calculation. If all values are weighted equally, the weighted average would be equal to the arithmetic average.

How Weighted Averages Are Used in Business the "Weight" Each Would Use

Weighted Average Cost of Capital: a calculation of a company's cost of capital; the sources of capital (debt, equity) are weighted by the percent of capital each contributes to the whole

Weighted Average Inventory: a measure of the cost items in inventory; items are weighted by the cost of each and then divided by the total number of items

Weighted Average Shares Outstanding: calculation incorporates changes in the number of outstanding shares due to repurchases, retiring shares, etc.; weighted by the portion of the period the shares were outstanding

A student had the following scores in her accounting class. Each assignment represents the percentage shown of the final grade. Calculate the student's final accounting grade.

Homework: 95 (30%), Quiz: 86 (30%), Test: 90 (40%)

To find the weighted average of all grades, we must multiple each score by the percentage it represents of the final grade. When multiplying by a percentage, don't forget to use its decimal form:

$$95\,(0.30) + 86\,(0.30) + 90\,(0.40) = 90.3$$

Therefore, the student's final grade is 90.3.

Percentile

A Percentile is a statistical value that describes where data points lie in a distribution. For example, the 40th percentile is a value where 40% of numbers in the data set are less than that value and 60% of the values are higher. The median is considered the 50th percentile, and each 25th percentile multiple is called a *quartile*.

Business Applications

The sales of a toy company in 2005 were $3.0 million, and this is to be the index base period. Find the simple index number for the following sales years.

a. 2006; $3.1 million
b. 2007; $3.5 million

The simple index number can be found by using the formula: $I_t = \frac{y_t}{y_0} \cdot 100$, where I_t is the index number at period t, y_t is the value of the time series at time t, and y_0 is the value of the time series at the index base period. The index base period is given as $3.0 million in 2005.

a. $I_{2006} = \frac{y_{2006}}{y_0} \cdot 100 = \frac{3.1}{3.0} \cdot 100 = 103.3$

b. $I_{2007} = \frac{y_{2007}}{y_0} \cdot 100 = \frac{3.5}{3.0} \cdot 100 = 116.7$

Using a Simple Index Number to Find the Percentage Growth

If simple index number from time 0 to time t is I, the percentage growth is $(I - 100)\%$. For example, let y_0 = $10 million, and the base year be 2006. If in 2008, y_{2008} = $12.5 million, then I_{2008} can be found using:

$$I_{2008} = \frac{y_{2008}}{y_0} \cdot 100 = \frac{12.5}{10.0} \cdot 100 = 125$$

The percentage growth from 2006 to 2008 is: (125 – 100)% = 25%.

Let 2007 be the Index Base Period. Find the Simple Index Number for Each Year in the Table Below.

Year	Value of Property
2007	$150,000
2008	$165,000
2009	$170,000
2010	$192,000

2008: $I_{2008} = \frac{y_{2008}}{y_0} \cdot 100 = \frac{165{,}000}{150{,}000} \cdot 100 = 110$

2009: $I_{2009} = \frac{y_{2009}}{y_0} \cdot 100 = \frac{170{,}000}{150{,}000} \cdot 100 = 113.3$

2010: $I_{2010} = \frac{y_{2010}}{y_0} \cdot 100 = \frac{192{,}000}{150{,}000} \cdot 100 = 128$

Using Simple Index Numbers to Find the Actual Percentage Growth Between Each Pair of Years.

Year	Index Number
2001	140.2
2002	174.0
2003	193.5

To determine the actual percentage growth, find the difference between the two index numbers, then divide the difference by the index number of the earlier year, and multiply by 100.

The actual percentage growth from 2001 to 2002 is:

$$\frac{174.0 - 140.2}{140.2} \cdot 100 = 24.1\%$$

The actual percentage growth from 2002 to 2003 is:

$$\frac{193.5 - 174.0}{174.0} \cdot 100 = 11.2\%$$

The actual percentage growth from 2003 to 2004 is:

$$\frac{201.6 - 193.5}{193.5} \cdot 100 = 4.2\%$$

Find the simple interest, *I*, for each of the given values of principal, *P*, yearly interest rate, *R*, and time, *T*

a. $P = \$4{,}000$; $R = 3.1\%$; $T = 26$ months
b. $P = \$26{,}400$; $R = 1.4\%$; $T = 8$ months
c. $P = \$130{,}000$; $R = 2.0\%$; $T = 10$ months

Simple interest can be calculated using the formula: $I = P \cdot R \cdot T$, where *P* is the principal, *I* is the yearly interest rate, and *T* is the time in years.

a. $I = (4{,}000)(0.031)\left(\frac{26}{12}\right) = \$268.67$
b. $I = (26{,}400)(0.014)\left(\frac{8}{12}\right) = \$246.40$
c. $I = (130{,}000)(0.020)\left(\frac{10}{12}\right) = \$2{,}166.67$

Find the maturity value of the loan, *M*, with each given principal, *P*, interest rate, *R*, and loan due date. The loan has simple interest.

a. $P = \$51{,}000$; $R = 5.8\%$; due in: 18 months
b. $P = \$280{,}200$; $R = 4.0\%$; due in: 120 months
c. $P = \$5{,}000$; $R = 8.5\%$; due in: 30 months

First, find the interest, using the formula for simple interest: $I = P \cdot R \cdot T$, where *P* is the principal, *R* is the yearly interest rate, and *T* is the time in years. Next, find the maturity value, *M*, using the formula: $M = P + I$.

a. $I = (51{,}000)(0.058)\left(\frac{18}{12}\right) = \$4{,}437.00$
$M = 51{,}000 + 4{,}437 = \$55{,}437.00$
b. $I = (280{,}200)(0.040)\left(\frac{120}{12}\right) = \$112{,}080.00$
$M = 280{,}200 + 112{,}080 = \$392{,}280.00$
c. $I = (5{,}000)(0.085)\left(\frac{30}{12}\right) = \$1{,}062.50$
$M = 5{,}000 + 1{,}062.50 = \$6{,}062.50$

FIND THE MATURITY VALUE OF THE INTEREST-BEARING ACCOUNTS BELOW. THE PRINCIPAL INVESTMENT IN THE ACCOUNT IS $150,000. ACCOUNT A EARNS ANNUAL SIMPLE INTEREST AT A RATE OF 2.5%, AND THE FUNDS ARE INVESTED FOR 8 YEARS.

To find the maturity value of an account with simple interest, use the formula: $M = P + I$, where the interest $I = P \cdot R \cdot T$ and P is the principal invested, R is the interest rate, and T is the time invested. Account A has annual simple interest, so the time will be in years. The funds in the account will have a maturity value of: $M = P + I = P + P \cdot R \cdot T = 150{,}000 + (150{,}000)(0.025)(8) = \$180{,}000.00$

FIND THE MATURITY VALUE OF A FUND WITH A PRINCIPAL INVESTMENT OF $20,000, INVESTED FOR 4 YEARS, WITH AN ANNUAL INTEREST RATE OF 1.5%. ACCOUNT A COMPOUNDS INTEREST ANNUALLY.

To find the maturity value of an account with compound interest, use the formula: $M = P(1 + i)^n$, where P is the principal invested, i is the interest rate per compounding period, and n is the total number of compounding periods. P = $20,000 and the annual interest rate is 1.5%. The interest in Account A is compounded annually, so the compounding periods will equal the number of years the funds are invested, or 4 years. The interest rate per compounding period will equal the annual interest rate, 1.5%.

$$M = P(1 + i)^n = 20{,}000(1 + 0.015)^4 = \$21{,}227.27$$

Identify the account with the higher maturation value. Both accounts have a principal investment of $45,000, and the funds are invested for 6 years.

a. Account A has interest compounded monthly at an annual rate of 2.1%.
b. Account B has interest compounded daily at an annual rate of 2.0%.

To find the maturity value of an account with compound interest, use the formula: $M = P(1 + i)^n$, where P is the principal invested, i is the interest rate per compounding period, and n is the total number of compounding periods. For each of the accounts, P = $45,000.

a. The interest in Account A is compounded monthly, or 12 times per year. The number of compounding periods will be twelve times the number of years, or: $12 \cdot 6 = 72$. The interest rate per compounding period will equal the annual interest rate, 2.1%, divided by 12: $0.021 \div 12 = 0.00175$.

$$M = P(1 + i)^n = 45{,}000(1 + 0.00175)^{72} = \$51{,}037.08$$

b. The interest in Account B is compounded daily. The number of compounding periods will be the number of days invested, or 365 times the number of years: $365 \cdot 6 = 2{,}190$. The interest rate per compounding period will equal the annual interest rate, 2.0%, divided by 365. Enter the expression: $\frac{0.02}{365}$ directly into the equation for the compounding interest rate to reduce rounding errors.

$$M = P(1 + i)^n = 45{,}000(1 + \frac{0.02}{365})^{2190} = \$50{,}737.19$$

Account A has a higher maturation value.

a. Describe straight-line depreciation and salvage value.
b. A laser copier is purchased in 2000 for $1,200.00. The useful life of the printer is 4 years, and the salvage value is $300.00. Assume that straight-line depreciation can be used.

Determine the annual rate of depreciation and annual amount of depreciation

a. Straight-line depreciation is a method of depreciation that assumes that an object loses value equally over each year of the object's useful life. Salvage value is the approximate value of an object when it has stopped being used (retired, traded, disposed of, or exhausted.)

b. The annual rate of depreciation is 1 divided by the number of years of useful life: $\frac{1}{4} = 25\%$. The annual depreciation amount, if the object loses value equally over each year of its life, will be the depreciation amount multiplied by the annual rate of depreciation. The amount to be depreciated can be found using the formula: amount to be depreciated = cost – salvage value.

Amount to be depreciated: $\$1{,}200.00 - \$300.00 = \$900.00$.

The annual depreciation amount is: $\$900.00 \cdot 0.25 = \$225.00$.

a. Describe the book value of an object.

b. Determine the book value of an object after 4 years with an initial value of $6,000.00, useful life of 10 years, and salvage value of $150.00.

a. The book value of an object is the declared value of an object after a given length of time. It can be found by determining the original cost minus the accumulated depreciation.

b. First, find the annual rate of depreciation. The total useful life of the object is 10 years, so the annual rate of depreciation is: $\frac{1}{10} = 10\%$. Next, determine the annual depreciation amount. The total amount to be depreciated is the original value minus the salvage value: $\$6{,}000.00 - \$150.00 = \$5{,}850.00$. The annual depreciation amount is the total depreciation amount times the annual rate of depreciation: $\$5{,}850.00 \cdot 0.10 = \$585.00$. Finally, to find the book value after 4 years, find the accumulated depreciation over the four years. Multiply the annual depreciation amount by the number of years: $\$585.00 \cdot 4 = \$2{,}340.00$. The book value after 4 years will be the original value minus the accumulated depreciation: $\$6{,}000.00 - \$2{,}340.00 = \$3{,}660.00$.

Relationship Between the Straight-Line Rate and Double-Declining Balance Rate

The double-declining balance rate is twice the straight-line rate. To find the value of depreciation using the double-declining balance method, first find the straight-line rate by dividing 1 by the number of years of useful life. The double-declining rate is two times the straight-line rate.

Double-Declining Balance Method

The declining balance method of depreciation reflects a change in depreciation over time. To find the depreciation for the first year, multiply the original value by the double-declining balance rate. This is the amount of depreciation for the first year. The book value of the object is the original value minus the amount of depreciation for the first year. The depreciation for each remaining year of the useful life is found similarly. Multiply the previous year's balance by the double-declining rate to find the amount of depreciation, and then subtract the new amount of depreciation from the previous year's book value.

Book Value vs. Salvage Value of an Object

The depreciation is subtracted from the original value of an object each year of its useful life until the salvage value is reached. If the salvage value is reached before the final year of life, the book value of the object is equal to the salvage value for all remaining years of life. The book value of the object can never be less than the salvage value. Similarly, if the amount of depreciation, when subtracted from the book value of an object, results in a book value that is less than the salvage value, then the depreciation will be equal to the difference between the previous year's book value and the salvage value.

An object has an initial value of $7,500.00, and a useful life of 8 years. Using the double-declining balance method, find the book value of the object after 1 and 2 years of life. The object's salvage value is $2,200.00.

The straight-line depreciation rate of the object is: $\frac{1}{8} = .125 = 12.5\%$. The double-declining balance rate is twice the straight-line rate: $12.5\% \cdot 2 = 25\%$. To find the book value after the first year, first find the depreciation by multiplying the rate by the original value of the object.

Year 1 depreciation: $7500 \cdot 0.25 = 1875$

The book value of the object is the original value minus the depreciation: $7500 - 1875 =$ $5,625.00.

Find the depreciation in year 2 by multiplying the book value after year 1 by the depreciation rate.

Year 2 depreciation: $5625 \cdot 0.25 = 1406.25$

The book value of the object after year 2 is the book value after year 1 minus the year 2 depreciation: $5625 - 1406.25 = \$4,218.75$

A manufacturer sells wheelbarrows to a local retailer. The manufacturer has a list price of $230.00 for the wheelbarrows, and sells to the retailer at a 30% trade discount. Find the price paid by the retailer to the manufacturer.

The trade discount is a discount given to the retailer by the manufacturer. The retailer pays the discounted price, or net price, to the manufacturer. To find the discounted, or net, price, subtract the discount from the list price. The discount is equal to the discount percent times the list price.

Discount: $\$230.00 \cdot 0.30 = \$69.00$

Net price: $\$230.00 - \$69.00 = \$161.00$

Complement of a Percent

The complement of a percent is the percent that when summed with the original percent equals 1, or 100%. For example, the complement of 40% is $100\% - 40\% = 60\%$, or $1 - 0.4 = 0.6$. If a 40% discount was offered, the complement of 40%, or 60% of the retail price, would be the amount paid for the item. Complements can be used to find a series discount. First the complement of each percent in the series, then find the product of the complements. Multiply this product by the list price to find the net cost of the item.

Using complements to find the series discounts below

a. List price: $40.00. Series discount: 10/30

b. List price: $510.00. Series discount: 5/20/25

a. The two percents in the series discount are 10% and 30%. The complement of 10% is: $1 - 0.10 = 0.90$. The complement of 30% is: $1 - 0.30 = 0.70$. The product of the complements: $0.90 \cdot 0.70 = 0.63$. The net price is:

$$\$40.00 \cdot 0.63 = \$25.20$$

b. The three percents in the series discount are 5%, 20%, and 25%. The complement of each percent is:

$$1 - 0.05 = 0.95$$
$$1 - 0.20 = 0.80$$
$$1 - 0.25 = 0.75$$

The product of the complements is: $0.95 \cdot 0.80 \cdot 0.75 = 0.57$

The net price is: $\$510.00 \cdot 0.57 = \$290.70$

An Invoice Dated 3/1 Lists the Following Terms: 3/15, Net 30. The Total Due for the Invoice Is $2,140.00.

a. Find the cash discount, and by which date the invoice must be paid to earn the discount.

b. Find the dates when the full invoice amount must be paid.

The information: 3/15, net 30, is describing the cash discount rate and terms, as well as the due date of the bill. The discount rate is 3% if the bill is paid within 15 days, and the total amount must be paid between 16 and 30 days from the date of the bill.

a. The discount is the discount rate times the total due for the invoice: $\$2{,}140.00 \cdot 0.03 = \$64.20$. To earn the discount, the bill must be paid by 3/16.

b. The total amount must be paid if the bill is paid between days 16 and 30 of the date on the bill. From 3/17 to 3/31, $2,140.00 must be paid.

An Invoice Provides the Information Below

Dated: 8/10, as of 8/15

Terms: 6/5, 4/15

Invoice Total: $580.00

Find the Discounted Balances and Due Dates for Each of the Terms.

The due dates will be calculated from the "as of" date, 8/15.

Term 6/5: 6% discount to be taken if paid within 5 days. The discounted percent paid is: $1 - 0.06 = 0.94$. The discount amount is: $\$580.00 \cdot 0.94 = \$545.20$. It is due 5 days from the as of date: $15 + 5 = 20$, on 8/20.

Term 4/15: 4% discount to be taken if paid within 15 days. The discounted percent paid is: $1 - 0.04 = 0.96$. The discounted amount is: $\$580.00 \cdot 0.96 = \$556.80$. It is due 15 days from the as of date: $15 + 15 = 30$, on 8/30.

THE FOLLOWING INFORMATION IS PROVIDED ON AN INVOICE:

DATED: 9/1

TERMS: 4/14, 3/21, 2/35, N/42

INVOICE TOTAL: $1,610.00

FIND THE DUE DATE OF EACH TERM, AND THE AMOUNT DUE IF THE INVOICE IS PAID ON 10/1.

Find the due dates of each of the terms, to identify which discount, if any, applies.

Term: 4/14; due date: 14 days from 9/1: $1 + 14 = 15$, 9/15.

Term: 3/21; due date: 21 days from 9/1: $1 + 21 = 22$, 9/22.

Term: 2/35: due date: 35 days from 9/1: $1 + 35 = 36$. The last day of September is 9/30, so the due date is: $36 - 30 = 6$ days from the last day of September, or 10/6.

Term: n/42: due date: 42 days from 9/1: $1 + 42 = 43$. The last day of September is 9/30, so the due date is: $43 - 30 = 13$ days from the last day of September, or 10/13.

The term 2/35 applies, so a 2% discount may be taken. The discounted percent paid will be: $1 - 0.02 = 0.98$. The discounted amount due is: $\$1{,}610.00 \cdot 0.98 = \$1{,}577.80$.

RELATIONSHIP BETWEEN A CASH PRICE, DOWN PAYMENT, AMOUNT FINANCED, INSTALLMENT PAYMENT, AND INSTALLMENT PRICE.

The cash price of an item is the price paid if the item is purchased at one time in full. The installment payment for an item is the incremental amount due for an item being paid over time. A down payment is the cash due up front for an item being paid in installments. The installment price is the total price of an item, including finance charges and the down payment, for paying for the item in installment payments, or incremental payments, over time. The amount financed is the difference between the installment price and cash price. In equations:

amount financed = cash price – down payment

installment price = total of installment payments + down payment

Use the information below to determine the installment price of each item.

a. Item A requires 10 installment payments of $35.00 each, and a down payment of $125.00.

b. Item B requires 24 installment payments of $82.00 each, and a down payment of $300.00.

a. The installment price will be the sum of the payments plus the down payment.

10 payments · $35.00/each = $350.00 in payments

Total installment price: $\$350.00 + \$125.00 = \$475.00$

b. The installment price will be the sum of the payments plus the down payment.

24 payments · $82.00/each = $1,968.00 in payments

Total installment price: $\$1{,}968.00 + \$300.00 = \$2{,}268.00$

THE TOTAL PRICE OF AN ITEM IS $520.00. THERE ARE A TOTAL OF 8 PAYMENTS DUE, AND THE DOWN PAYMENT IS $130.00. FIND THE INSTALLMENT PAYMENT AMOUNT FOR THE ITEM.

To find the installment payment amount, first find the total amount paid in the installment payments. The amount paid installments is the total installment price less the down payment: $\$520.00 - \$130.00 = \$390.00$. To find the installment payment, divide the total amount paid in payments by the number of payments: $\$390.00 \div 8 = \$48.75$.

THE CASH PRICE OF AN ITEM IS $74.00, AND THE FINANCE CHARGE IS $6.00. THERE ARE 5 INSTALLMENT PAYMENTS DUE, AND $25.00 DOWN. FIND THE INSTALLMENT PAYMENT AMOUNT.

To find the installment payment amount, first find the installment price. The installment price is the cash price plus the finance charge: $\$74.00 + \$6.00 = \$80.00$. Next, find the amount paid in installments, by subtracting the down payment from the installment price: $\$80.00 - \$25.00 = \$55.00$. Find the installment payment amount by dividing this amount by the number of payments: $\$55.00 \div 5 = \$11.00$.

RELATIONSHIP BETWEEN COST, MARKUP, AND SELLING PRICE, WHERE MARKUP IS ON COST

The cost is the amount a business pays for an item. The selling price is the amount the business charges a consumer to purchase the item. The difference between the business's cost and selling price is the markup. Markup based on cost is expressed as a percentage, where the cost is 100%, markup is a rate or percentage of the cost, and the selling price is the sum of the two percentages. For example, if the cost of an item is $100.00, and the markup is 20%, the selling price can be determined as follows

Markup: $0.20 \cdot \text{cost} = 0.20 \cdot \$100.00 = 20.00$

Selling price: $\$100.00 + \$20.00 = \$120.00$

Selling price is $120.00, or $100\% + 20\% = 120\%$ of cost.

Use information about cost, markup, and selling price to solve the following problems. Markup is on cost.

a. The cost is $20.00, and the selling price is $25.00. Find the percent of markup.

b. The cost is $84.00, and the markup is 30%. Find the selling price.

a. The markup is the percent increase from the cost to the selling price, based on the cost. First, find the difference between the selling price and the cost.
Selling price – cost = $\$25.00 - \$20.00 = \$5.00$
Next, find the markup as a percent of the cost: $\frac{\text{Markup}}{\text{Cost}} = \frac{5}{20} = 0.25 = 25\%$
b. The dollar amount of markup is the cost times the markup percentage.
Cost · markup percentage = $\$84.00 \cdot 0.30 = \$25.20$
The selling price is the cost plus the markup dollar amount.
Cost + markup = $\$84.00 + \$25.20 = \$109.20$

Find the cost and selling price for items with the following markup rate and dollar value. Markup is on cost.

a. Markup rate: 40%; markup: \$124.80

b. Markup rate: 55%; markup: \$4.40

The markup is a percentage of the cost. Solve for the cost using the given rate and dollar amounts. Cost · markup rate = markup, and therefore cost= $\frac{\text{Markup}}{\text{Markup Rate}}$. The selling price will be the cost plus the markup, or cost + markup = selling price.

a. cost= $\frac{\text{Markup}}{\text{Markup Rate}} = \frac{\$124.80}{0.40} = \$312.00$
Selling price = cost + markup = $\$312.00 + \$124.80 = \$436.80$
b. cost= $\frac{\text{Markup}}{\text{Markup Rate}} = \frac{\$4.40}{0.55} = \$8.00$
Selling price = cost + markup = $\$8.00 + \$4.40 = \$12.40$

Difference Between Markup Based on Cost and Markup as a Percent of Selling Price

Markup based on cost can be expressed as a percentage of the cost of an item. If markup is a percentage of selling price, selling price is expressed at 100%, and the cost and markup are each a percentage portion of the selling price.

For example, the cost of an item is \$10.00, and the markup is \$4.00, and the selling price is \$14.00. The markup based on cost is: $\frac{\text{markup}}{\text{cost}} = \frac{4}{10} = 0.40 = 40\%$. The markup based on selling price is: $\frac{\text{markup}}{\text{selling price}} = \frac{4}{14} = .286 = 28.6\%$.

Solve the following

a. Cost: \$38.00; markup: \$12.00. Find the selling price and the percent of markup on selling price.

b. Markup: \$30.00; percent of markup on selling price: 37.5%. Find the cost and the selling price.

a. The selling price is the sum of the cost and markup: $\$38.00 + \$12.00 = \$50.00$.
The percent of markup on selling price is the markup divided by the selling price, expressed as a percent: $\frac{\text{markup}}{\text{selling price}} = \frac{12}{50} = 0.24 = 24\%$

b. Use the information to find the selling price. Set up a fraction relating the selling price, markup, and markup percentage of selling price: $\frac{\text{markup}}{\text{selling price}}$ =percent markup, and $\frac{\text{markup}}{\text{percent markup}}$ =selling price. Thus selling price = $\frac{\$30.00}{0.375} = \$80.00$. The cost will be the difference between the selling price and the markup: $\$80.00 - \$30.00 = \$50.00$.

Markdown of a Selling Price

A markdown of a selling price is a reduction of the selling price to a new reduced sale price. As dollar amounts: selling price – markdown = reduced price. Markdown can also be expressed as a percentage of the selling price: $\frac{\text{markdown}}{\text{selling price}}$ = percent markdown.

For example, if the selling price of an item is \$100.00, and a 10% markdown is taken, the amount of the markdown can be found by determining 10% of \$100: $\$100.00 \cdot 0.10 = \$10.00$. The new reduced price will be the selling price minus the markdown: $\$100.00 - \$90.00 = \$10.00$.

Another way to use the given markdown percentage is to identify the reduced price as a percentage of the selling price. The reduced price percentage of the selling price will be the complement of the markdown percentage: reduced price percentage = 1 – markdown percentage.

To use the given information, that a 10% markdown was made on a \$100.00 item, first find the complement of 10%: $1 - 0.10 = 0.90$. The reduced price will equal this percentage times the selling price: $\$100.00 \cdot 0.90 = \$90.00$.

Use the given information to solve each problem

a. The selling price of a sofa is \$810.00. A markdown of 8% is offered. Find the markdown amount and the reduced price.

b. A computer is marked down by 15% for a markdown amount of \$187.50. Determine the selling price and the reduced price of the computer.

a. The markdown amount is the markdown percent times the selling price: $\$810.00 \cdot 0.08 = \$64.80$. One way of determining the reduced price is to subtract the markdown amount from the selling price: $\$810.00 - \$64.80 = \$745.20$.

b. Use the percentage and markdown amount to find the selling price. The markdown percentage times the selling price is the markdown amount. Solve for selling price, therefore selling price is the markdown divided by the markdown percent: $\frac{\$187.50}{0.15} = \$1{,}250.00$. The reduced price can be found by subtracting the markdown from the selling price: $\$1{,}250.00 - \$187.50 = \$1{,}062.50$.

Four Main Components of Determining Income Tax Responsibility

1. Find adjusted gross income.
2. Find taxable income.
3. Determine tax due.
4. Identify if taxes are owed or if a refund is due.

Adjusted Gross Income

Adjusted gross income (AGI) is the sum of income, such as wages, tips, interest, dividends, etc., minus certain adjustments, such as IRA (individual retirement account) contributions and alimony payments. For example, if an individual has a W-2 indicating that \$34,200 was made in income, but \$2,310 was deposited into an IRA, the AGI would be: $\$34{,}200 - \$2{,}310 = \$31{,}890$.

Taxable Income

Taxable income is the AGI less either the standard deduction or itemized deductions, whichever is greater. The standard deduction is based on the filing status of the individual, with additional standard deductions available. The filing statuses are single, married filing jointly or qualifying widow, married filing separately, and head of household. Also subtract any deductions for exemptions, with 1 exemption for the individual (or one each for married individual filing jointly) and 1 each for any dependents. Itemized deductions are deductions that can be made for items such as medical expenses, charitable contributions, qualified real estate interest, taxes other than federal income or gasoline, unreimbursed casualty or theft losses, and other miscellaneous deductions.

Determining Tax Due

The tax due amount is dependent on the taxable income. The percentage of taxable income owed in taxes is dependent on the taxable income amount. There are different income spans which each have different percentages owed in income tax. As the income in the span increases, the percentage of income due in income tax also increases. Use the amount withheld throughout the year and the total amount due to determine if excess was paid or if additional funds are due to the IRS. If the difference: taxes due – taxes withheld is positive, then the difference is owed to the IRS. If the difference is negative, then the difference is owed to the individual as a refund from the IRS.

Determine the number of personal exemptions for each of the following income tax returns. If the deduction per exemption is $3,300, find the total deduction.

a. Mark and Ryan Stevens, married filing jointly, 2 dependents.

b. Bella Lang, single, no dependents.

c. Jonah Case, head of household, 1 dependent.

a. One exemption for each member of the married couple, and one exemption for each dependent, for a total of 4 exemptions. The total deduction is the number of exemptions times the deduction per exemption: $4 \cdot \$3{,}300 = \$13{,}200$.
b. Only one exemption for the individual filing the return, so 1 exemption. The total deduction is: $1 \cdot \$3{,}300 = \$3{,}300$.
c. One exemption for the head of household, and one of the dependent, for a total of 2 exemptions. The total deduction is: $2 \cdot \$3{,}300 = \$6{,}600$.

Gross Earnings vs. Net Pay

Gross earnings are the total funds earned through tips and wages. Before being paid, deductions are often taken from the total funds earned. Common deductions are Social Security, Medicare tax, federal withholding tax, state withholding tax, and other withholdings, such as retirement contributions, union dues, health insurance, life insurance, etc. The difference between the gross earnings and these deductions is the actual pay received, or net pay.

Fixed and Variable Costs

Fixed costs are charges that remain steady over time. For example, a monthly lease is a fixed cost, because each month that the business is in operation, the monthly lease will need to be paid. The amount of the lease will also remain constant (at least for some foreseeable time in the future, as is the case with leases on spaces where a contract is signed keeping the lease amount fixed for a period of time, such as 12 months). A variable cost is a charge that changes over time, such as a business's monthly shipping expenditures. Some months may require more shipping expenses than others, depending on the business demands each month. Often variable costs are tied into the number of units sold or produced, where fixed costs are the same rate regardless of units sold or produced.

Describe the Formula Used to Perform Break-Even Analysis. Include Profit, Units Sold, the Price per Unit, the Variable Costs, and the Fixed Costs, and Describe Methods for Analyzing the Formula.

The formula for break-even analysis is: $P = u(p - v) - F$, where P is the profit, u is the units produced, p is the price of each unit, v is the variable costs per unit, and F is the fixed costs. Another way to write the formula is to consider the profit, P, as zero, since when the profit equals zero, or income equals costs (expenses), a business is breaking even. If the fixed costs, F, are moved to the left side of the equation, the equation to determine the break-even point would be: $F = u(p - v)$. Break-even analysis can also be performed by looking at two separate equations for costs and for income. The equation for costs would include the fixed costs, F, and the variable costs per unit, v, as well as the number of units sold, u. The equation for income would include the price per unit, p, and the number of units sold, u.

$$\text{Total costs} = uv + F$$

$$\text{Total income} = up$$

Use algebraic representations to determine the number of units, *u*, that need to be sold each month to break-even in each of the following scenarios.

a. Company A charges \$15 per unit. The monthly fixed costs are \$3,240, and the variable costs per unit are \$3.

b. Company B charges \$802 per unit. The monthly fixed costs are \$6,560, and the variable costs per unit are \$618.

To determine the number of units that need to be sold to break even, find the value of *u* that makes profit, *P*, equal zero, in the formula: $P = u(p - v) - F$. *F* is the fixed costs, *v* are the variable costs per unit, and *p* is the price of each unit. In each scenario, *F* will be the monthly fixed costs, and *u* will be the number of units to sell each month. If *P* equals zero, the equation can be rewritten as $F = u(p - v)$.: Solve for *u*, since this is the unknown quantity in each scenario: $u(p - v) = F$ thus $u = \frac{F}{(p-v)}$. Replace *F*, *p*, and *v* with the given quantities to solve scenarios above:

a. $u = \frac{F}{(p-v)} = \frac{3240}{(15-3)} = 270$
270 units must be sold by Company A each month to break even.
b. $u = \frac{F}{(p-v)} = \frac{6560}{(802-618)} = 35.65 \approx 36$
Approximately 36 units must be sold by Company B each month to break even.

A Company Projects That It Will Sell 500 Units Next Quarter. The Company's Fixed Quarterly Costs Are \$14,300, and the Variable Costs per Unit Are \$86. Use a Graphical Representation to Identify Which Price Charged per Unit Will Allow Them to Break Even for the Quarter.

Use a pair of equations, one representing costs, and one representing income, to perform a break-even analysis. The first equation for total costs is: total costs = *uv* + *F*, where *u* is the number of units sold, *v* is the variable costs per unit, and *F* is the fixed costs. Since the information is given per quarter, the units sold and fixed costs will be per quarter. The second equation, for total income is: total income = *up*, where *p* is the price per unit, and *u* is the number of units sold. Replace the known quantities for the variables in each equation.

Total costs = $uv + F = (500) \cdot (86) + 14{,}300 = 57{,}300$

The total costs will be a projected fixed amount, since the unit production is projected at a fixed quantity.

Total income = $up = (500) \cdot p = 500p$

Graphing both equations gives:

The intersection of the two equations is the break-even point, or where income equals costs. When *x*, or the price per unit is approximately \$114, the total income will equal the total costs. The price should be greater than \$114 if the company intends to make a profit.

Financial Ratios That Measure the Liquidity of a Firm

The liquidity of a firm is the firm's ability to raise cash quickly without having to sell assets, or the firm's ability to meet current financial obligations using current assets. The current ratio, read as "current assets to current liabilities", is one ratio measuring the liquidity of a firm. A benchmark for an acceptable current ratio is a 2 to 2.1. Current ratio=$\frac{\text{current assets}}{\text{current liabilities}}$.

Another ratio that measures liquidity is the acid-test ratio. While the current ratio, in the current assets, includes inventory, this ratio only includes liquid assets. A benchmark for an acceptable acid-test ratio is 1. Acid-test ratio=$\frac{\text{liquid assets}}{\text{current liabilities}}$.

Ratio of Net Income After Taxes to Average Owners' Equity

The average owners' equity is the sum of the owners' equity at the beginning of the year and the owners' equity at the end of the year, divided by 2. When the net income after taxes is divided by this value, the rate should be higher than the interest paid on savings accounts or other low-risk investments, like government bonds, to indicate that the investment in the company carries higher risk, and consequently higher reward, than other investments.

Find the current ratio and acid-test ratio for Company X using the information from a consolidated statement of income below. Determine if they meet the acceptable benchmarks.

Company X (values in thousands of dollars)

Current assets:

Cash and short-term investments: $87

Accounts receivable and other: $125

Inventory: $210

Current liabilities: $198

Current ratio=$\frac{\text{current assets}}{\text{current liabilities}}$.

Current assets is the sum of the cash and short-term investments, accounts receivable and other, and inventory. Current liabilities are as listed.

$$\text{Current ratio}=\frac{87+125+210}{198}=2.13$$

$$\text{Acid-test ratio}=\frac{\text{liquid assets}}{\text{current liabilities}}.$$

The liquid assets are the current assets less the inventory.

$$\text{Acid-test ratio}=\frac{87+125}{198}=1.07$$

Both ratios slightly exceed the acceptable benchmarks of 2.0 to 2.1 and 1.0, respectively.

Determining the Total Installment Cost, Finance Charge, and Amount Financed of an Installment Loan

The total installment cost of an installment loan is the cost of the amount paid in payments plus the down payment: total installment cost = payment amount · number of payments + down payment. The finance charge is the difference between the total installment amount and the cash price of the item: finance charge = total installment cost – cash price. The amount financed is the difference between the cash price and the down payment: amount financed = cash price – down payment.

Find the total installment cost, finance charge, and amount financed for an installment loan to pay for a dining set. Cash price of dining set: $1,200.00, number of installments: 18, cash down: 20% of cash price. Each installment is $75.00.

The amount financed is the cash price less the down payment. The down payment is 20% of the cash price, or: $\$1{,}200.00 \cdot 0.20 = \$240.00$. Thus amount financed = cash price – down payment = $\$1{,}200.0 - \$240.00 = \$960.00$. The total installment cost is: payment amount · number of payments + down payment = $\$75.00 \cdot 18 + \$240.00 = \$1{,}590.00$. The finance charge is the difference between paying the cash price and paying the installments: $\$1{,}590.00 - \$1{,}200.00 = \$390.00$.

Calculating the approximate annual percentage rate (APR) for a loan paid in monthly payments

To calculate the approximate APR for a loan, first determine the finance charge (by using the formula: finance charge = total installment cost – cash price) and next determined the amount financed (by using the formula: amount financed = cash price – down payment). Using these two quantities, and the total number of payments, calculate the approximate APR as follows:

$$\text{Approximate APR}=\frac{24\cdot\text{finance charge}}{\text{amount financed}\cdot(1+\text{number of payments})}$$

Find the total installment cost, finance charge, amount financed, and approximate APR for an installment loan to pay for a used car. The cash price is $4,800.00. The down payment is 15% of the cash price. The loan is paid in 36 installments, at $135.00 each.

The down payment is 15% of the cash price: $\$4{,}800.00 \cdot 0.15 = \$720.00$.

Thus the amount financed = cash price – down payment = $\$4{,}800.00 - \$720.00 = \$4{,}080.00$. Total installment cost = payment amount · number of payments + down payment = $\$135.00 \cdot 36 + \$720.00 = \$5{,}580.00$. Finance charge = total installment cost – cash price = $\$5{,}580.00 - \$4{,}800.00 = \$780.00$. Therefore the approximate APR is

$$\frac{24\cdot\text{finance charge}}{\text{amount financed}\cdot(1+\text{number of payments})}=\frac{24\cdot 780}{4080(1+36)}=0.124=12.4\%$$

To pay for a new home, the Fosters borrow $210,000 at 6.0% for 30 years, with a monthly payment of $1,260.00. Using simple interest calculations, find the amount paid towards principal and the amount paid towards interest after the first month's payment.

Using a simple interest calculation, the interest, I, is: $I = PRT$, where P is the principal, R, is the interest rate, and T is the time in years. The principal is the amount borrowed, \$210,000, the R is the interest rate, 6.0% = 0.06, and T is $\frac{1}{12}$. $I = PRT = 210{,}000(.06)\left(\frac{1}{12}\right) = \$1{,}050.00$. Find the amount the payment reduces the principal by deducting the first month's interest from the first month's payment: $\$1{,}260.00 - \$1{,}050.00 = \$210.00$. The principal remaining is the original principal less the principal paid after the first month: $\$210{,}000.00 - \$210.00 = \$209{,}790.00$. After the first month, \$1,050.00 is paid towards interest, and \$209,790.00 of the principal remains.

PROMISSORY NOTE

A promissory note is an item where a maker of the note, or borrower, promises to repay money to the bearer of the note (lender) at a specific date. The date is called the maturity date or due date of the promissory note. The amount written on the note is the face value of the note, or principal of the loan. If the note is interest bearing, the maturity value of the note will equal the principal plus the interest due at the maturity date.

THE TABLE BELOW SHOWS THE NUMBER OF ITEMS PURCHASED BY 20 CUSTOMERS AT A RETAIL STORE

Customer	Number of Items Purchased
1	3
2	2
3	5
4	8
5	1
6	4
7	6
8	1
9	5
10	4
11	1
12	3
13	1
14	2
15	2
16	1
17	2
18	3
19	1
20	3

Create a frequency distribution of the data.

In a frequency distribution, list the range of number of items purchased. Here, the range is from 1 to 8 items. Then identify the number of customers purchasing that many items.

Number of Items Purchased	Frequency
1	6
2	4
3	4
4	2
5	2
6	1
7	0
8	1

A RETAIL STORE TRACKS THE TOTAL PURCHASE AMOUNT OF 30 INDIVIDUAL CUSTOMERS. USE THE FREQUENCY DISTRIBUTION BELOW TO CREATE A FREQUENCY HISTOGRAM OF THE DATA

Purchase amount	Frequency
\$0.00 - \$15.00	7
\$15.01 - \$30.00	2
\$30.01 - \$45.00	3
\$45.01 - \$50.00	9
\$50.01 - \$65.00	6
Over \$65.01	3

The purchase amount ranges will be the labels on the *x*-axis. The frequency will be the quantities on the *y*-axis.

A CUSTOMER SERVICE CENTER TRACKS THE WAIT TIME OF A RANDOM SAMPLE OF CALLERS. THE DATA IS LISTED IN THE FREQUENCY DISTRIBUTION BELOW.

Wait Time (in seconds)	Frequency
0 - 30	18
31 - 60	26
61 - 90	39
91 - 120	42
121 - 150	44
Over 150	31

Create a frequency histogram showing the relationship between the wait time and the relative frequency distribution.

First find the relative frequency of each wait time. Divide the frequency of each wait time divided by the total of the frequencies, or the total number of callers. The total frequency is: $18 + 26 + 39 + 42 + 44 + 31 = 200$.

Wait Time (in seconds)	Relative frequency
0 - 30	$18/200 = 0.09$
31 - 60	$26/200 = 0.13$
61 - 90	$39/200 = 0.195$
91 - 120	$42/200 = 0.21$
121 - 150	$44/200 = 0.22$
Over 150	$31/200 = 0.155$

Create a frequency histogram with the wait times as the labels on the *x*-axis and the relative frequency values in the *y*-axis.

A BUSINESS IDENTIFIES ITS QUARTERLY FIXED COSTS AS LISTED BELOW. CREATE A PIE CHART SHOWING THE DISTRIBUTION OF THE QUARTERLY FIXED COSTS.

Cost	Quarterly amount
Rent	\$18,000
Utilities	\$2,700

Cost	Quarterly amount
Salaries	$34,500
Insurance	$3,180
Other	$1,620

First, identify the percentage of each cost of the total fixed quarterly costs. The sum of the quarterly costs is: $18,000 + $2,700 + $34,500 + $3,180 + $1,620 = $60,000. The percent of each cost is the quarterly amount divided by the total fixed quarterly costs.

Cost	Percent of total quarterly costs
Rent	$18,000/$60,000 = 0.30 = 30%
Utilities	$2,700/$60,000 = 0.045 = 4.5%
Salaries	$34,500/$60,000 = 0.575 = 57.5%
Insurance	$3,180/$60,000 = 0.053 = 5.3%
Other	$1,620/$60,000 = 0.027 = 2.7%

The percentage of each cost will represent the percent of the pie chart that represents that item.

LINE CHART DISPLAYING THE CHANGE IN SALES OVER TIME

Year	Total Sales (in thousands)
2000	$1,040
2001	$905
2002	$1,129
2003	$1,350
2004	$1,508
2005	$1,490
2006	$1,758
2007	$2,003
2008	$1,800
2009	$1,720
2010	$1,880

Create a graph with the years as the values in the x-axis, and the total sales amounts in the y-axis. Each point on the graph will be of the form (year, total sales). The points will be connected to show the change in sales over time.

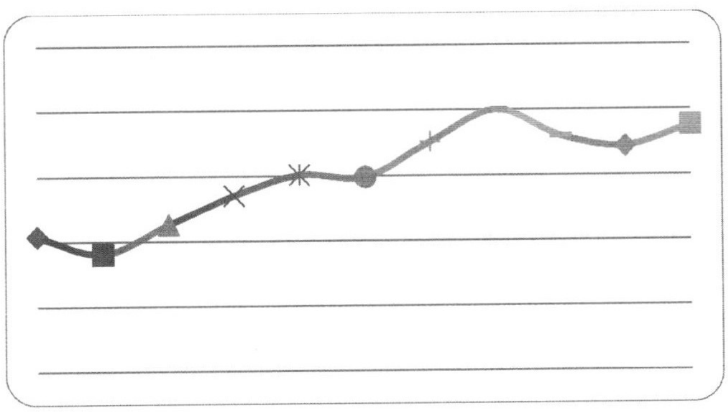

COMPARING TWO GRAPHS CAN BE MISLEADING

In order to properly compare two graphical representations, the scales and the ranges on both the x- and y-axes should be identical. Otherwise, the shape of the graphs could be misleading. For example, it could appear that one graph grows at a faster rate, or is steeper, than another, when the scales of the two graphs are not the same.

Convert the following units to meters

a. 35 mm

b. 218 cm

c. 0.35 km

Identify the relationship between each of the given units and the desired units, meters. Use this to create a ratio relating the two units. The given units should be in the denominator of the ratio, and the desired units in the numerator. Multiply the given units by the ratio to convert to the desired units.

a. 1 m = 1,000 mm, therefore 35 mm$\cdot\frac{1\text{ m}}{1000\text{ mm}}$ = 0.035 m

b. 1 m = 100 cm, therefore 218$\cdot\frac{1\text{ m}}{100\text{ cm}}$ = 2.18 m.

c. 1000 m = 1 km, therefore 0.35 km$\cdot\frac{1000\text{ m}}{1\text{ km}}$ = 350 m.

Convert each of the given units to feet

a. 52 inches

b. 0.4 yards

c. 0.08 miles

Identify the relationship between each of the given units and the desired units, feet. Use this to create a ratio relating the two units. The given units should be in the denominator of the ratio, and the desired units in the numerator. Multiply the given units by the ratio to convert to the desired units.

a. There are 12 inches in 1 foot, therefore 52 in $\cdot\frac{1\text{ ft}}{12\text{ in}}$ = 4.33 ft.

b. There are 3 feet in 1 yard, therefore 0.4 yd $\cdot\frac{3\text{ ft}}{1\text{ yd}}$ = 1.2 ft.

c. There are 5,280 feet in 1 mile, therefore 0.08 mi $\cdot\frac{5280\text{ ft}}{1\text{ mi}}$ = 422.4 ft.

GIVEN 1 METER = 3.281 FEET, CONVERT 13 INCHES TO METERS

The ratio of meters to feet is given as $\frac{1\text{ m}}{3.281\text{ ft}}$. The ratio of feet to inches is $\frac{1\text{ ft}}{12\text{ in}}$. Therefore 13 in = $\frac{1\text{ ft}}{12\text{ in}}\cdot\frac{1\text{ m}}{3.281\text{ ft}}$ = 0.33 m.

GIVEN 1 METER = 3.281 FEET, CONVERT 19 KM TO MILES

The ratio of meters to feet is given as $\frac{1\text{ m}}{3.281\text{ ft}}$. The ratio of feet to miles is $\frac{5280\text{ ft}}{1\text{ mi}}$. There are 1,000 meters in 1 km. Therefore 19 km = $\frac{1000\text{ m}}{1\text{ km}}\cdot\frac{3.281\text{ ft}}{1\text{ m}}\cdot\frac{1\text{ mi}}{5280\text{ ft}}$ = 11.81 mi.

Price/earnings (p/e) ratio

The price/earnings ratio, or p/e ratio, is a measure of the company's profits versus the current market price. The p/e ratio is calculated by finding the ratio of the current market price of the stock to the earnings per share, or EPS: $p/e = \frac{\text{current market price per share}}{\text{EPS}}$. The EPS is a reflection on the profitability of the company, and the EPS for a period can be found as: EPS = $\frac{\text{net income}}{\text{outstanding shares}}$. In general, a higher p/e ratio indicates that higher future earnings growth is expected, as compared to a similar company in a similar industry with a lower p/e ratio.

DIVIDEND YIELD RATIO

The dividend yield ratio measures the dividend earned by investors. It only measures the income from dividends, or the portion of a company's earnings distributed per share to shareholders, and not the income from any increase in share price. It also doesn't take into account any broker commission fees to purchase the stock. The dividend yield ratio is $\frac{\text{dividend per share}}{\text{market price per share}}$.

Find the dividend yield for each of the situations below.

a. Sixty shares of stock are purchased at $92.00 a share. The total commission fee paid to a broker is $35.00. The annual dividend of the stock is $3.15.

b. One hundred forty shares of stock are purchased at $6.25 a share. The total commission fee paid to a broker is $42.00. The annual dividend of the stock is $0.80.

The dividend yield can be found by dividing the total annual dividends divided by the total cost of the stock, including the broker fee or commission.

a. The total cost of the stock is the cost of the shares plus the broker fee: (60 shares · $92.00 per share) + $35.00 fee = $5,555.00. The annual dividends from the stock are the annual dividends per stock multiplied by the number of shares held: 60 shares · $3.15 dividend per share = $189.00. Therefore the dividend yield is: $\frac{\text{annual dividends}}{\text{total cost of stock}} = \frac{\$189.00}{\$5,555.00} = 0.034 = 3.4\%$

b. The total cost of the stock is: $(140\ shares\ \cdot\ \$6.25\ per\ share)\ +\ \$42.00\ fee\ =\ \$917.00$. The annual dividends from the stock are: $0.80 per share · 140 shares = $112.00. Therefore the dividend yield is: $\frac{\text{annual dividends}}{\text{total cost of stock}} = \frac{\$112.00}{\$912.00} = 0.122 = 12.2\%$

ROI

The return on investment, or ROI, is a percentage of return based on the capital invested, and measures the rate of return so that different investments with different capital investments and returns can be compared. To calculate the ROI, evaluate the formula ROI = $\frac{\text{return(gain)from investment-capital investment}}{\text{capital investment}}$.

For example, if the capital investment of a stock is $100, and the yield of the investment after a year is $105, then ROI = $\frac{105\text{-}100}{100} = 0.05 = 5\%$

Find the ROI for each of the stocks below.

a. Capital investment: $2,050.00; Gain from investment: $2,310.00.

b. Capital investment: $860.00; Gain from investment: $1,020.00.

c. Capital investment: $10,700.00; Gain from investment: $11,140.00.

a. ROI = $\frac{\text{return(gain)from investment-capital investment}}{\text{capital investment}} = \frac{2310-2050}{2050} = 0.127 = 12.7\%$

b. ROI = $\frac{\text{return(gain)from investment-capital investment}}{\text{capital investment}} = \frac{1020-860}{860} = 0.186 = 18.6\%$

c. ROI = $\frac{\text{return(gain)from investment-capital investment}}{\text{capital investment}} = \frac{11,140-10,700}{10,700} = 0.041 = 4.1\%$

Inventory Turnover

Inventory turnover is a measure of the efficiency of a company. Holding inventory ties up cash (or bank loans). Having excess inventory of a product may result in having to sell the product at a reduced price to unload the inventory to free up cash and selling space for a new product. Inventory turnover measures the number of times a retailer's average turnover is turned over, or sold, in a year. A retailer with a lower turnover may be poorly managed or having difficulty selling goods. The inventory turnover of a retailer of non-perishable goods will be much lower than the inventory turnover of a retailer of perishable goods. There are two measures of inventory turnover; turnover at retail, based on the retail price, and turnover at cost, based on the cost of goods to the retailer:

$$\text{Turnover at retail} = \frac{\text{retail sales}}{\text{average inventory at retail}}$$

$$\text{Turnover at cost} = \frac{\text{cost of goods sold}}{\text{average inventory at cost}}$$

Theoretically, the two measures should be equal, but shrinkage (loss of merchandise due to theft, markdowns, or unsalable merchandise) causes the turnover at cost to typically be higher than the turnover at retail.

Find the inventory turnover at retail and inventory turnover at cost for the following scenario. Autoparts Plus sells auto parts. Retail sales over the past quarter was $38,830, and the average retail inventory is $4,010. Autoparts Plus uses a markup of 35% on selling price. The cost of goods sold was $25,429.00.

The turnover at retail can be calculated with the retail sales and the average retail inventory. Turnover at retail $= \frac{\text{retail sales}}{\text{average inventory at retail}} = \frac{38{,}830}{4010} = 9.68$. Over the quarter, the inventory was turned over approximately 9.68 times. The turnover at cost can be calculated with the cost of goods sold and the average inventory at cost. The average inventory at cost can be calculated using the markup information. The cost of goods sold would be $1 - 0.35 = 0.65$ of the retail price, or $\$4{,}010 \cdot 0.65 = \$2{,}606.50$. Turnover at cost $= \frac{\text{cost of goods sold}}{\text{average inventory at cost}} = \frac{25{,}429}{2606.50} = 9.76$

High Inventory Turnover

Benefits

High inventory turnover may indicate that the needs of the customers are being readily met by the products offered. Less capital is tied up in investing in the inventory, because it is quickly being turned into a profit. Less costs are being allocated to storage space and other funds related to holding inventory until it can be distributed and sold. If products are being sold quickly, there is less need to discount the products to move merchandise out of inventory.

Problems

High inventory turnover may indicate that not all demand is being met. There may be additional goods to be sold, but because inventory isn't readily available to consumers, it is not being sold. Customers could be dissatisfied with the retail establishment if desired products are frequently unavailable.

FIND THE MATURITY VALUE OF THE INTEREST-BEARING ACCOUNTS BELOW. THE PRINCIPAL INVESTMENT IN THE ACCOUNTS IS $150,000. ACCOUNT B EARNS INTEREST COMPOUNDED ANNUALLY AT A RATE OF 2.0%, AND THE FUNDS ARE INVESTED FOR 8 YEARS.

To find the maturity value of an account with compound interest, use the formula: $M = P(1 + i)^n$, where P is the principal invested, i is the interest rate per compounding period, and n is the total number of compounding periods. Account B has annual compound interest, so the number of compounding periods will be the time in years. The interest rate per compounding period is equal to the annual interest rate. The funds in the account will have a maturity value of: $M = P(1 + i)^n = 150{,}000(1 + 0.02)^8 = \$175{,}748.91$

Find the maturity value of a fund with a principal investment of $20,000, invested for 4 years, with an annual interest rate of 1.5%, in each of the following accounts:

a. Account B compounds interest semiannually.

b. Account C compounds interest quarterly.

To find the maturity value of an account with compound interest, use the formula: $M = P(1 + i)^n$, where P is the principal invested, i is the interest rate per compounding period, and n is the total number of compounding periods. For each of the accounts, P = $20,000 and the annual interest rate is 1.5%.

a. The interest in Account B is compounded semiannually, or twice a year. The number of compounding periods will equal twice the number of years, or: $4 \cdot 2 = 8$. The interest rate per compounding period will equal the annual interest rate, 1.5%, divided by 2: $0.015 \div 2 = 0.0075$. $M = P(1 + i)^n = 20{,}000(1 + 0.0075)^8 = \$21{,}231.98$.

b. The interest in Account C is compounded quarterly, or four times a year. The number of compounding periods will equal four times the number of years, or: $4 \cdot 4 = 16$. The interest rate per compounding period will equal the annual interest rate, 1.5%, divided by 4: $0.015 \div 4 = 0.00375$. $M = P(1 + i)^n = 20{,}000(1 + 0.00375)^{16} = \$21{,}234.35$

A SERIES DISCOUNT OF 10/20/10 IS GIVEN ON AN ITEM WITH A NET PRICE OF $55.08. FIND THE LIST PRICE OF THE ITEM.

To find the list price of an item, first find the complement of each percent in the series discount. The product of the complements is the percent of the list price paid, or net cost. If given the percent and net cost, the list price can be found by solving the equation for the list price:

Net price = list price ·percent of list price paid, thus list price = $\frac{\text{net price}}{\text{percent of list price paid}}$.

Find the percent of the list price paid by finding the product of the complements of the series discounts.

$$1 - 0.10 = 0.90$$
$$1 - 0.20 = 0.80$$
$$1 - 0.10 = 0.90$$

Percent of list price paid: $0.90 \cdot 0.80 \cdot 0.90 = 0.648$. Therefore list price = $\frac{\text{net price}}{\text{percent of list price paid}} = \frac{55.08}{0.648} = \$85.00$.

An invoice provides the information below.

Dated: 8/10, as of 8/15.
Terms: 2/30, n/60.
Invoice total: $580.00

Find the discounted balances and due dates for each of the terms.

The due dates will be calculated from the "as of" date, 8/15.

Term 2/30: 2% discount to be taken if paid within 15 days. The discounted percent paid is: $1 - 0.02 = 0.98$. The discounted amount is: $\$580.00 \cdot 0.98 = \$568.40$. It is due 30 days from the as of date: $15 + 30 = 45$. There are 31 days in August. The difference between the last day of August and the due date is: $45 - 31 = 14$. The due date is 14 days from the last day of August, or 9/14.

Term n/60: The net amount, or invoice total, is due 60 days from the as of date, 8/15: $15 + 60 = 75$. There are 31 days in August. The difference between the last day of August and the due date is: $75 - 31 = 44$. There are 30 days in September. The difference between the last day of September and the due date is: $44 - 30 = 14$. The due date is 14 days from the last day of September, or 10/14.

Open-End Credit

Open-end credit, unlike an installment loan, has no regular monthly payments. A credit amount, usually identified as the credit limit, is extended to a consumer, and up to this amount may be spent in all or in part. Consumers then pay towards the credit used. Additional credit is typically available before the credit used is paid. An interest rate is charged on credit used while it is being paid off.

Use information about cost, markup, and selling price to solve the following problem. Markup is on cost. The markup is 18%, and the selling price is $300.40. Find the cost.

The selling price is cost plus the markup dollar amount. In percentage, the selling price is 100% (the cost) + the markup, which equals: $100\% + 18\% = 118\%$. This percentage times the cost equals the selling price: $118\% \cdot \text{cost} = \text{selling price}$. To find the cost, divide the selling price by 118%: $\frac{\$300.40}{1.18} = \$254.58$.

Financial Mathematics

Annuity

An annuity is a series of equal payments occurring at equal periods of time.

An ordinary annuity occurs when the cash flow is at the end of a period. When unspecified, the term "annuity" refers to ordinary annuity.

An annuity due occurs when the cash flow is at the beginning of the period, such as a rent payment.

Present Value

The present value of an annuity is the current value of a stream of money paid or received in equal amounts over future periods. The present value of an annuity can be calculated using the following formula: $PV = PMT\frac{[1-(1+i)^{-n}]}{i}$

where:

PV = Present Value

PMT = Payment (annuity amount)

i = interest rate

n = number of periods

Amortization

Amortization is the gradual reduction of the book value of an asset and represents the usage and obsolescence of the asset. Amortization is a way to spread the assets costs over its useful life. In addition, since amortization is an expense, it reduces a firm's taxable income. Amortization is similar to depreciation, but amortization typically refers to intangible assets, such as goodwill, patents, or copyrights, while depreciation refers to tangible assets.

Future Value

The Future Value is the equivalent amount of present cash flows at some time in the future. The future value of a present amount is found using the following formula: $FV = PV\,(1 + i)^n$

where:

FV = Future Value

PV = Present Value

i = interest rate

n = number of periods

If you invest $1000 today at an annual interest rate of 4%, calculate the future value of your investment in 20 years.

1. First, define your known variables:

PV = $1000

i= 4% = 0.04

n = 20

2. Next, choose the appropriate formula: $FV = PV\,(1 + i)^n$

3. Finally, calculate the result: $FV = 1000\,(1 + 0.04)^{20} = 2191$

The future value of the investment is $2,191.

APR

The Annual Percentage Rate, or APR, is the annual interest rate plus the added costs of a loan or investment. Examples of extra costs added to the interest rate include application fees, processing fees, and closing costs. When borrowing money, the APR represents the cost of the loan. When using APR in calculations, remember it represents an annual rate. In order to use the future value, present value, and annuity formulas, the period must match the compounding of the interest rate.

Effective Annual Rate

The Effective Annual Rate expresses a loan or investment's interest rate when compounding occurs more frequently than once per year. The following formula is used to calculate the effective annual rate:

$$EAR = \left(1 + \frac{i}{n}\right)^n - 1$$

where:

EAR = Effective Annual Rate

i = annual interest rate

n = number of compounding period

DSST Practice Test

Want to take this practice test in an online interactive format?
Check out the online resources page, which includes interactive practice questions and much more: **mometrix.com/resources719/dsstbusmath**

1. Determine the number of diagonals of a dodecagon.

a. 12
b. 24
c. 54
d. 108

2. A circular bracelet contains 5 charms, A, B, C, D, and E, attached at specific points around the bracelet, with the clasp located between charms A and B. The bracelet is unclasped and stretched out into a straight line. On the resulting linear bracelet, charm C is between charms A and B, charm D is between charms A and C, and charm E is between charms C and D. Which of these statements is (are) necessarily true?

I. The distance between charms B and E is greater than the distance between charms A and D.
II. Charm E is between charms B and D.
III. The distance between charms D and E is less than the distance of bracelet between charms A and C.

a. I, II, and III
b. II and III
c. II only
d. None of these is necessarily true.

3. In a town of 35,638 people, about a quarter of the population is under the age of 35. Of those, just over a third attend local K-12 schools. If the number of students in each grade is about the same, how many fourth graders likely reside in the town?

a. Fewer than 100
b. Between 200 and 300
c. Between 300 and 400
d. More than 400

4. Identical rugs are offered for sale at two local shops and one online retailer, designated Stores A, B, and C, respectively. The rug's regular sales price is $296 at Store A, $220 at Store B, and $198.00 at Store C. Stores A and B collect 8% in sales tax on any after-discount price, while Store C collects no tax but charges a $35 shipping fee. A buyer has a 30% off coupon for Store A and a $10 off coupon for Store B. Which of these lists the stores in order of lowest to highest final sales price after all discounts, taxes, and fees are applied?

a. Store A, Store B, Store C
b. Store B, Store A, Store C
c. Store B, Store C, Store A
d. Store C, Store A, Store B

5. Two companies offer monthly cell phone plans, both of which include free text messaging. Company A charges a $25 monthly fee plus five cents per minute of phone conversation, while Company B charges a $50 monthly fee and offers unlimited calling. Both companies charge the same amount when the total duration of monthly calls is

a. 500 hours.
b. 8 hours and 33 minutes.
c. 8 hours and 20 minutes.
d. 5 hours.

6. A dress is marked down by 20% and placed on a clearance rack, on which is posted a sign reading, "Take an extra 25% off already reduced merchandise." What fraction of the original price is the final sale price of the dress?

a. $\frac{1}{4}$
b. $\frac{2}{5}$
c. $\frac{3}{5}$
d. $\frac{9}{20}$

7. On a floor plan drawn at a scale of 1:100, the area of a rectangular room is 30 cm^2. What is the actual area of the room?

a. 30,000 cm^2
b. 3,000 cm^2
c. 3,000 m^2
d. 30 m^2

8. The ratio of employee wages and benefits to all other operational costs of a business is 2:3. If a business's total expenses are $130,000 per month, how much money does the company spend on employee wages and benefits?

a. $43,333.33
b. $86,666.67
c. $52,000.00
d. $78,000.00

9. The path of ball thrown into the air is modeled by the first quadrant graph of the equation $h = -16t^2 + 64t + 5$, where h is the height of the ball in feet and t is time in seconds after the ball is thrown. What is the average rate of change in the ball's height with respect to time over the interval [1, 3]?

a. 0 feet/second
b. 48 feet/second
c. 53 feet/second
d. 96 feet/second

10. Zeke drove from his house to a furniture store in Atlanta and then back home along the same route. It took Zeke three hours to drive to the store. By driving an average of 20 mph faster on his return trip, Zeke was able to save an hour of diving time. What was Zeke's average driving speed on his round trip?

a. 24 mph
b. 48 mph
c. 50 mph
d. 60 mph

11. Aaron goes on a run every morning down the straight country road that he lives on. The graph below shows Aaron's distance from home at times throughout his morning run. Which of the following statements is (are) true?

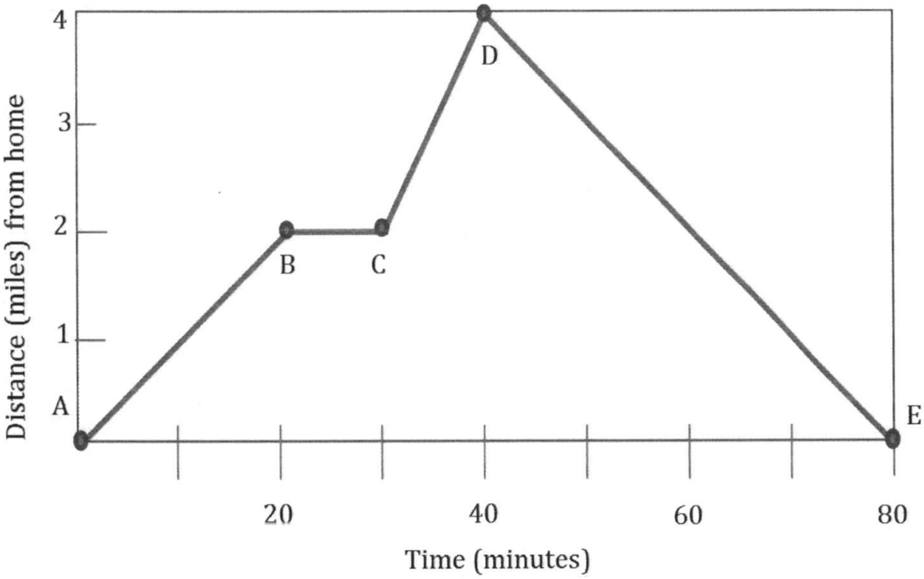

I. Aaron's average running speed was 6 mph.
II. Aaron's running speed from point A to point B was the same as his running speed from point D to E.
III. Aaron ran a total distance of four miles.

a. I only
b. II only
c. I and II
d. I, II, and III

12. Use the operation table to determine $(a * b) * (c * d)$.

$*$	a	b	c	d
a	d	a	b	c
b	a	b	c	d
c	b	c	d	a
d	c	d	a	b

a. a
b. b
c. c
d. d

13. Complete the analogy.

x^3 is to $\sqrt[3]{y}$ as ...

a. $x + a$ is to $x - y$.
b. e^x is to $ln\, y, y > 0$.
c. $\frac{1}{x}$ is to $y, x, y \neq 0$.
d. $sin\, x$ is to $cos\, y$.

14. Which of these statements is (are) true for deductive reasoning?

I. A general conclusion is drawn from specific instances.
II. If the premises are true and proper reasoning is applied, the conclusion must be true.

a. Statement I is true
b. Statement II is true
c. Both statements are true
d. Neither statement is true

15. Given that premises "all *a* are *b*," "all *b* are *d*," and "no *b* are *c*" are true and that premise "all *b* are *e*" is false, determine the validity and soundness of the following arguments:

Argument I: All a are b. No b are c. Therefore, no a are c.
Argument II: All a are b. All d are b. Therefore, all d are a.
Argument III: All a are b. All b are e. Therefore, all a are e.

a.

	Invalid	Valid	Sound
Argument I		X	X
Argument II	X		
Argument III		X	

b.

	Invalid	Valid	Sound
Argument I	X		
Argument II		X	X
Argument III	X		

c.

	Invalid	Valid	Sound
Argument I		X	X
Argument II		X	X
Argument III	X		

d.

	Invalid	Valid	Sound
Argument I		X	X
Argument II	X		
Argument III	X		

16. If $p \rightarrow q$ is true, which of these is also necessarily true?

a. $q \rightarrow p$
b. $\sim p \rightarrow \sim q$
c. $\sim q \rightarrow \sim p$
d. None of these

17. Given statements p and q, which of the following is the truth table for the statement $q \leftrightarrow \sim(p \wedge q)$?

a.

p	q	$q \leftrightarrow \sim(p \wedge q)$
T	T	F
T	F	T
F	T	T
F	F	T

b.

p	q	$q \leftrightarrow \sim(p \wedge q)$
T	T	T
T	F	T
F	T	T
F	F	F

c.

p	q	$q \leftrightarrow \sim(p \wedge q)$
T	T	F
T	F	F
F	T	F
F	F	T

d.

p	q	$q \leftrightarrow \sim(p \wedge q)$
T	T	F
T	F	F
F	T	T
F	F	F

18. Which of the following is the truth table for logic circuit shown below?

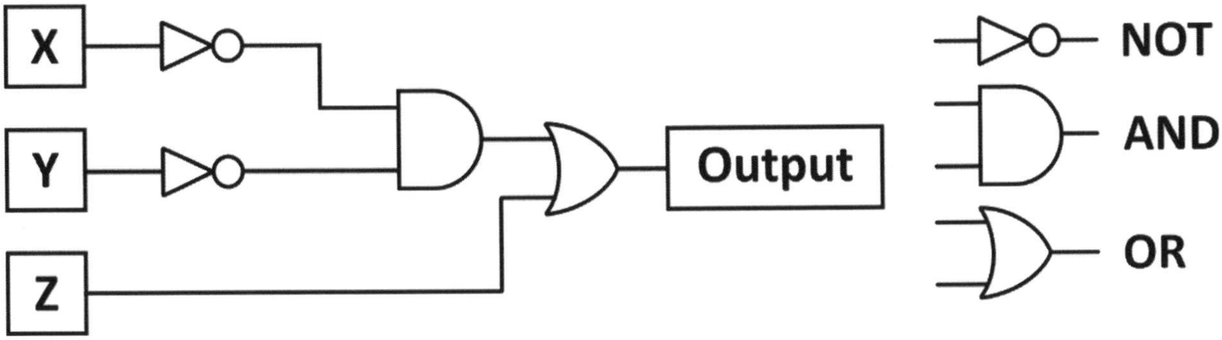

a.

X	Y	Z	Output
0	0	0	1
0	0	1	0
0	1	0	0
0	1	1	0
1	0	0	0
1	0	1	0
1	1	0	0
1	1	1	1

b.

X	Y	Z	Output
0	0	0	0
0	0	1	1
0	1	0	1
0	1	1	1
1	0	0	1
1	0	1	1
1	1	0	1
1	1	1	1

c.

X	Y	Z	Output
0	0	0	0
0	0	1	0
0	1	0	0
0	1	1	1
1	0	0	1
1	0	1	1
1	1	0	1
1	1	1	0

d.

X	Y	Z	Output
0	0	0	0
0	0	1	0
0	1	0	0
0	1	1	0
1	0	0	1
1	0	1	1
1	1	0	1
1	1	1	0

19. Which of these is a major contribution of the Babylonian civilization to the historical development of mathematics?

a. The division of an hour into 60 minutes, and a minute into 60 seconds, and a circle into 360 degrees
b. The development of algebra as a discipline separate from geometry
c. The use of deductive reasoning in geometric proofs
d. The introduction of Boolean logic and algebra

20. Which mathematician is responsible for what is often called the most remarkable and beautiful mathematical formula, $e^{i\pi} + 1 = 0$?

a. Pythagoras
b. Euclid
c. Euler
d. Fermat

21. Which of these demonstrates the relationship between the sets of prime numbers, real numbers, natural numbers, complex numbers, rational numbers, and integers?

$\mathbb{P}$ - Prime; $\mathbb{R}$ - Real; $\mathbb{N}$ - Natural; $\mathbb{C}$ - Complex; $\mathbb{Q}$ - Rational; $\mathbb{Z}$ - Integer

a. $\mathbb{P} \subseteq \mathbb{Q} \subseteq \mathbb{R} \subseteq \mathbb{Z} \subseteq \mathbb{C} \subseteq \mathbb{N}$
b. $\mathbb{P} \subseteq \mathbb{N} \subseteq \mathbb{Z} \subseteq \mathbb{Q} \subseteq \mathbb{R} \subseteq \mathbb{C}$
c. $\mathbb{C} \subseteq \mathbb{R} \subseteq \mathbb{Q} \subseteq \mathbb{Z} \subseteq \mathbb{N} \subseteq \mathbb{P}$
d. None of these

22. To which of the following sets of numbers does -4 NOT belong?

a. The set of whole numbers
b. The set of rational numbers
c. The set of integers
d. The set of real numbers

23. Which of these forms a group?

a. The set of prime numbers under addition
b. The set of negative integers under multiplication
c. The set of negative integers under addition
d. The set of non-zero rational numbers under multiplication

24. Simplify $\frac{2+3i}{4-2i}$.

a. $\frac{1}{10} + \frac{4}{5}i$
b. $\frac{1}{10}$
c. $\frac{7}{6} + \frac{2}{3}i$
d. $\frac{1}{10} + \frac{3}{10}i$

25. Simplify $|(2-3i)^2 - (1-4i)|$.

a. $\sqrt{61}$
b. $-6-8i$
c. $6+8i$
d. 10

26. Which of these sets forms a group under multiplication?

a. $\{-i, 0, i\}$
b. $\{-1, 1, i, -i\}$
c. $\{i, 1\}$
d. $\{i, -i, 1\}$

27. The set $\{a, b, c, d\}$ forms a group under operation #. Which of these statements is (are) true about the group?

#	a	b	c	d
a	c	d	b	a
b	d	c	a	b
c	b	a	d	c
d	a	b	c	d

I. The identity element of the group is d.
II. The inverse of c is c.
III. The operation # is commutative.

a. I
b. III
c. I, III
d. I, II, III

28. If the square of twice the sum of x and three is equal to the product of twenty-four and x, which of these is a possible value of x?

a. $6 + 3\sqrt{2}$
b. $\frac{3}{2}$
c. $-3i$
d. -3

29. Given that x is a prime number and that the greatest common factor of x and y is greater than 1, compare the two quantities.

Quantity A	Quantity B
y	the least common multiple of x and y

a. Quantity A is greater.
b. Quantity B is greater.
c. The two quantities are the same.
d. The relationship cannot be determined from the given information.

30. If a, b, and c are even integers and $3a^2 + 9b^3 = c$, which of these is the largest number which must be factor of c?

a. 2
b. 3
c. 6
d. 12

31. Which of these relationships represents *y* as a function of *x*?

a. $x = y^2$

b. 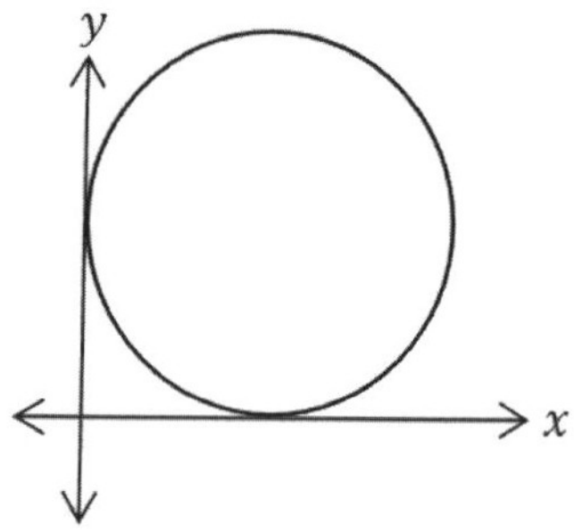

c. $y = [\![x]\!]s$

d. 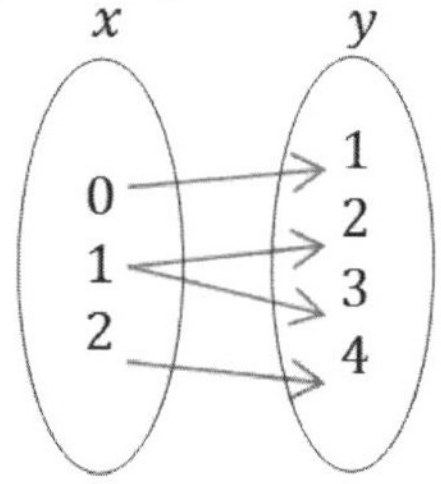

32. Express the area of the given triangle as a function of *x*.

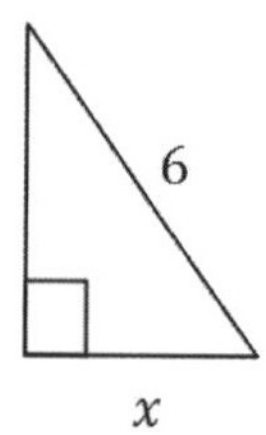

a. $A(x) = 3x$
b. $A(x) = \frac{x\sqrt{36-x^2}}{2}$
c. $A(x) = \frac{x^2}{2}$
d. $A(x) = 18 - \frac{x^2}{2}$

33. Find $[g \circ f\,]x$ when $f(x) = 2x + 4$ and $g(x) = x^2 - 3x + 2$.

a. $4x^2 + 10x + 6$
b. $2x^2 - 6x + 8$
c. $4x^2 + 13x + 18.$
d. $2x^2 - 3x + 6$

34. Given the partial table of values for $f(x)$ and $g(x)$, find $f(g(-4))$. (Assume that $f(x)$ and $g(x)$ are the simplest polynomials that fit the data.)

x	$f(x)$	$g(x)$
-2	8	1
-1	2	3
0	0	5
1	2	7
2	8	9

a. 69
b. 31
c. 18
d. 9

35. If $f(x)$ and $g(x)$ are inverse functions, which of these is the value of x when $f(g(x)) = 4$?

a. -4
b. $\frac{1}{4}$
c. 2
d. 4

36. Determine which pair of equations are NOT inverses.

a. $y = x + 6; y = x - 6$
b. $y = 2x + 3; y = 2x - 3$
c. $y = \frac{2x+3}{x-1}; y = \frac{x+3}{x-2}$
d. $y = \frac{x-1}{2}; y = 2x + 1$

37. Which of these statements is (are) true for function $g(x)$?

$$g(x) = \begin{cases} 2x - 1 & x \geq 2 \\ -x + 3 & x < 2 \end{cases}$$

I. $g(3) = 0$
II. The graph of $g(x)$ is discontinuous at $x = 2$.
III. The range of $g(x)$ is all real numbers.

a. II
b. III
c. I, II
d. II, III

38. Which of the following piecewise functions can describe the graph below?

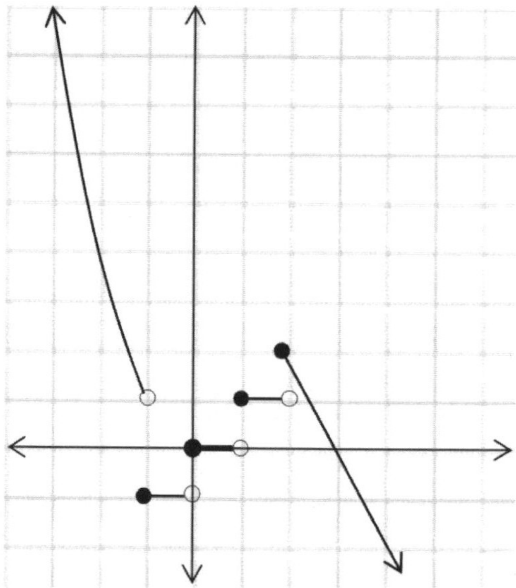

a. $f(x) = \begin{cases} x^2 & x < -1 \\ [\![x]\!] & -1 \le x < 2 \\ -2x + 6 & x \ge 2 \end{cases}$

b. $f(x) = \begin{cases} x^2 & x \le -1 \\ [\![x]\!] & -1 \le x \le 2 \\ -2x + 6 & x > 2 \end{cases}$

c. $f(x) = \begin{cases} (x+1)^2 & x < -1 \\ [\![x]\!] + 1 & -1 \le x < 2 \\ -2x + 6 & x \ge 2 \end{cases}$

d. $f(x) = \begin{cases} (x+1)^2 & x < -1 \\ [\![x - 1]\!] & -1 \le x < 2 \\ -2x + 6 & x \ge 2 \end{cases}$

39. Which of the following could be the graph of $y = a(x + b)(x + c)^2$ if $a > 0$?

a.

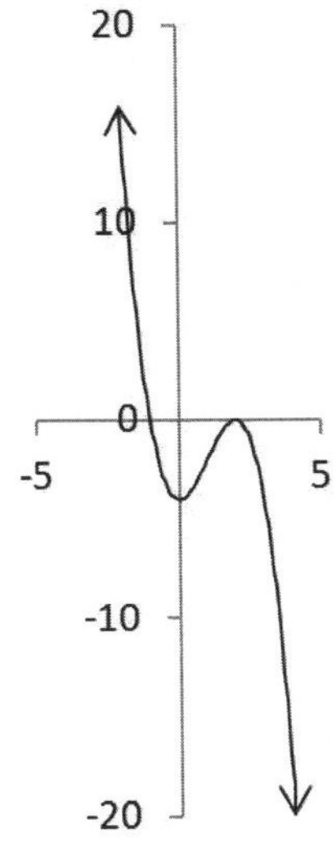

c.

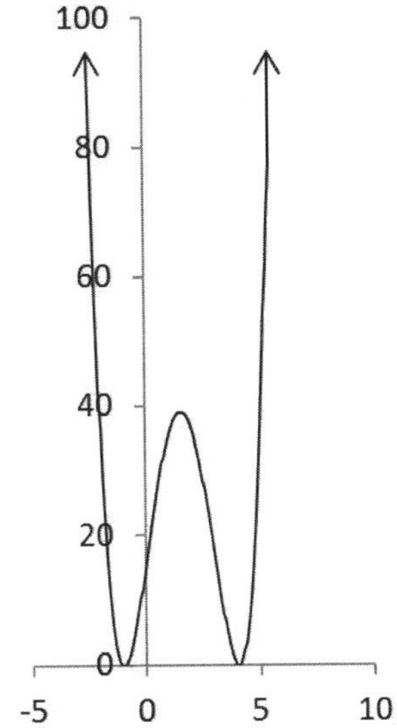

b.

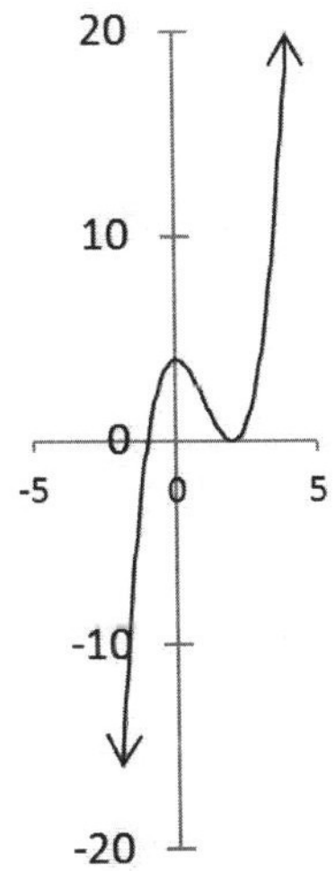

d.

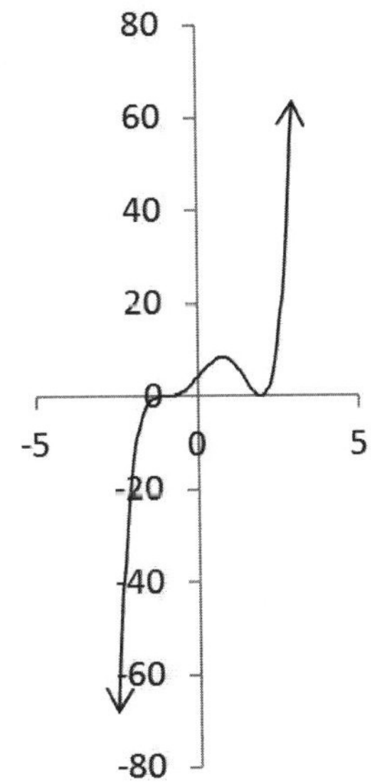

40. A school is selling tickets to its production of *Annie Get Your Gun*. Student tickets cost $3 each, and non-student tickets are $5 each. In order to offset the costs of the production, the school must earn at least $300 in ticket sales. Which graph shows the number of tickets the school must sell to offset production costs?

a.

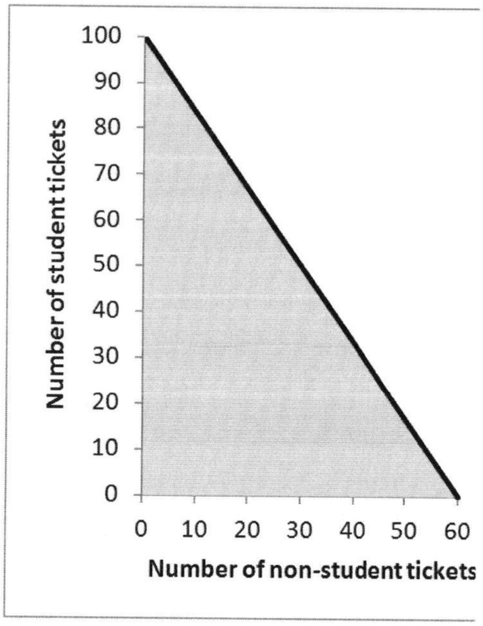

c.

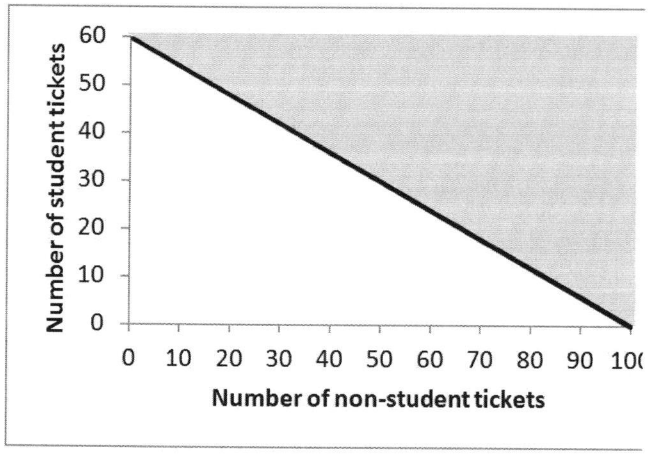

b.

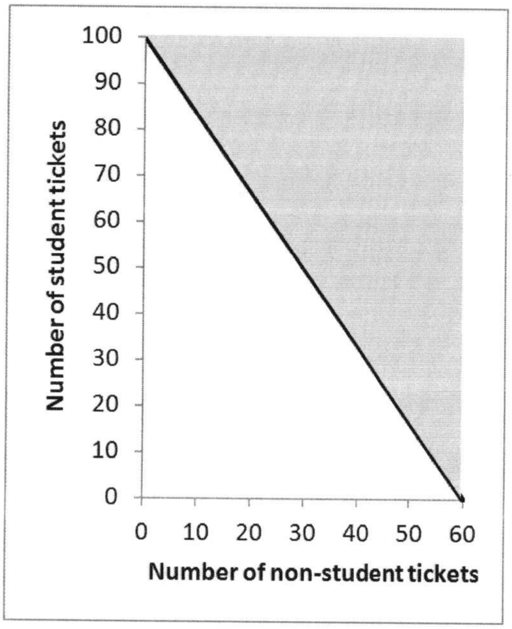

d.

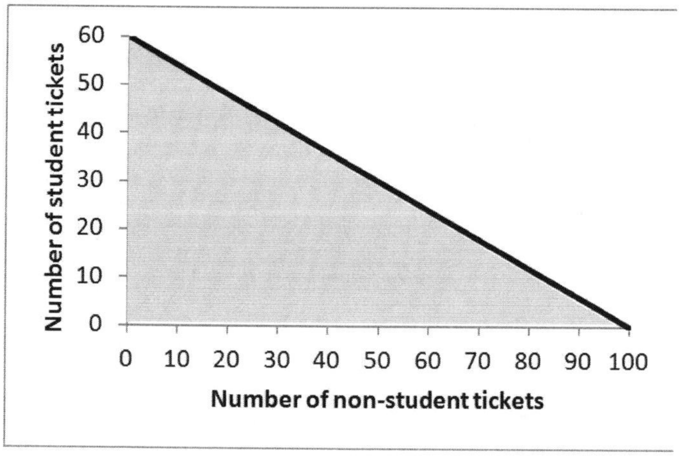

41. Which of these is the equation graphed below?

a. $y = -2x^2 - 4x + 1$
b. $y = -x^2 - 2x + 5$
c. $y = -x^2 - 2x + 2$
d. $y = -\frac{1}{2}x^2 - x + \frac{5}{2}$

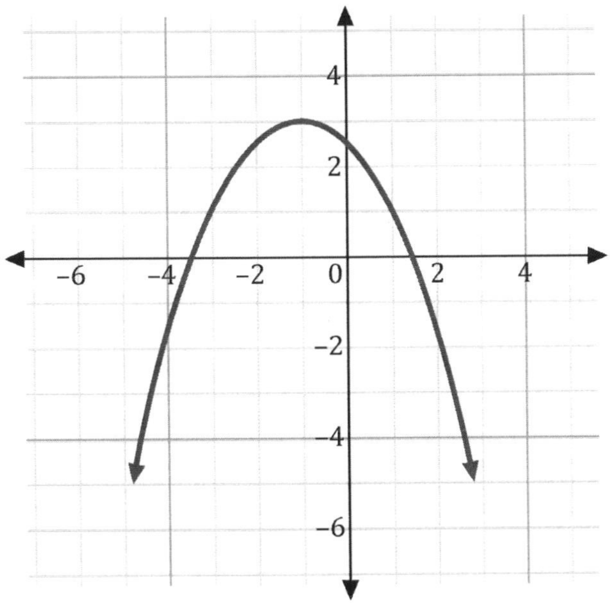

42. Solve $7x^2 + 6x = -2$.

a. $x = \frac{-3 \pm \sqrt{23}}{7}$
b. $x = \pm i\sqrt{5}$
c. $x = \pm \frac{2i\sqrt{2}}{7}$
d. $x = \frac{-3 \pm i\sqrt{5}}{7}$

43. Solve the system of equations.

$$3x + 4y = 2$$
$$2x + 6y = -2$$

a. $\left(0, \frac{1}{2}\right)$
b. $\left(\frac{2}{5}, \frac{1}{5}\right)$
c. $(2, -1)$
d. $\left(-1, \frac{5}{4}\right)$

44. Which system of linear inequalities has no solution?

a. $x - y < 3$
$x - y \geq -3$

b. $y \leq 6 - 2x$
$\frac{1}{3}y + \frac{2}{3}x \geq 2$

c. $6x + 2y \leq 12$
$3x \geq 8 - y$

d. $x + 4y \leq -8$
$y + 4x > -8$

45. The cost of admission to a theme park is shown below.

Under age 10	Ages 10-55	Over age 65
$15	$25	$20

Yesterday, the theme park sold 810 tickets and earned $14,500. There were twice as many children under 10 at the park as there were other visitors. If x, y, and z represent the number of $15, $25, and $20 tickets sold, respectively, which of the following matrix equations can be used to find the number of each type of ticket sold?

a. $\begin{bmatrix} 1 & 1 & 1 \\ 15 & 25 & 20 \\ 1 & -2 & -2 \end{bmatrix} \begin{bmatrix} x \\ y \\ z \end{bmatrix} = \begin{bmatrix} 810 \\ 14500 \\ 0 \end{bmatrix}$

b. $\begin{bmatrix} 1 & 1 & 1 \\ 15 & 25 & 20 \\ 1 & -2 & -2 \end{bmatrix} \begin{bmatrix} 810 \\ 14500 \\ 0 \end{bmatrix} = \begin{bmatrix} x \\ y \\ z \end{bmatrix}$

c. $\begin{bmatrix} 1 & 15 & 1 \\ 1 & 25 & -2 \\ 1 & 20 & -2 \end{bmatrix} \begin{bmatrix} x \\ y \\ z \end{bmatrix} = \begin{bmatrix} 810 \\ 14500 \\ 0 \end{bmatrix}$

d. $\begin{bmatrix} 1 & 15 & 1 \\ 1 & 25 & -2 \\ 1 & 20 & -2 \end{bmatrix} \begin{bmatrix} 810 \\ 14500 \\ 0 \end{bmatrix} = \begin{bmatrix} x \\ y \\ z \end{bmatrix}$

46. Solve the system of equations.

$$2x - 4y + z = 10$$
$$-3x + 2y - 4z = -7$$
$$x + y - 3z = -1$$

a. $(-1, -3, 0)$
b. $(1, -2, 0)$
c. $(-\frac{3}{4}, -\frac{21}{8}, -1)$
d. No solution

47. Solve $x^4 + 64 = 20x^2$.

a. $x = \{2, 4\}$
b. $x = \{-2, 2, -4, 4\}$
c. $x = \{2i, 4i\}$
d. $x = \{-2i, 2i, -4i, 4i\}$

48. Solve $3x^3y^2 - 45x^2y = 15x^3y - 9x^2y^2$ for x and y.

a. $x = \{0, -3\},\ y = \{0, 5\}$
b. $x = \{0\},\ y = \{0\}$
c. $x = \{0, -3\},\ y = \{0\}$
d. $x = \{0\},\ y = \{0, 5\}$

49. Which of these statements is true for functions $f(x)$, $g(x)$, and $h(x)$?

$$f(x) = 2x - 2$$
$$g(x) = 2x^2 - 2$$
$$h(x) = 2x^3 - 2$$

a. The degree of each polynomial function is 2.
b. The leading coefficient of each function is -2.
c. Each function has exactly one real zero at $x = 1$.
d. None of these is true for functions $f(x)$, $g(x)$, and $h(x)$.

50. Which of these can be modeled by a quadratic function?

a. The path of a sound wave
b. The path of a bullet
c. The distance an object travels over time when the rate is constant
d. Radioactive decay

51. Which of these is equivalent to $\log_y 256$ if $2\log_4 y + \log_4 16 = 3$ if y is positive?

a. 16
b. 8
c. 4
d. 2

52. Simplify $\frac{(x^2y)(2xy^{-2})^3}{16x^5y^2} + \frac{3}{xy}$

a. $\frac{3x+24y^6}{8xy^7}$
b. $\frac{x+6y^6}{2xy^7}$
c. $\frac{x+24y^5}{8xy^6}$
d. $\frac{x+6y^5}{2xy^6}$

53. Given: $f(x) = 10^x$. If $f(x) = 5$, which of these approximates x?

a. 100,000
b. 0.00001
c. 0.7
d. 1.6

54. Which of these could be the equation of the function graphed below?

a. $f(x) = x^2$
b. $f(x) = \sqrt{x}$
c. $f(x) = 2^x$
d. $f(x) = log_2 x$

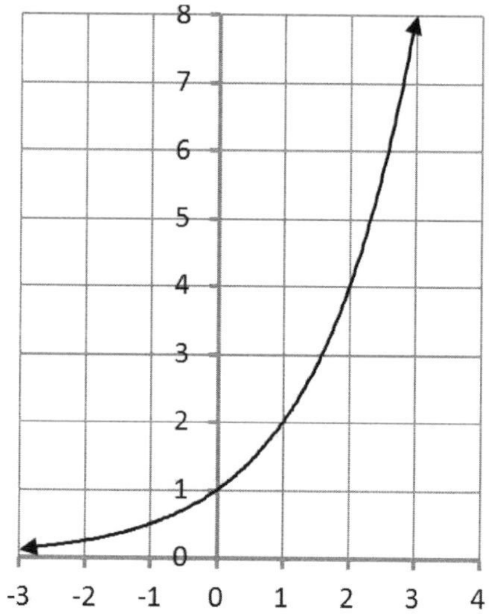

55. Which of these statements is NOT necessarily true when $f(x) = \log_b x$ and $b > 1$?

a. The x-intercept of the graph of $f(x)$ is 1.
b. The graph of $f(x)$ passes through $(b, 1)$
c. $f(x) < 0$ when $x < 1$
d. If $g(x) = b^x$, the graph of $f(x)$ is symmetric to the graph of $g(x)$ with respect to $y = x$.

56. A colony of *Escherichia coli* is inoculated from a Petri dish into a test tube containing 50 mL of nutrient broth. The test tube is placed in a 37°C incubator/shaker; after one hour, the number of bacteria in the test tube is determined to be 8×10^6. Given that the doubling time of *E. coli* is 20 minutes with agitation at 37°C, approximately how many bacteria should the test tube contain after eight hours of growth?

a. 2.56×10^8
b. 2.05×10^9
c. 1.7×10^{10}
d. 1.7×10^{13}

57. The strength of an aqueous acid solution is measured by pH. $\text{pH} = -\log[\text{H}^+]$, where $[\text{H}^+]$ is the molar concentration of hydronium ions in the solution. A solution is acidic if its pH is less than 7. The lower the pH, the stronger the acid; for example, gastric acid, which has a pH of about 1, is a much stronger acid than urine, which has a pH of about 6. How many times stronger is an acid with a pH of 3 than an acid with pH of 5?

a. 2
b. 20
c. 100
d. 1000

58. Simplify $\sqrt{\frac{-28x^6}{27y^5}}$.

a. $\frac{2x^3 i\sqrt{21y}}{9y^3}$
b. $\frac{2x^3 i\sqrt{21y}}{27y^4}$
c. $\frac{-2x^3\sqrt{21y}}{9y^3}$
d. $\frac{12x^3 yi\sqrt{7}}{27y^2}$

59. Which of these does NOT have a solution set of $\{x: -1 \leq x \leq 1\}$?

a. $-4 \leq 2 + 3(x-1) \leq 2$
b. $-2x^2 + 2 \geq x^2 - 1$
c. $\frac{11-|3x|}{7} \geq 2$
d. $3|2x| + 4 \leq 10$

60. Solve the equation $2 - \sqrt{x} = \sqrt{x - 20}$.

a. $x = 6$
b. $x = 36$
c. $x = 144$
d. No solution

61. Solve $\frac{x-2}{x-1} = \frac{x-1}{x+1} + \frac{2}{x-1}$.

a. $x = 2$
b. $x = -5$
c. $x = 1$
d. No solution

62. Which of these equations is represented by the graph below?

a. $y = \frac{3}{x^2-x-2}$
b. $y = \frac{3x+3}{x^2-x-2}$
c. $y = \frac{1}{x+1} + \frac{1}{x-2}$
d. None of these

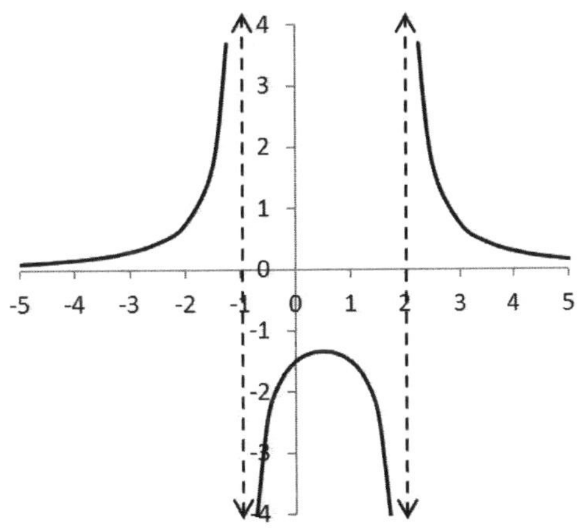

63. Which of the graphs shown represents $f(x) = -2|-x + 4| - 1$?

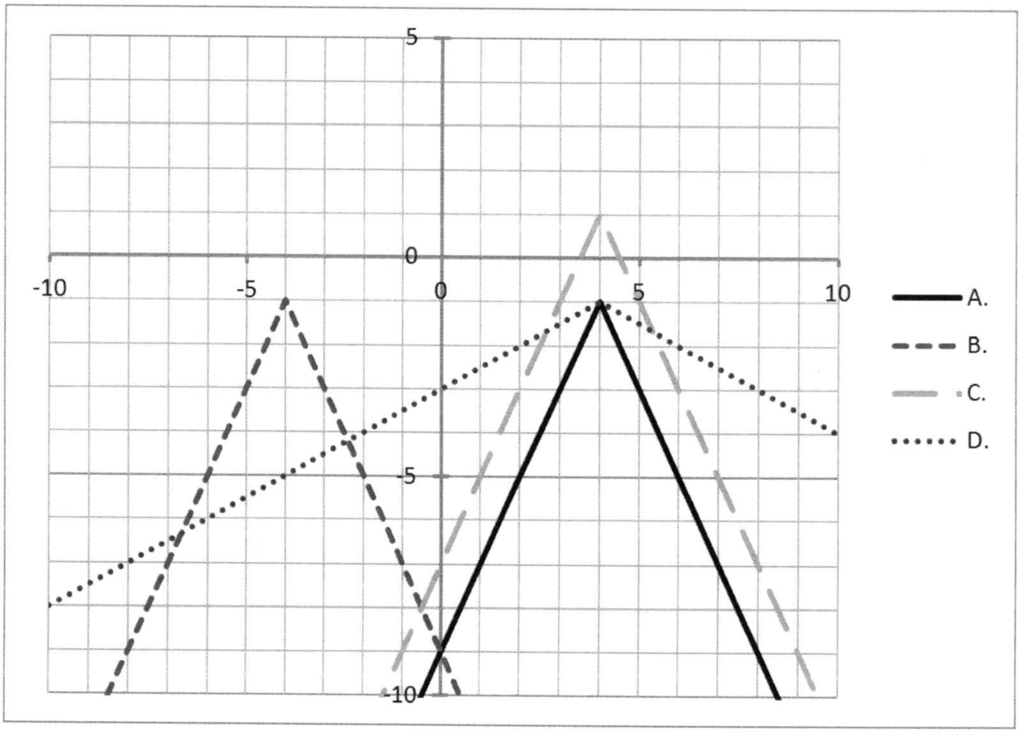

64. Which of these functions includes 1 as an element of the domain and 2 as an element of the range?

a. $y = \frac{1}{x-1} + 1$
b. $y = -\sqrt{x+2} - 1$
c. $y = |x + 2| - 3$
d. $y = \begin{cases} x & x < -1 \\ -x - 3 & x \geq -1 \end{cases}$

65. Which of the following statements is (are) true when $f(x) = \frac{x^2-x-6}{x^3+2x^2-x-2}$?

I. The graph $f(x)$ has vertical asymptotes at $x = -2, x = -1$, and $x = 1$.
II. The x- and y-intercepts of the graph of $f(x)$ are both 3.

a. I
b. II
c. I and II
d. Neither statement is true.

66. In the 1600s, Galileo Galilei studied the motion of pendulums and discovered that the period of a pendulum, the time it takes to complete one full swing, is a function of the square root of the length of its string: $2\pi\sqrt{\frac{L}{g}}$, where L is the length of the string and g is the acceleration due to gravity.

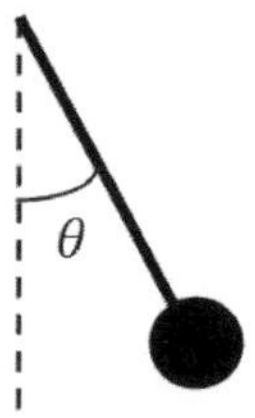

Consider two pendulums released from the same pivot point and at the same angle, $\theta = 30°$. Pendulum 1 has a mass of 100 g, while Pendulum 2 has a mass of 200 g. If Pendulum 1 has a period four times the period of Pendulum 2, what is true of the lengths of the pendulums' strings?

a. The length of Pendulum 1's string is four times the length of Pendulum 2's string.
b. The length of Pendulum 1's string is eight times the length of Pendulum 2's string.
c. The length of Pendulum 1's string is sixteen times the length of Pendulum 2's string.
d. The length of Pendulum 1's string is less than the length of Pendulum 2's string.

67. At today's visit to her doctor, Josephine was prescribed a liquid medication with instructions to take 25 cc's every four hours. She filled the prescription on her way to work, but when it came time to take the medicine, she realized that the pharmacist did not include a measuring cup. Josephine estimated that the plastic spoon in her desk drawer was about the same size as a teaspoon and decided to use it to measure the approximate dosage. She recalled that one cubic centimeter (cc) is equal to one milliliter (mL) but was not sure how many milliliters were in a teaspoon. So, she noted that a two-liter bottle of soda contains about the same amount as a half-gallon container of milk and applied her knowledge of the customary system of measurement to determine how many teaspoons of medicine to take. Which of these calculations might she have used to approximate her dosage?

a. $25 \cdot \frac{1}{1000} \cdot \frac{2}{0.5} \cdot 16 \cdot 48$
b. $25 \cdot \frac{1}{100} \cdot \frac{0.5}{2} \cdot 16 \cdot 4 \cdot 12$
c. $\frac{1000}{25} \cdot \frac{0.5}{2} \cdot 16 \cdot 4 \cdot 12$
d. $\frac{25}{1000} \cdot \frac{1}{4} \cdot 16 \cdot 48$

68. If 1 inch on a map represents 60 feet, how many yards apart are two points if the distance between the points on the map is 10 inches?

a. 1,800 yards
b. 600 yards
c. 200 yards
d. 2 yards

69. Roxana walks x meters west and $x + 20$ meters south to get to her friend's house. On a neighborhood map which has a scale of 1cm:10 m, the distance between Roxana's house and her friend's house is 10 cm. How far did Roxana walk to her friend's house?

a. 60 m
b. 80 m
c. 100 m
d. 140 m

70. For ΔABC, what is AB?

a. 3
b. 10
c. 12
d. 15

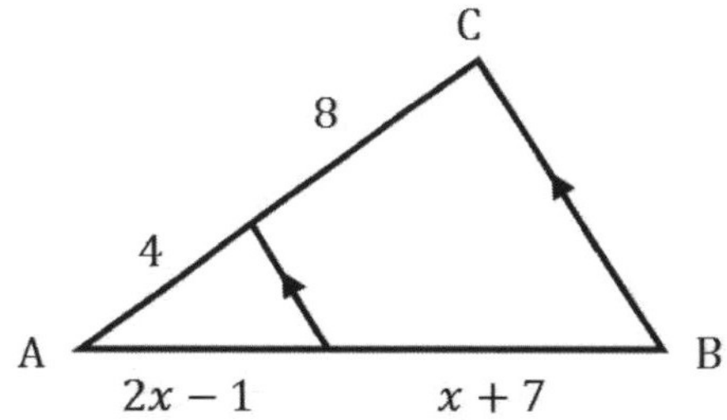

71. To test the accuracy and precision of two scales, a student repeatedly measured the mass of a 10 g standard and recorded these results.

	Trial 1	Trial 2	Trial 3	Trial 4
Scale 1	9.99 g	9.98 g	10.02g	10.01g
Scale 2	10.206 g	10.209 g	10.210 g	10.208 g

Which of these conclusions about the scales is true?

a. Scale 1 has an average percent error of 0.15%, and Scale 2 has an average percent error of 2.08%. Scale 1 is more accurate and precise than Scale 2.
b. Scale 1 has an average percent error of 0.15%, and Scale 2 has an average percent error of 2.08%. Scale 1 is more accurate than Scale 2; however, Scale 2 is more precise.
c. Scale 1 has an average percent error of 0%, and Scale 2 has an average percent error of 2.08%. Scale 1 is more accurate and precise than Scale 2.
d. Scale 1 has an average percent error of 0%, and Scale 2 has an average percent error of 2.08%. Scale 1 is more accurate than Scale 2; however, Scale 2 is more precise.

72. A developer decides to build a fence around a neighborhood park, which is positioned on a rectangular lot. Rather than fencing along the lot line, he fences x feet from each of the lot's boundaries. By fencing a rectangular space 141 yd^2 smaller than the lot, the developer saves \$432 in fencing materials, which cost \$12 per linear foot. How much does he spend?

a. \$160
b. \$456
c. \$3,168
d. The answer cannot be determined from the given information.

73. Natasha designs a square pyramidal tent for her children. Each of the sides of the square base measures x ft, and the tent's height is h feet. If Natasha were to increase by 1 ft the length of each side of the base, how much more interior space would the tent have?

a. $\frac{h(x^2+2x+1)}{3}$ ft^3
b. $\frac{h(2x+1)}{3}$ ft^3
c. $\frac{x^2h+3}{3}$ ft^3
d. 1 ft^3

74. A rainbow pattern is designed from semi-circles as shown below.

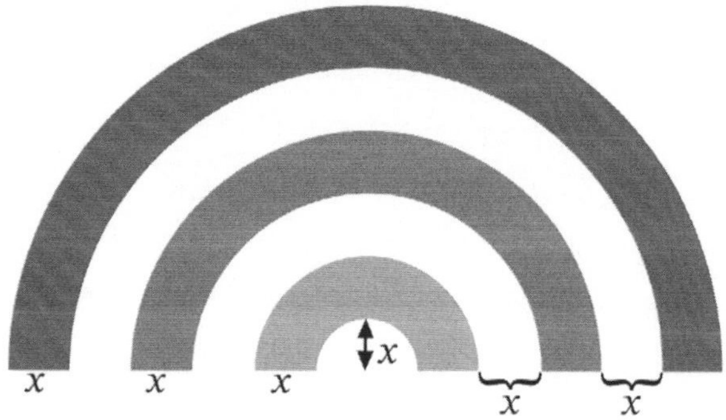

Which of the following gives the area A of the shaded region as a function of x?

a. $A = \frac{21x^2\pi}{2}$
b. $A = 21x^2\pi$
c. $A = 42x^2\pi$
d. $A = 82x^2\pi$

75. Categorize the following statements as axioms of Euclidean, hyperbolic, or elliptical geometry.

I. In a plane, for any line l and point *A* not on l, no lines which pass through *A* intersect l.
II. In a plane, for any line l and point *A* not on l, exactly one line which passes through *A* does not intersect l.
III. In a plane, for any line l and point *A* not on l, all lines which pass through *A* intersect l.

a.

Statement I	Elliptical geometry
Statement II	Euclidean geometry
Statement III	Hyperbolic geometry

b.

Statement I	Hyperbolic geometry
Statement II	Euclidean geometry
Statement III	Elliptical geometry

c.

Statement I	Hyperbolic geometry
Statement II	Elliptical geometry
Statement III	Euclidean geometry

d.

Statement I	Elliptical geometry
Statement II	Hyperbolic geometry
Statement III	Euclidean geometry

76. As shown below, four congruent isosceles trapezoids are positioned such that they form an arch. Find *x* for the indicated angle.

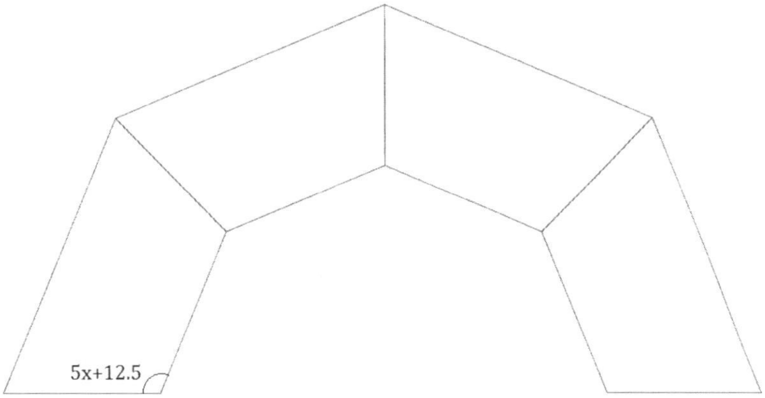

a. $x = 11$
b. $x = 20$
c. $x = 24.5$
d. The value of x cannot be determined from the information given.

77. A circle is inscribed inside quadrilateral *ABCD*. $\overline{CD}$ is bisected by the point at which it is tangent to the circle. If $AB = 14, BC = 10, DC = 8$, then

a. $AD = 11$
b. $AD = 2\sqrt{34}$
c. $AD = 12$
d. $AD = 17.5$

78. Which of the following equations gives the area *A* of the triangle below as a function of *a* and *b*?

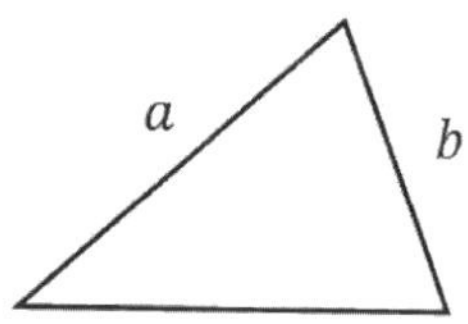

a. $\frac{2a^2-b^2}{4}$
b. $\frac{ab-a^2}{2}$
c. $\frac{b\sqrt{a^2-b^2}}{2}$
d. $\frac{b\sqrt{4a^2-b^2}}{4}$

79. Given the figure and the following information, find DE to the nearest tenth.

$\overline{AD}$ is an altitude of ΔABC

$\overline{DE}$ is an altitude of triangle ΔADC

$BD \cong DC$

$BC = 24; AD = 5$

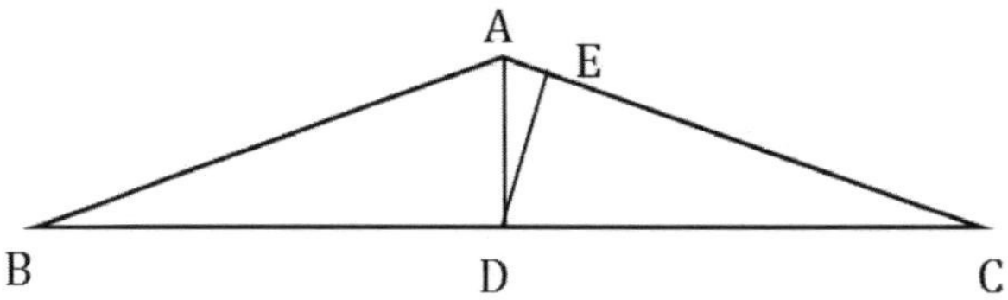

a. 4.2
b. 4.6
c. 4.9
d. 5.4

80. A cube inscribed in a sphere has a volume of 64 cubic units. What is the volume of the sphere in cubic units?

a. $4\pi\sqrt{3}$
b. $8\pi\sqrt{3}$
c. $32\pi\sqrt{3}$
d. $256\pi\sqrt{3}$

Questions 81 and 82 are based on the following proof:

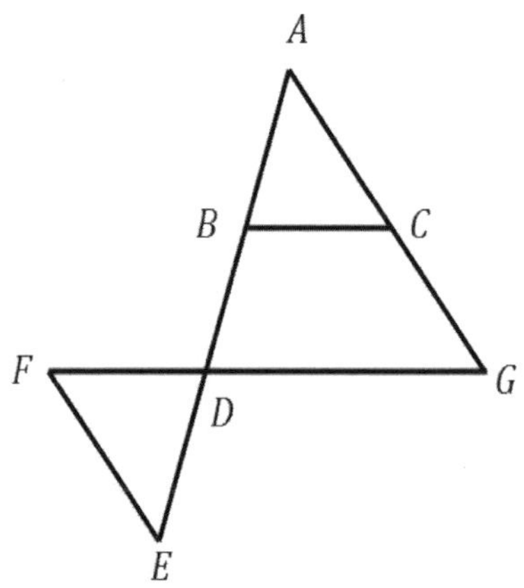

Statement	Reason
1. $\overline{BC} \| \overline{FG}$	Given
2.	
3. $\overline{FD} \cong \overline{BC}$	Given
4. $\overline{AB} \cong \overline{DE}$	Given
5. $\Delta ABC \cong \Delta EDF$	81.
6. 82.	
7. $\overline{FE} \| \overline{AG}$	

Given: $\overline{BC} \| \overline{FG}$; $\overline{FD} \cong \overline{BC}$; $\overline{AB} \cong \overline{DE}$
Prove: $\overline{FE} \| \overline{AG}$

81. Which of the following justifies step 5 in the proof?

a. AAS
b. SSS
c. ASA
d. SAS

82. Step 6 in the proof should contain which of the following statements?

a. $\angle BAC \cong \angle DEF$
b. $\angle ABC \cong \angle EDF$
c. $\angle ACB \cong \angle EFD$
d. $\angle GDA \cong \angle EDF$

83. Which of these is NOT a net of a cube?

a.
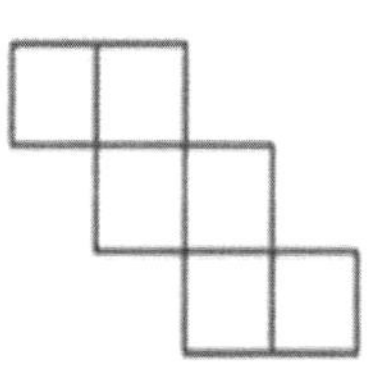

b.
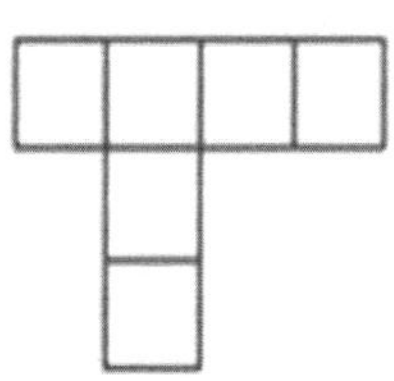

c.
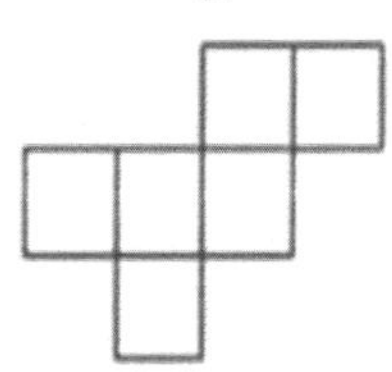

d.
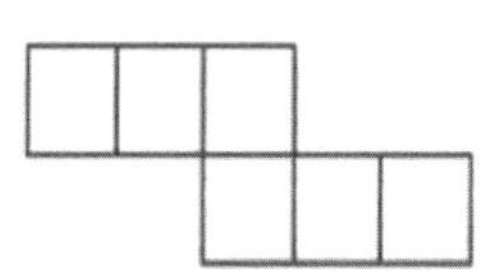

84. Identify the cross-section polygon formed by a plane containing the given points on the cube.

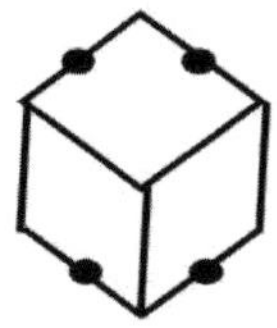

a. Rectangle
b. Trapezoid
c. Pentagon
d. Hexagon

85. Which of these represents the equation of a sphere which is centered in the xyz-space at the point (1, 0, -2) and which has a volume of 36π cubic units?

a. $x^2 + y^2 + z^2 - 2x + 4z = 4$
b. $x^2 + y^2 + z^2 + 2x - 4z = 4$
c. $x^2 + y^2 + z^2 - 2x + 4z = -2$
d. $x^2 + y^2 + z^2 + 2x - 4z = 2$

86. A triangle has vertices $(0, 0, 0)$, $(0, 0, 4)$, and $(0, 3, 0)$ in the xyz-space. In cubic units, what is the difference in the volume of the solid formed by rotating the triangle about the z-axis and the solid formed by rotating the triangle about the y-axis?

a. 0
b. 4π
c. 5π
d. 25

87. If the midpoint of a line segment graphed on the xy-coordinate plane is $(3, -1)$ and the slope of the line segment is -2, which of these is a possible endpoint of the line segment?

a. $(-1,1)$
b. $(0,-5)$
c. $(7,1)$
d. $(5,-5)$

88. The vertices of a polygon are $(2, 3)$, $(8, 1)$, $(6, -5)$, and $(0, -3)$. Which of the following describes the polygon most specifically?

a. Parallelogram
b. Rhombus
c. Rectangle
d. Square

89. What is the radius of the circle defined by the equation $x^2 + y^2 - 10x + 8y + 29 = 0$?

a. $2\sqrt{3}$
b. $2\sqrt{5}$
c. $\sqrt{29}$
d. 12

90. Which of these describes the graph of the equation $2x^2 - 3y^2 - 12x + 6y - 15 = 0$?

a. Circular
b. Elliptical
c. Parabolic
d. Hyperbolic

91. The graph of $f(x)$ is a parabola with a focus of (a, b) and a directrix of $y = -b$, and $g(x)$ represents a transformation of $f(x)$. If the vertex of the graph of $g(x)$ is $(a, 0)$, which of these is a possible equation for $g(x)$ for nonzero integers a and b?

a. $g(x) = f(x) + b$
b. $g(x) = -f(x)$
c. $g(x) = f(x + a)$
d. $g(x) = f(x - a) + b$

92. A triangle with vertices $A(-4, 2)$, $B(-1, 3)$, and $C(-5, 7)$ is reflected across $y = x + 2$ to give $\Delta A'B'C'$, which is subsequently reflected across the y-axis to give $\Delta A''B''C''$. Which of these statements is true?

a. A 90° rotation of ΔABC about (−2,0) gives ΔA″B″C″.
b. A reflection of ΔABC about the x-axis gives ΔA″B″C″.
c. A 270° rotation of ΔABC about (0,2) gives ΔA″B″C″.
d. A translation of ΔABC two units down gives ΔA″B″C″.

93. For which of these does a rotation of 120° about the center of the polygon map the polygon onto itself?

a. Square
b. Regular hexagon
c. Regular octagon
d. Regular decagon

94. Line segment $\overline{PQ}$ has endpoints (a, b) and (c, b). If $\overline{P'Q'}$ is the translation of $\overline{PQ}$ along a diagonal line such that P' is located at point (c, d), what is the area of quadrilateral $PP'Q'Q$?

a. $|a - c| \cdot |b - d|$
b. $|a - b| \cdot |c - d|$
c. $|a - d| \cdot |b - c|$
d. $(a - c)^2$

95. For the right triangle below, which of the following is a true statement of equality?

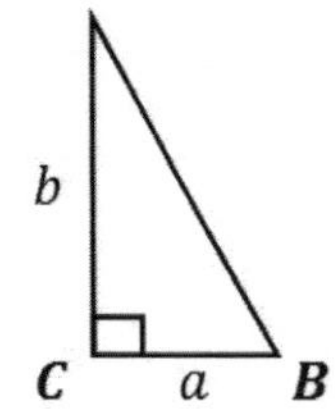

a. $\tan B = \frac{a}{b}$
b. $\cos B = \frac{a\sqrt{a^2+b^2}}{a^2+b^2}$
c. $\sec B = \frac{\sqrt{a^2+b^2}}{b}$
d. $\csc B = \frac{a^2+b^2}{b}$

96. A man looks out of a window of a tall building at a 45° angle of depression and sees his car in the parking lot. When he turns his gaze downward to a 60° angle of depression, he sees his wife's car. If his car is parked 60 feet from his wife's car, about how far from the building did his wife park her car?

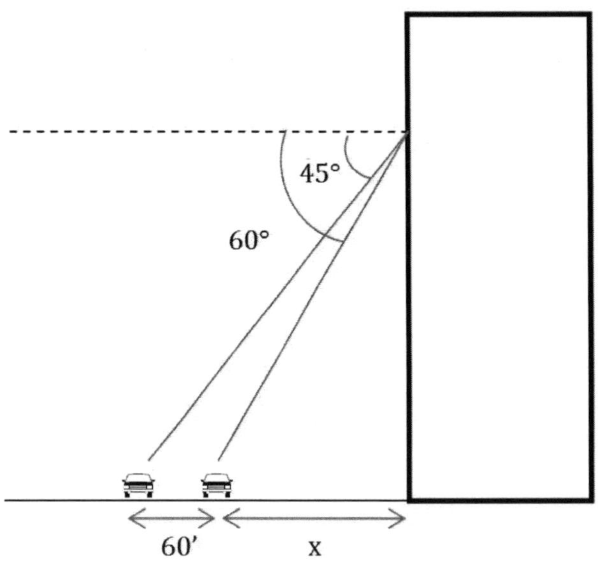

a. 163 feet
b. 122 feet
c. 82 feet
d. 60 feet

97. What is the exact value of $\tan(-\frac{2\pi}{3})$?

a. $\sqrt{3}$
b. $-\sqrt{3}$
c. $\frac{\sqrt{3}}{3}$
d. 1

98. If $\sin\theta = \frac{1}{2}$ when $\frac{\pi}{2} < \theta < \pi$, what is the value of θ?

a. $\frac{\pi}{6}$
b. $\frac{\pi}{3}$
c. $\frac{2\pi}{3}$
d. $\frac{5\pi}{6}$

99. Which of the following expressions is equal to $\cos\theta\cot\theta$?

a. $sin\,\theta$
b. $sec\,\theta\ tan\,\theta$
c. $csc\,\theta - sin\,\theta$
d. $sec\,\theta - sin\,\theta$

100. Solve $\sec^2\theta = 2\tan\theta$ for $0 < \theta \le 2\pi$.

a. $\theta = \frac{\pi}{6}$ or $\frac{7\pi}{6}$
b. $\theta = \frac{\pi}{4}$ or $\frac{5\pi}{4}$
c. $\theta = \frac{3\pi}{4}$ or $\frac{7\pi}{4}$
d. There is no solution to the equation.

101. A car is driving along the highway at a constant speed when it runs over a pebble, which becomes lodged in one of the tire's treads. If this graph represent the height *h* of the pebble above the road in inches as a function of time *t* in seconds, which of these statements is true?

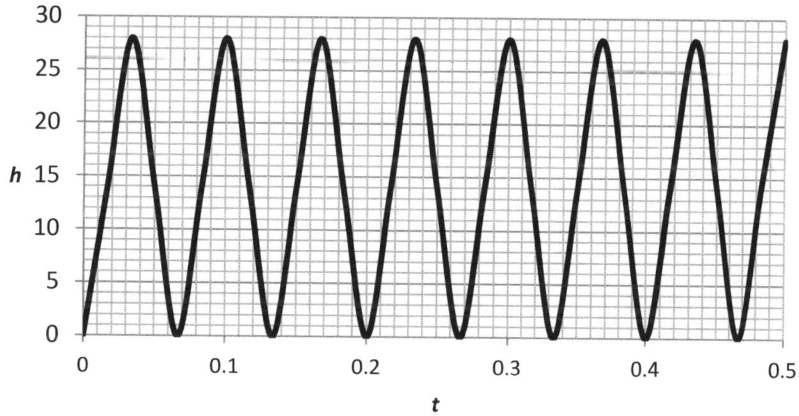

a. The outer radius of the tire is 14 inches, and the tire rotates 900 times per minute.
b. The outer radius of the tire is 28 inches, and the tire rotates 900 times per minute.
c. The outer radius of the tire is 14 inches, and the tire rotates 120 times per minute.
d. The outer radius of the tire is 28 inches, and the tire rotates 120 times per minute.

Below are graphed functions $f(x) = a_1 \sin(b_1 x)$ and $g(x) = a_2 \cos(b_2 x)$; a_1 and a_2 are integers, and b_1 and b_2 are positive rational numbers. Use this information to answer questions 102-103:

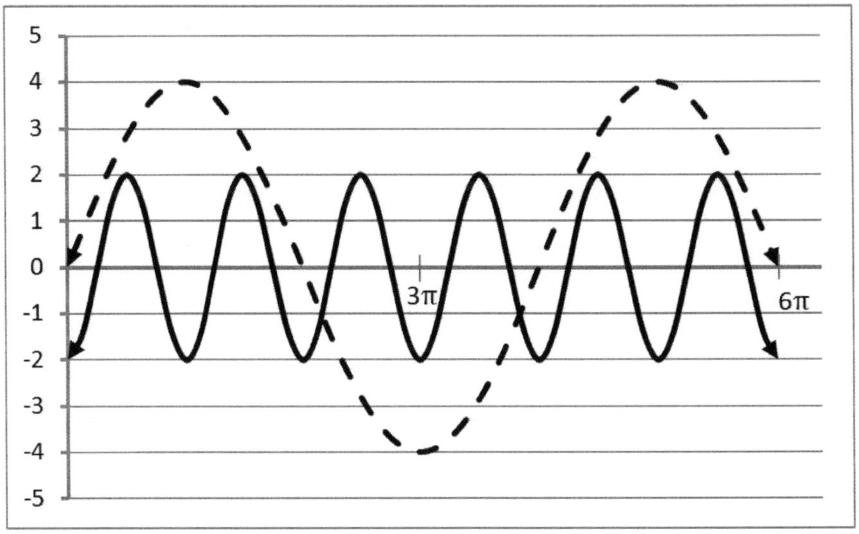

102. Which of the following statements is true?

a. The graph of $f(x)$ is represented by a solid line.
b. The amplitude of the graph of $g(x)$ is 4.
c. $0 < b_1 < 1$.
d. $b_2 = \pi$.

103. Which of the following statements is true?

a. $0 < a_2 < a_1$
b. $a_2 < 0 < a_1$
c. $0 < a_1 < a_2$
d. $a_2 < a_1 < 0$

104. A weight suspended on a spring is at its equilibrium point five inches above the top of a table. When the weight is pulled down two inches, it bounces above the equilibrium point and returns to the point from which it was released in one second. Which of these can be used to model the weight's height h above the table as a function of time t in seconds?

a. $h = -2\cos(2\pi t) + 5$
b. $h = 5\sin(t) - 2$
c. $h = -2\sin(2\pi t) + 5$
d. $h = -2\cos(0.5\pi t) + 3$

105. Evaluate $\lim_{x \to -3} \frac{x^3+3x^2-x-3}{x^2-9}$.

a. 0
b. $\frac{1}{3}$
c. $-\frac{4}{3}$
d. ∞

106. Evaluate $\lim_{x\to\infty} \frac{x^2+2x-3}{2x^2+1}$.

a. 0
b. $\frac{1}{2}$
c. -3
d. ∞

107. Evaluate $\lim_{x\to 3^+} \frac{|x-3|}{3-x}$.

a. 0
b. -1
c. 1
d. ∞

108. If $f(x) = \frac{1}{4}x^2 - 3$, find the slope of the line tangent to graph of $f(x)$ at $x = 2$.

a. -2
b. 0
c. 1
d. 4

109. If $f(x) = 2x^3 - 3x^2 + 4$, what is $\lim_{h\to 0} \frac{f(2+h)-f(2)}{h}$?

a. -4
b. 4
c. 8
d. 12

110. Find the derivative of $f(x) = e^{3x^2-1}$.

a. $6xe^{6x}$
b. e^{3x^2-1}
c. $(3x^2-1)e^{3x^2-2}$
d. $6xe^{3x^2-1}$

111. Find the derivative of $f(x) = \ln(2x+1)$.

a. $\frac{1}{2x+1}$
b. $2e^{2x+1}$
c. $\frac{2}{2x+1}$
d. $\frac{1}{2}$

112. For functions $f(x)$, $g(x)$, and $h(x)$, determine the limit of the function as x approaches 2 and the continuity of the function at $x = 2$.

a.

$\lim_{x\to 2+} f(x) = 4$ $\lim_{x\to 2-} f(x) = 2$ $f(2) = 2$	$\lim_{x\to 2} f(x)$ DNE	The function $f(x)$ is discontinuous at 2.
$\lim_{x\to 2+} g(x) = 2$ $\lim_{x\to 2-} g(x) = 2$ $g(2) = 4$	$\lim_{x\to 2} g(x) = 2$	The function $g(x)$ is discontinuous at 2.
$\lim_{x\to 2+} h(x) = 2$ $\lim_{x\to 2-} h(x) = 2$ $h(2) = 2$	$\lim_{x\to 2} h(x) = 2$	The function $h(x)$ is continuous at 2.

b.

$\lim_{x\to 2+} f(x) = 4$ $\lim_{x\to 2-} f(x) = 2$ $f(2) = 2$	$\lim_{x\to 2} f(x)$ DNE	The function $f(x)$ is continuous at 2.
$\lim_{x\to 2+} g(x) = 2$ $\lim_{x\to 2-} g(x) = 2$ $g(2) = 4$	$\lim_{x\to 2} g(x)$ DNE	The function $g(x)$ is continuous at 2.
$\lim_{x\to 2+} h(x) = 2$ $\lim_{x\to 2-} h(x) = 2$ $h(2) = 2$	$\lim_{x\to 2} h(x) = 2$	The function $h(x)$ is continuous at 2.

c.

$\lim_{x\to 2+} f(x) = 4$ $\lim_{x\to 2-} f(x) = 2$ $f(2) = 2$	$\lim_{x\to 2} f(x) = 2$	The function $f(x)$ is continuous at 2.
$\lim_{x\to 2+} g(x) = 2$ $\lim_{x\to 2-} g(x) = 2$ $g(2) = 4$	$\lim_{x\to 2} g(x) = 2$	The function $g(x)$ is discontinuous at 2.
$\lim_{x\to 2+} h(x) = 2$ $\lim_{x\to 2-} h(x) = 2$ $h(2) = 2$	$\lim_{x\to 2} h(x) = 2$	The function $h(x)$ is continuous at 2.

d.

$\lim_{x\to 2+} f(x) = 4$ $\lim_{x\to 2-} f(x) = 2$ $f(2) = 2$	$\lim_{x\to 2} f(x) = 2$	The function $f(x)$ is discontinuous at 2.
$\lim_{x\to 2+} g(x) = 2$ $\lim_{x\to 2-} g(x) = 2$ $g(2) = 4$	$\lim_{x\to 2} g(x) = 2$	The function $g(x)$ is discontinuous at 2.
$\lim_{x\to 2+} h(x) = 2$ $\lim_{x\to 2-} h(x) = 2$ $h(2) = 2$	$\lim_{x\to 2} h(x) = 2$	The function $h(x)$ is continuous at 2.

113. Find $f''(x)$ if $f(x) = 2x^4 - 4x^3 + 2x^2 - x + 1$.

a. $24x^2 - 24x + 4$
b. $8x^3 - 12x^2 + 4x - 1$
c. $32x^2 - 36x^2 + 8$
d. $\frac{2}{5}x^5 - x^4 + \frac{2}{3}x^3 - \frac{1}{2}x^2 + x + c$

114. If $f(x) = 4x^3 - x^2 - 4x + 2$, which of the following statements is(are) true of its graph?

I. The point $\left(-\frac{1}{2}, 3\frac{1}{4}\right)$ is a relative maximum.

II. The graph of f is concave upward on the interval $(-\infty, \frac{1}{2})$.

a. I
b. II
c. I and II
d. Neither I nor II

115. Suppose the path of a baseball hit straight up from three feet above the ground is modeled by the first quadrant graph of the function $h = -16t^2 + 50t + 3$, where t is the flight time of the ball in seconds and h is the height of the ball in feet. What is the velocity of the ball two seconds after it is hit?

a. 39 ft/s upward
b. 19.5 ft/s upward
c. 19.5 ft/s downward
d. 14 ft/s downward

116. A manufacturer wishes to produce a cylindrical can which can hold up to 0.5 L of liquid. To the nearest tenth, what is the radius of the can which requires the least amount of material to make?

a. 2.8 cm
b. 4.3 cm
c. 5.0 cm
d. 9.2 cm

117. Approximate the area A under the curve by using a Riemann sum with $\Delta x = 1$.

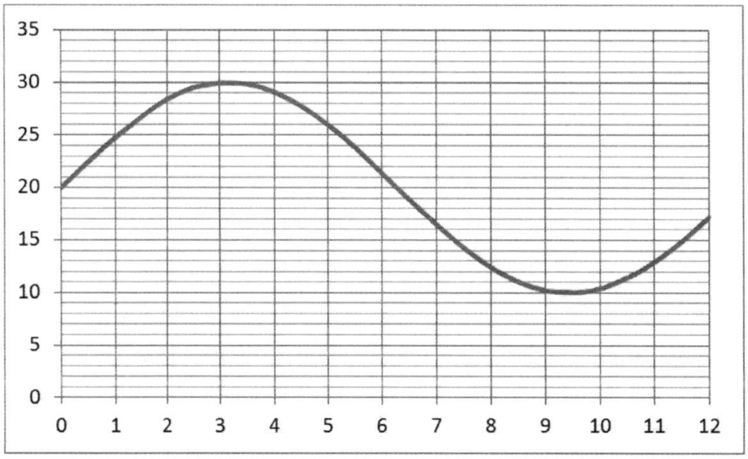

a. $209 < A < 211$
b. $230 < A < 235$
c. $238 < A < 241$
d. $246 < A < 250$

118. To the nearest hundredth, what is the area in square units under the curve of $f(x) = \frac{1}{x}$ on [1,2]?

a. 0.50
b. 0.69
c. 1.30
d. 1.50

119. Calculate $\int 3x^2 + 2x - 1\ dx$.

a. $x^3 + x^2 - x + c$
b. $6x^2 + 2$
c. $\frac{3}{2}x^3 + 2x^2 - x + c$
d. $6x^2 + 2 + c$

120. Calculate $\int 3x^2 e^{x^3}\ dx$

a. $x^3 e^{x^3} + c$
b. $e^{x^3} + c$
c. $x^3 e^{\frac{x^4}{4}} + c$
d. $ln\, x^3 + c$

121. Find the area A of the finite region between the graphs of $y = -x + 2$ and $y = x^2 - 4$.

a. 18
b. $\frac{125}{6}$
c. $\frac{45}{2}$
d. 25

122. The velocity of a car which starts at position 0 at time 0 is given by the equation $v(t) = 12t - t^2$ for $0 \leq t \leq 12$. Find the position of the car when its acceleration is 0.

a. 18
b. 36
c. 144
d. 288

123. Which of these graphs is NOT representative of the data set shown below?

Stem	Leaves
3	6 7 9 9
4	2 3 8 8 9
5	0 1 1 1 5 7
6	0 0 1 2 3

Key
2|1 2 3 = 21, 22, 23

a. 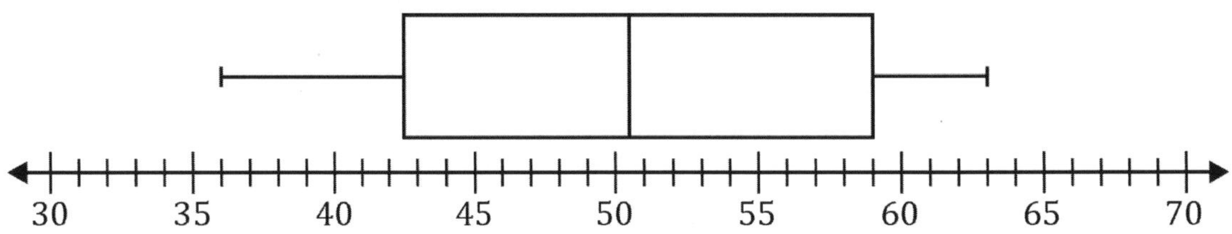

b. 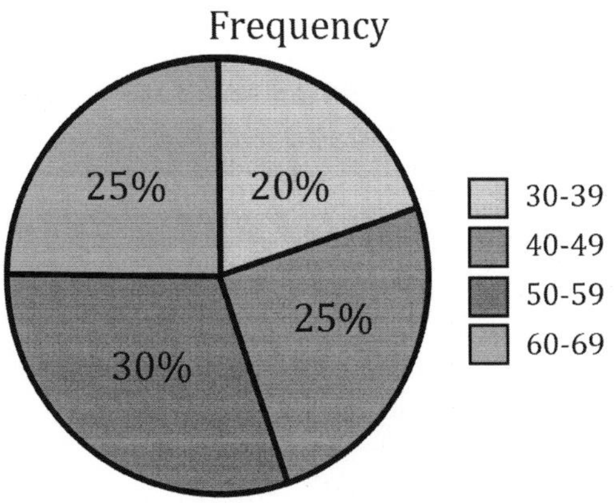

c. 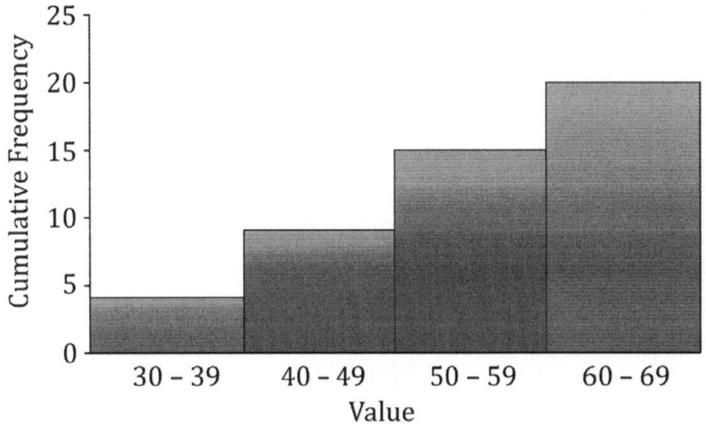

d. All of these graphs represent the data set.

124. Which of these would best illustrate change over time?

a. Pie chart
b. Line graph
c. Box-and-whisker plot
d. Venn diagram

125. Which of these is the least biased sampling technique?

a. To assess his effectiveness in the classroom, a teacher distributes a teacher evaluation to all of his students. Responses are anonymous and voluntary.
b. To determine the average intelligence quotient (IQ) of students in her school of 2,000 students, a principal uses a random number generator to select 300 students by student identification number and has them participate in a standardized IQ test.
c. To determine which video game is most popular among his fellow eleventh graders at school, a student surveys all of the students in his English class.
d. Sixty percent of students at the school have a parent who is a member of the Parent-Teacher Association (PTA). To determine parent opinions regarding school improvement programs, the Parent-Teacher Association (PTA) requires submission of a survey response with membership dues.

126. Which of these tables properly displays the measures of central tendency which can be used for nominal, interval, and ordinal data?

a.

	Mean	Median	Mode
Nominal			x
Interval	x	x	x
Ordinal		x	x

b.

	Mean	Median	Mode
Nominal			x
Interval	x	x	x
Ordinal	x	x	x

c.

	Mean	Median	Mode
Nominal	x	x	x
Interval	x	x	x
Ordinal	x	x	x

d.

	Mean	Median	Mode
Nominal			x
Interval	x	x	
Ordinal	x	x	x

Use the following data to answer questions 127-129:

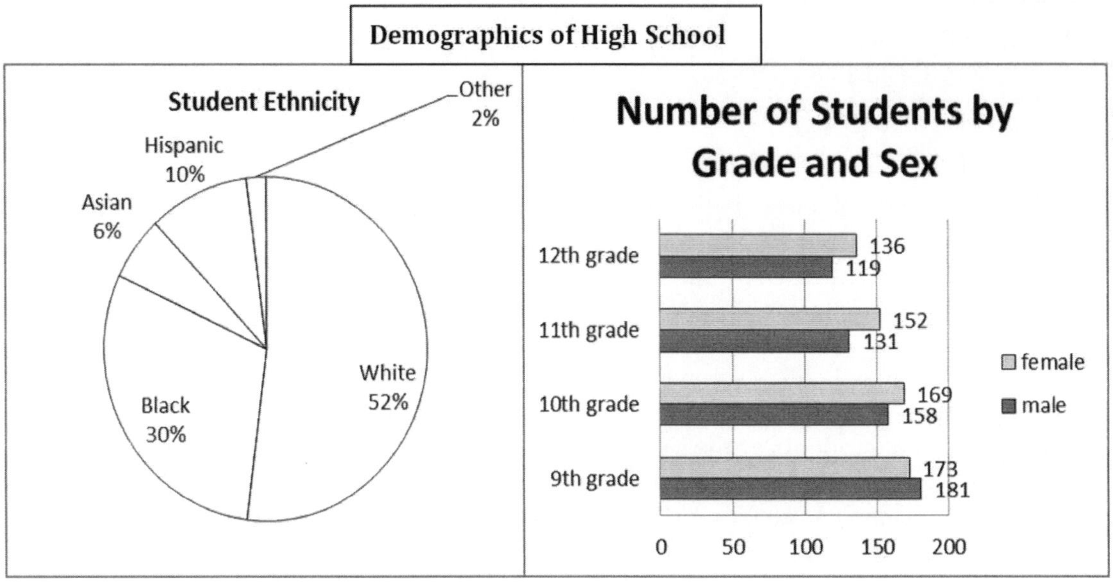

127. Which of these is the greatest quantity?

a. The average number of male students in the 11th and 12th grades
b. The number of Hispanic students at the school
c. The difference in the number of male and female students at the school
d. The difference in the number of 9th and 12th grade students at the school

128. Compare the two quantities.

Quantity A	Quantity B
The percentage of white students at the school, rounded to the nearest whole number	The percentage of female students at the school, rounded to the nearest whole number

a. Quantity A is greater.
b. Quantity B is greater.
c. The two quantities are the same.
d. The relationship cannot be determined from the given information.

129. An eleventh grader is chosen at random to represent the school at a conference. What is the approximate probability that the student is male?

a. 0.03
b. 0.11
c. 0.22
d. 0.46

The box-and-whisker plot displays student test scores by class period. Use the data to answer questions 130 through 132:

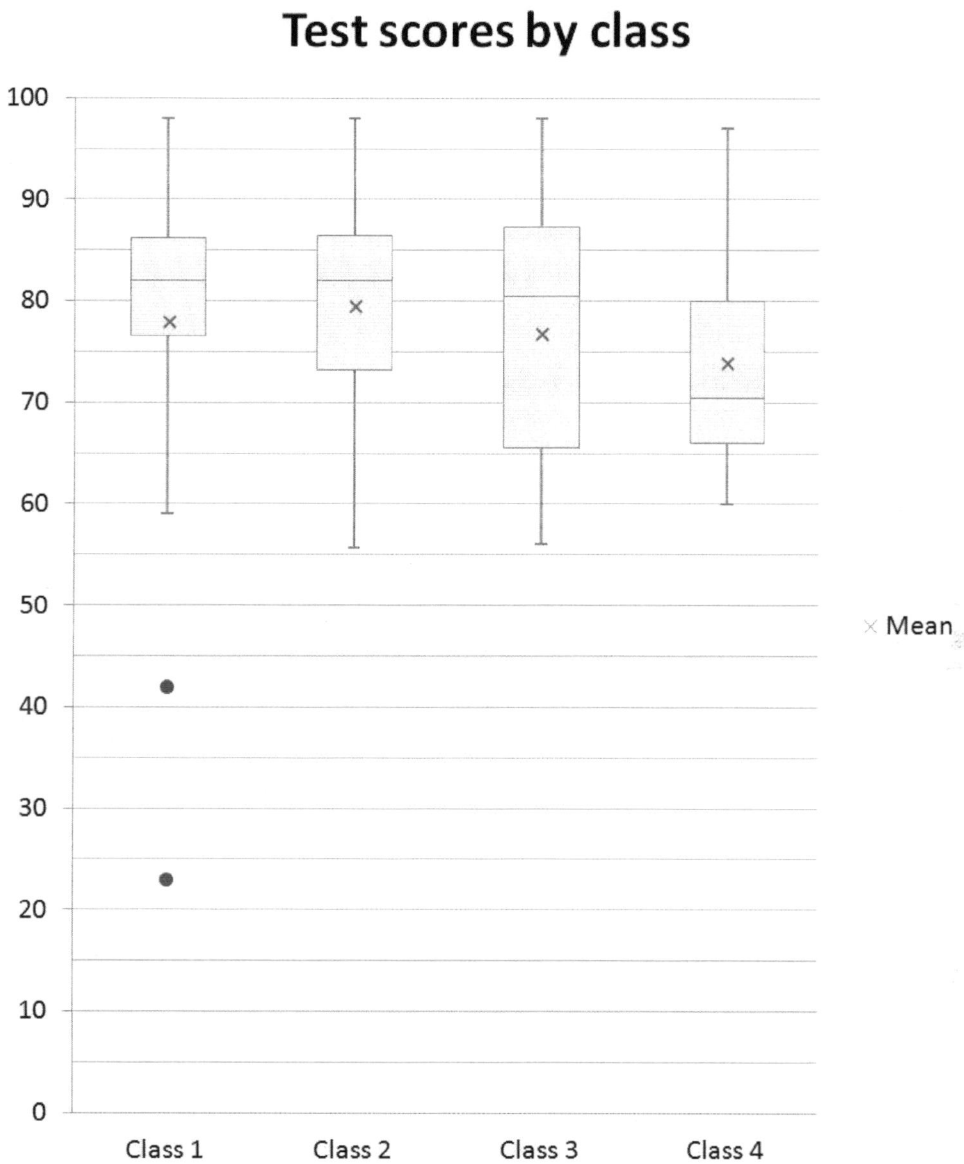

130. Which class has the greatest range of test scores?

a. Class 1
b. Class 2
c. Class 3
d. Class 4

131. What is the probability that a student chosen at random from class 2 made above a 73 on this test?

a. 0.25
b. 0.5
c. 0.6
d. 0.75

132. Which of the following statements is true of the data?

a. The mean better reflects student performance in class 1 than the median.
b. The mean test score for class 1 and 2 is the same.
c. The median test score for class 1 and 2 is the same.
d. The median test score is above the mean for class 4.

133. In order to analyze the real estate market for two different zip codes within the city, a realtor examines the most recent 100 home sales in each zip code. She considered a house which sold within the first month of its listing to have a market time of one month; likewise, she considered a house to have a market time of two months if it sold after having been on the market for one month but by the end of the second month. Using this definition of market time, she determined the frequency of sales by the number of months on the market. The results are displayed below.

Which of the following is a true statement for these data?

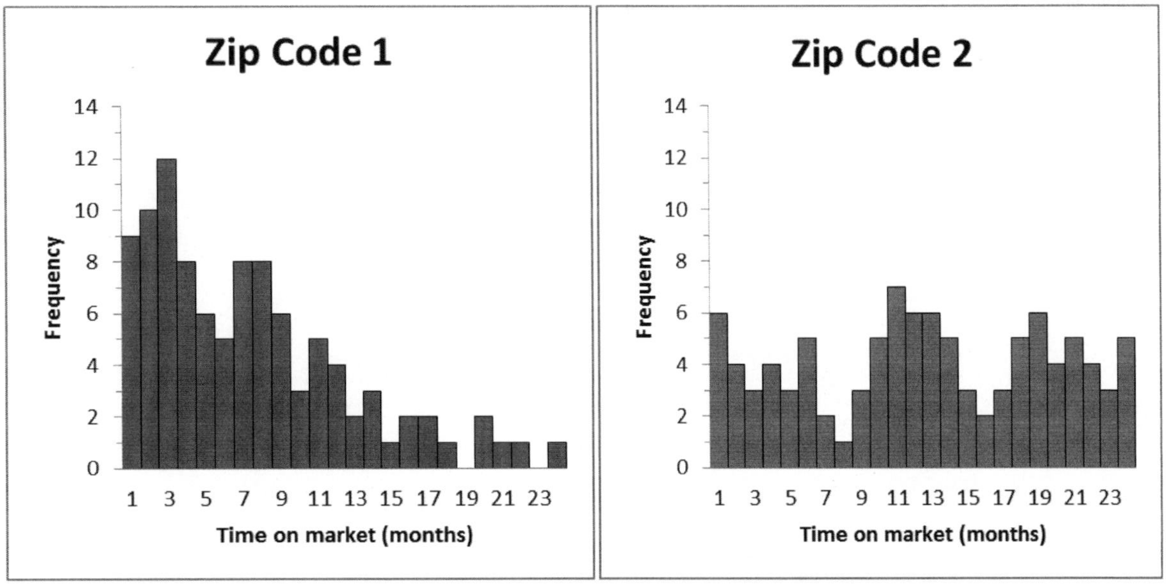

a. The median time a house spends on the market in Zip Code 1 is five months less than Zip Code 2
b. On average, a house spent seven months longer on the market in Zip Code 2 than in Zip Code 1.
c. The mode time on the market is higher for Zip Code 1 than for Zip Code 2.
d. The median time on the market is less than the mean time on the market for Zip Code 1.

134. Attending a summer camp are 12 six-year-olds, 15 seven-year-olds, 14 eight-year-olds, 12 nine-year-olds, and 10 ten-year-olds. If a camper is randomly selected to participate in a special event, what is the probability that he or she is at least eight years old?

a. $\frac{2}{9}$
b. $\frac{22}{63}$
c. $\frac{4}{7}$
d. $\frac{3}{7}$

135. A small company is divided into three departments as shown. Two individuals are chosen at random to attend a conference. What is the approximate probability that two women from the same department will be chosen?

	Department 1	Department 2	Department 3
Women	12	28	16
Men	18	14	15

a. 8.6%
b. 10.7%
c. 11.2%
d. 13.8%

136. A random sample of 90 students at an elementary school were asked these three questions:

Do you like carrots?
Do you like broccoli?
Do you like cauliflower?

The results of the survey are shown below. If these data are representative of the population of students at the school, which of these is most probable?

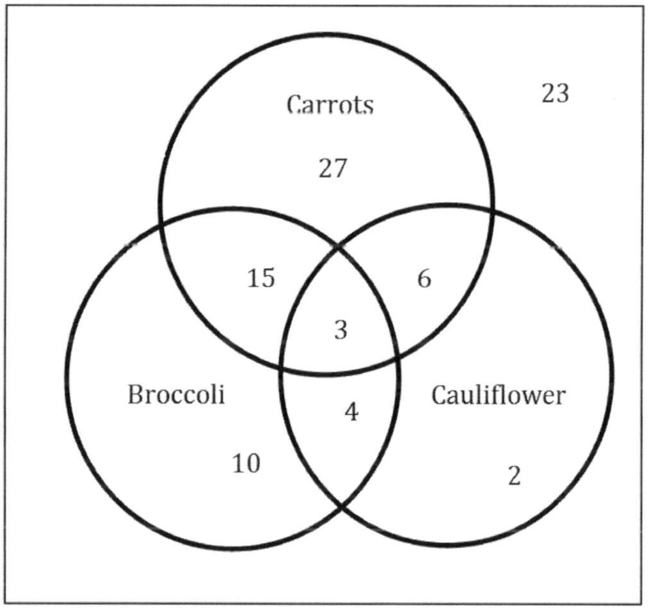

a. A student chosen at random likes broccoli.
b. If a student chosen at random likes carrots, they will also like at least one other vegetable.
c. If a student chosen at random likes cauliflower and broccoli, they will also like carrots.
d. A student chosen at random does not like carrots, broccoli, or cauliflower.

Use the information below to answer questions 137 and 138:

Each day for 100 days, a student tossed a single misshapen coin three times in succession and recorded the number of times the coin landed on heads. The results of his experiment are shown below.

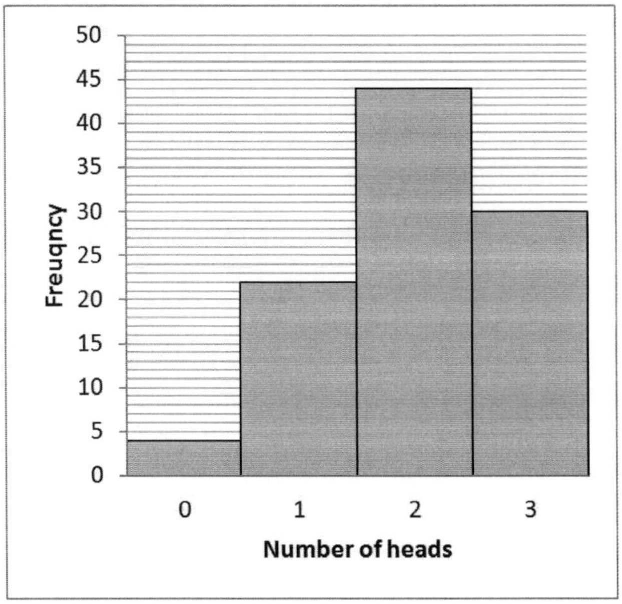

137. Given these experimental data, which of these approximates P(heads) for a single flip of this coin.

a. 0.22
b. 0.5
c. 0.67
d. 0.74

138. Which of these shows the graphs of the probability distributions from ten flips of this misshapen coin and ten flips of a fair coin?

a.

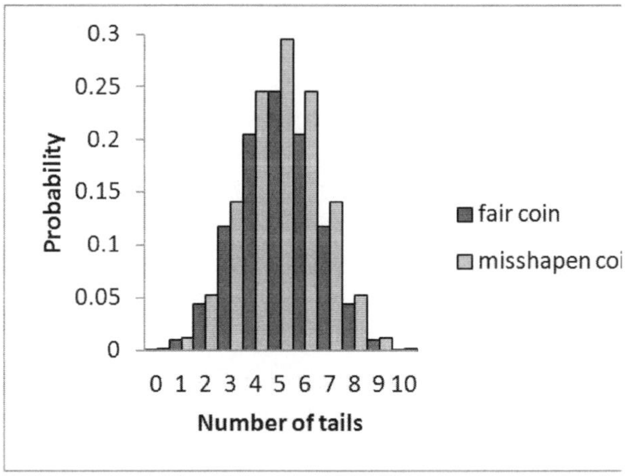

b.

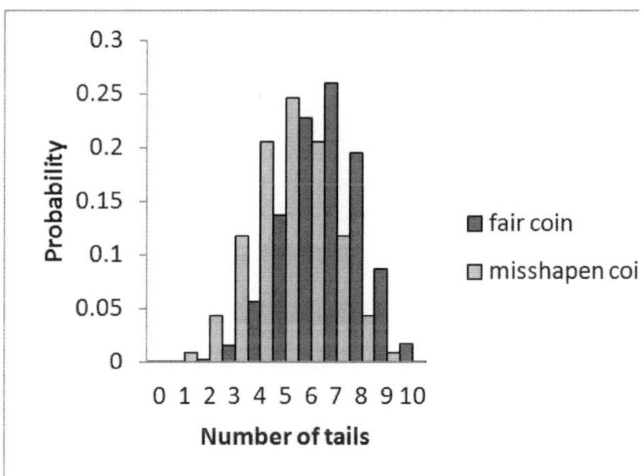

c.

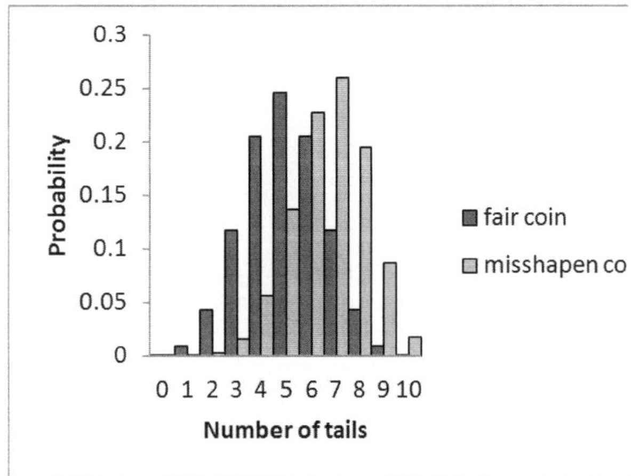

d.

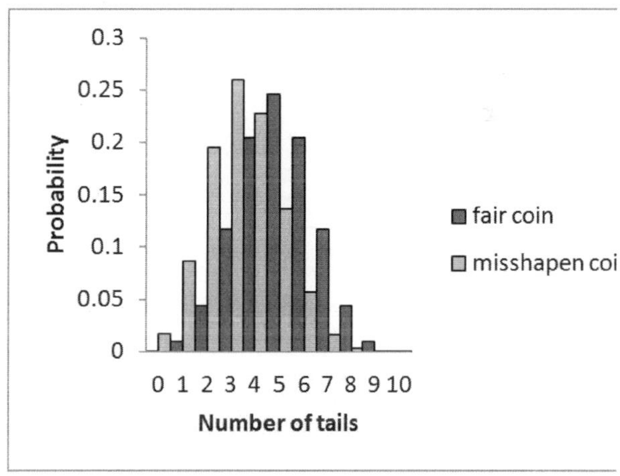

139. Which of these does NOT simulate randomly selecting a student from a group of 11 students?

a. Assigning each student a unique card value of A, 1, 2, 3, 4, 5, 6, 7, 8, 9, or J, removing queens and kings from a standard deck of 52 cards, shuffling the remaining cards, and drawing a single card from the deck
b. Assigning each student a unique number 0-10 and using a computer to randomly generate a number within that range
c. Assigning each student a unique number from 2 to 12 ; rolling two dice and finding the sum of the numbers on the dice
d. All of these can be used as a simulation of the event.

140. Gene P has three possible alleles, or gene forms, called a, b and c. Each individual carries two copies of Gene P, one of which is inherited from his or her mother and the other of which is inherited from his or her father. If the two copies of Gene P are of the same form, the individual is homozygous for that allele; otherwise, the individual is heterozygous. A simulation is performed to determine the genotypes, or genetic make-ups, of 500 individuals selected at random from the population. 500 two-digit numbers are generator using a random number generator. Based on the relative frequencies of each allele, the digit 0 is assigned to represent allele a, the digits 1 and 2 to represent allele b, and the digits 3-9 to represent allele c.

28 93 97 37 92 00 27 21 87 13 62 62 15 31 55 09 47 07 54 88 38 88 10
98 34 01 45 14 34 46 38 61 93 22 37 39 57 03 93 50 53 16 28 65 81 60
21 12 13 10 19 91 04 18 49 01 99 30 11 16 00 48 04 63 59 24 02 42 23
06 32 52 19 18 94 94 46 63 87 41 79 39 85 20 43 20 15 03 39 33 77 45
66 77 70 92 25 27 68 71 89 35 98 55 85 47 60 97 12 92 53 44 45 41 51
22 09 23 81 33 04 35 43 48 32 80 36 95 64 56 34 74 55 37 64 84 51 50
25 99 51 94 19 46 10 44 17 25 75 52 47 35 70 65 08 50 98 09 02 24 30
59 00 03 21 40 30 86 16 53 91 28 17 97 58 75 76 73 83 54 40 54 13 38
36 67 74 80 63 12 41 27 96 61 66 05 60 69 96 15 56 82 57 31 83 26 24
78 42 76 49 56 06 57 78 67 02 96 40 82 29 14 07 29 62 90 31 08 26 71
61 18 22 84 23 33 49 29 90 07 08 05 14 59 72 86 44 69 68 99 06 11 95
43 72 58 28 93 97 37 92 00 27 21 87 13 62 62 15 31 55 09 47 07 54 88
38 88 10 98 34 01 45 14 34 46 38 61 93 22 37 39 57 03 93 50 53 16 28
65 81 60 21 12 13 10 19 91 04 18 49 01 99 30 11 16 00 48 04 63 59 24
02 42 23 06 32 52 19 18 94 94 46 63 87 41 79 39 85 20 43 20 15 03 39
33 77 45 66 77 70 92 25 27 68 71 89 35 98 55 85 47 60 97 12 92 53 44
45 41 51 22 09 23 81 33 04 35 43 48 32 80 36 95 64 56 34 74 55 37 64
84 51 50 25 99 51 94 19 46 10 44 17 25 75 52 47 35 70 65 08 50 98 09
02 24 30 59 00 03 21 40 30 86 16 53 91 28 17 97 58 75 76 73 83 54 40
54 13 38 36 67 74 80 63 12 41 27 96 61 66 05 60 69 96 15 56 82 57 31
83 26 24 78 42 76 49 56 06 57 78 67 02 96 40 82 29 14 07 29 62 90 31
08 26 71 61 18 22 84 23 33 49 29 90 07 08 05 14 59

Using the experimental probability that an individual will be homozygous for allele a (light grey) or for allele b (dark grey), predict the number of individuals in a population of 100,000 who will be homozygous for either allele.

a. 2,800
b. 5,000
c. 5,400
d. 9,000

141. The intelligence quotients (IQs) of a randomly selected group of 300 people are normally distributed with a mean IQ of 100 and a standard deviation of 15. In a normal distribution, approximately 68% of values are within one standard deviation of the mean. About how many individuals from the selected group have IQs of at least 85?

a. 96
b. 200
c. 216
d. 252

142. How many different seven-digit telephone numbers can be created in which no digit repeats and in which zero cannot be the first digit?

a. 5,040
b. 35,280
c. 544,320
d. 3, 265,920

143. A teacher wishes to divide her class of twenty students into four groups, each of which will have three boys and two girls. How many possible groups can she form?

a. 248
b. 6,160
c. 73,920
d. 95,040

144. In how many distinguishable ways can a family of five be seated a circular table with five chairs if Tasha and Mac must be kept separated?

a. 6
b. 12
c. 24
d. 60

145. Which of these defines the recursive sequence $a_1 = -1, a_{n+1} = a_n + 2$ explicitly?

a. $a_n = 2n - 3$
b. $a_n = -n + 2$
c. $a_n = n - 2$
d. $a_n = -2n + 3$

146. What is the sum of the series 200 + 100 + 50 + 25 + ...?

a. 300
b. 400
c. 600
d. The sum is infinite.

147. For vector $v = (4, 3)$ and vector $w = (-3, 4)$, find $2(v + w)$.

a. $(2, 14)$
b. $(14, -2)$
c. $(1,7)$
d. $(7, -1)$

148. Simplify $[2 \quad 0 \quad -5]\left(\begin{bmatrix} 4 \\ 2 \\ -1 \end{bmatrix} - \begin{bmatrix} 3 \\ 5 \\ -5 \end{bmatrix}\right)$.

a. [-18]
b. $\begin{bmatrix} 2 \\ 0 \\ -20 \end{bmatrix}$
c. $[2 \quad 0 \quad -20]$
d. $\begin{bmatrix} 2 & 0 & -5 \\ -6 & 0 & 15 \\ 8 & 0 & -20 \end{bmatrix}$

149. Consider three sets, of which one contains the set of even integers, one contains the factors of twelve, and one contains elements 1, 2, 4, and 9. If each set is assigned the name A, B, or C, and $A \cap B \subseteq B \cap C$, which of these must be set C?

a. The set of even integers
b. The set of factors of 12
c. The set $\{1, 2, 4, 9\}$
d. The answer cannot be determined from the given information.

150. Last year, Jenny tutored students in math, in chemistry, and for the ACT. She tutored ten students in math, eight students in chemistry, and seven students for the ACT. She tutored five students in both math and chemistry, and she tutored four students both in chemistry and for the ACT, and five students both in math and for the ACT. She tutored three students in all three subjects. How many students did Jenny tutor last year?

a. 34
b. 25
c. 23
d. 14

Answer Key and Explanations

1. C: Because drawing a dodecagon and counting its diagonals is an arduous task, it is useful to employ a different problem-solving strategy. One such strategy is to draw polygons with fewer sides and look for a pattern in the number of the polygons' diagonals.

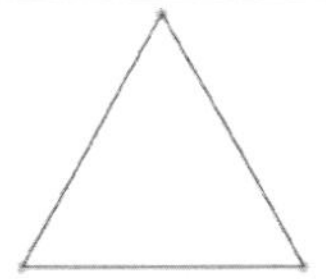	3	0
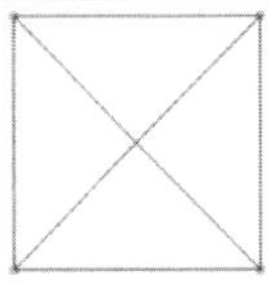	4	2
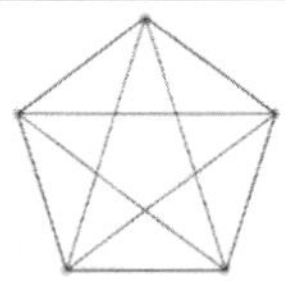	5	5
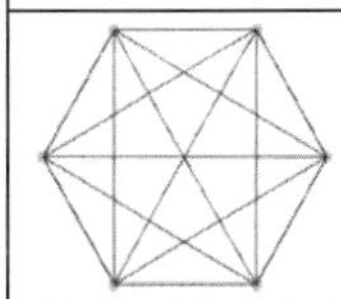	6	9
Heptagon	7	14
Octagon	8	20

A quadrilateral has two more diagonals than a triangle, a pentagon has three more diagonals than a quadrilateral, and a hexagon has four more diagonals than a pentagon. Continue this pattern to find that a dodecagon has 54 diagonals.

2. B: The problem does not give any information about the size of the bracelet or the spacing between any of the charms. Nevertheless, creating a simple illustration which shows the order of the charms will help when approaching this problem. For example, the circle below represents the bracelet, and the dotted line between A and B represents the clasp. On the right, the line shows the stretched-out bracelet and possible positions of charms C, D, and E based on the parameters.

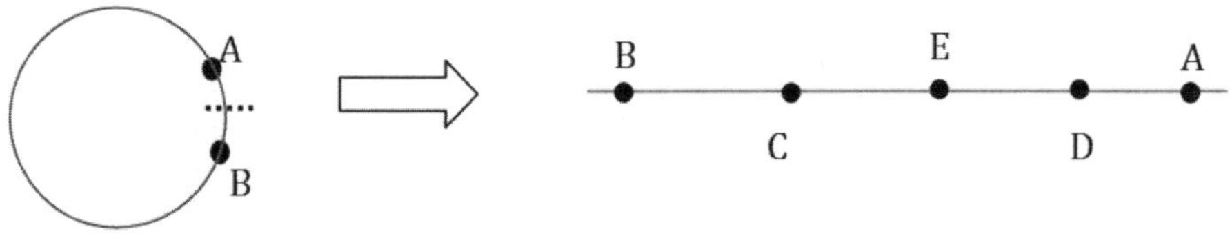

From the drawing above, it appears that statement I is true, but it is not necessarily so. The alternative drawing below also shows the charms ordered correctly, but the distance between B and E is now less than that between D and A.

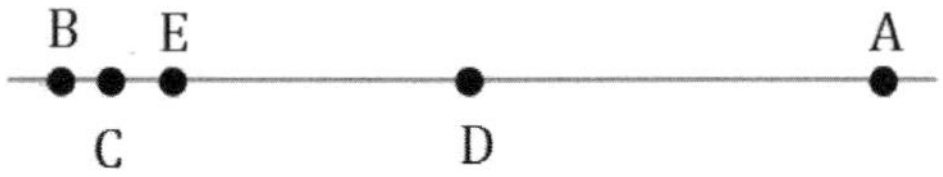

Statement II must be true: charm E must lie between B and D. Statement III must also be true: the distance between charms E and D must be less than that between C and A, which includes charms E and D in the space between them.

3. B: The population is approximately 36,000, so one quarter of the population consists of about 9,000 individuals under age 35. A third of 9,000 is 3,000, the approximate number of students in grades K-12. Since there are thirteen grades, there are about 230 students in each grade. So, the number of fourth graders is between 200 and 300.

4. A: Calculate the final sales price of the rug at each store. Please note that the explanation below uses 1.08 instead of 0.08 for tax in order to avoid having to perform addition later. If 0.08 were to be used, only the amount of tax charged would result instead of the total cost of the product with tax included. Thus, 1.08 is used to make sure 108% of the product price is calculated.

$$1.08(0.7 \times \$296) = \$223.78 \text{ at Store A}$$
$$1.08(\$220 - \$10) = \$226.80 \text{ at Store B}$$
$$\$198 + \$35 = \$233 \text{ at Store C}$$

Therefore, the stores in order of lowest to highest prices are Store A, Store B, Store C.

5. C: The expression representing the monthly charge for Company A is $\$25 + \$0.05m$, where m is the time in minutes spent talking on the phone. Set this expression equal to the monthly charge for Company B, which is $50. Solve for m to find the number of minutes for which the two companies charge the same amount:

$$\$25 + \$0.05m = \$50$$
$$\$0.05m = \$25$$
$$m = 500$$

Notice that the answer choices are given in hours, not in minutes. Since there are 60 minutes in an hour, $m = \frac{500}{60}$ hours = $8\frac{1}{3}$ hours. One-third of an hour is twenty minutes, so m = 8 hours and 20 minutes.

6. C: When the dress is marked down by 20%, the cost of the dress is 80% of its original price. Since a percentage can be written as a fraction by placing the percentage over 100, the reduced price of the dress can be written as $\frac{80}{100}x$, or $\frac{4}{5}x$, where x is the original price. When discounted an extra 25%, the dress costs 75% of the reduced price. This results in the expression $\frac{75}{100}\left(\frac{4}{5}x\right)$, which can be simplified to $\frac{3}{4}\left(\frac{4}{5}x\right)$, or $\frac{3}{5}x$. So the final price of the dress is three-fifths of the original price.

7. D: Since there are 100 cm in a meter, on a 1:100 scale drawing, each centimeter represents one meter. Therefore, an area of one square centimeter on the drawing represents one square meter in actuality. Since the area of the room in the scale drawing is 30 cm^2, the room's actual area is 30 m^2.

Another way to determine the area of the room is to write and solve an equation, such as this one:

$\frac{l}{100} \cdot \frac{w}{100} = 30 \text{ cm}^2$, where l and w are the dimensions of the actual room

$$\frac{lw}{10{,}000} = 30 \text{ m}^2$$

$$lw = 300{,}000 \text{ cm}^2$$

$$\text{Area} = 300{,}000 \text{ cm}^2$$

Since this is not one of the answer choices, convert cm^2 to m^2: $300{,}000 \text{ cm}^2 \cdot \frac{1 \text{ m}}{100 \text{ cm}} \cdot \frac{1 \text{ m}}{100 \text{ cm}} = 30 \text{ m}^2$.

8. C: Since the ratio of wages and benefits to other costs is 2:3, the amount of money spent on wages and benefits is $\frac{2}{(2+3)} = \frac{2}{5}$ of the business's total expenditure. $\left(\frac{2}{5}\right) \times \$130{,}000 = \$52{,}000$.

9. A: The height of the ball is a function of time, so the equation can be expressed as $f(t) = -16t^2 + 64t + 5$, and the average rate of change can be found by calculating $\frac{f(3)-f(1)}{3-1}$.

$$\frac{-16(3)^2 + 64(3) + 5 - [-16(1)^2 + 64(1) + 5]}{2} = \frac{-144 + 192 + 5 - (-16 + 64 + 5)}{2} = \frac{0}{2} = 0$$

Alternatively, the rate of change can be determined by finding the slope of the secant line through points $(1, f(1))$ and $(3, f(3))$. Notice that this is a horizontal line, which has a slope of 0.

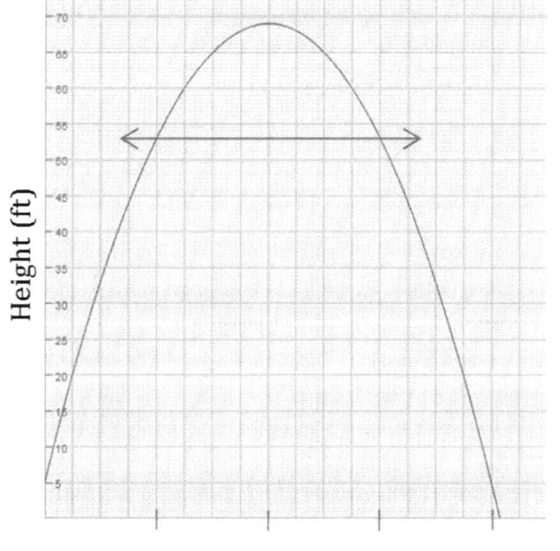

Time (sec)

10. B: Since rate in mph $= \frac{\text{distance in miles}}{\text{time in hours}}$, Zeke's driving speed on the way to Atlanta and home from Atlanta in mph can be expressed as d/3 and d/2, respectively, when d=distance between Zeke's house and his destination . Since Zeke drove 20 mph faster on his way home, $\frac{d}{2} - \frac{d}{3} = 20$.

$$6\left(\frac{d}{2} - \frac{d}{3} = 20\right)$$

$$3d - 2d = 120$$

$$d = 120$$

Since the distance between Zeke's house and the store in Atlanta is 120 miles, Zeke drove a total distance of 240 miles in five hours. Therefore, his average speed was $\frac{240 \text{ miles}}{5 \text{ hours}} = 48$ mph.

11. C: Aaron ran four miles from home and then back again, so he ran a total of eight miles. Therefore, statement III is false. Statements I and II, however, are both true. Since Aaron ran eight miles in eighty minutes, he ran an average of one mile every ten minutes, or six miles per hour; he ran two miles from point A to B in 20 minutes and four miles from D to E in 40 minutes, so his running speed between both sets of points was the same.

12. D: First, use the table to determine the values of $(a * b)$ and $(c * d)$.

$*$	a	b	c	d
a	d	a	b	c
b	a	b	c	d
c	b	c	d	a
d	c	d	a	b

$(a * b) = a$ and $(c * d) = a$, so $(a * b) * (c * d) = a * a$, which is equal to d.

13. B: When $y = x^3$, $x = \sqrt[3]{y}$. Similarly, when $y = e^x$, $x = \ln y$ for $y > 0$. On the other hand, when $y = x + a$, $x = y - a$; when $y = 1/x$, $x = 1/y$ for $x, y \neq 0$; and when $y = \sin x$, $x = \sin^{-1} y$.

14. B: Deductive reasoning moves from one or more general statements to a specific, while inductive reasoning makes a general conclusion based on a series of specific instances or observations. Whenever the premises used in deductive reasoning are true, the conclusion drawn is necessarily true. In inductive reasoning, it is possible for the premises to be true and the conclusion to be false since there may exist an exception to the general conclusion drawn from the observations made.

15. A: The first argument's reasoning is valid, and since its premises are true, the argument is also sound. The second argument's reasoning is invalid; that the premises are true is irrelevant. (For example, consider the true premises "all cats are mammals" and "all dogs are mammals;" it cannot be logically concluded that all dogs are cats.) The third argument's reasoning is valid, but since one of its premises is false, the argument is not sound.

16. C: The logical representation $p \rightarrow q$ means that p implies q. In other words, if p, then q. Unlike the contrapositive (Choice C), neither the converse (choice A) nor the inverse (choice B) is necessarily true. For example, consider this statement: all cats are mammals. This can be written as an if/then statement: if an animal is a cat, then the animal is a mammal. The converse would read, "If an animal is a mammal, then the animal is a cat;" of course, this is not necessarily true since there are many mammals other than cats. The inverse statement, "If an animal is not a cat, then the animal is not a mammal," is false. The contrapositive, "If an animal is not a mammal, then the animal is not a cat" is true since there are no cats which are not mammals.

17. D: The symbol $\wedge$ is the logical conjunction symbol. In order for statement $(p \wedge q)$ to be true, both statements p and q must be true. The $\sim$ symbol means "not," so if $(p \wedge q)$ is true, then $\sim(p \wedge q)$ is false, and if $(p \wedge q)$ is false, then $\sim(p \wedge q)$ is true. The statement $q \leftrightarrow \sim(p \wedge q)$ is true when the value of q is the same as the value of $\sim(p \wedge q)$.

p	q	$(p \wedge q)$	$\sim(p \wedge q)$	$q \leftrightarrow \sim(p \wedge q)$
T	T	T	F	F
T	F	F	T	F
F	T	F	T	T
F	F	F	T	F

18. D: The value "0" means "false," and the value "1" means "true." For the logical disjunction "or," the output value is true if either or both input values are true, else it is false. For the logical conjunction "and," the output value is true only if both input values are true. "Not *A*" is true when *A* is false and is false when *A* is true.

X	Y	Z	not Y	not Z	not Y or not Z	X and (not Y or not Z)
0	0	0	1	1	1	0
0	0	1	1	0	1	0
0	1	0	0	1	1	0
0	1	1	0	0	0	0
1	0	0	1	1	1	1
1	0	1	1	0	1	1
1	1	0	0	1	1	1
1	1	1	0	0	0	0

19. A: The Babylonians used a base-60 numeral system, which is still used in the division of an hour into 60 minutes, a minute into 60 seconds, and a circle into 360 degrees. (The word "algebra" and its development as a discipline separate from geometry are attributed to the Arabic/Islamic civilization. The Greek philosopher Thales is credited with using deductive reasoning to prove geometric concepts. Boolean logic and algebra was introduced by British mathematician George Boole.)

20. C: Leonhard Euler made many important contributions to the field of mathematics. One such contribution, Euler's formula $e^{i\varphi} = \cos\varphi + i\sin\varphi = 0$, can be written as $e^{i\pi} + 1 = 0$ when $\varphi = \pi$. This identity is considered both mathematically remarkable and beautiful, as it links together five important mathematical constants, $e, i, \pi, 0$ and 1.

21. B: The notation $\mathbb{P} \subset \mathbb{N} \subseteq \mathbb{Z} \subseteq \mathbb{Q} \subseteq \mathbb{R} \subseteq \mathbb{C}$ means that the set of prime numbers is a subset of the set natural numbers, which is a subset of the set of integers, which is a subset of the set of rational numbers, which is a subset of the set real numbers, which is a subset of the set of complex numbers.

22. A: The set of whole numbers, $\{0, 1, 2, 3, \dots\}$, does not contain the number -4. Since -4 is an integer, it is also a rational number and a real number.

23. D: In order for a set to be a group under operation $*$,

1. The set must be closed under that operation. In other words, when the operation is performed on any two members of the set, the result must also be a member of that set.
2. The set must demonstrate associativity under the operation: $a * (b * c) = (a * b) * c$
3. There must exist an identity element e in the group: $a * e = e * a = a$
4. For every element in the group, there must exist an inverse element in the group: $a * b = b * a = e$

Note: the group need not be commutative for every pair of elements in the group. If the group demonstrates commutativity, it is called an abelian group.

The set of prime numbers under addition is not closed. For example, 3+5=8, and 8 is not a member of the set of prime numbers. Similarly, the set of negative integers under multiplication is not closed since the product of two negative integers is a positive integer. Though the set of negative integers under addition is closed and is associative, there exists no identity element (the number zero in this case) in the group. The set of positive rational numbers under multiplication is closed and associative; the multiplicative identity 1 is a member of the group, and for each element in the group, there is a multiplicative inverse (reciprocal).

24. A: First, multiply the numerator and denominator by the denominator's conjugate, $4 + 2i$. Then, simplify the result and write the answer in the form $a + bi$.

$$\frac{2+3i}{4-2i} \cdot \frac{4+2i}{4+2i} = \frac{8+4i+12i+6i^2}{16-4i^2} = \frac{8+16i-6}{16+4} = \frac{2+16i}{20} = \frac{1}{10} + \frac{4}{5}i$$

25. D: First, simplify the expression within the absolute value symbol.

$$|(2-3i)^2 - (1-4i)|$$
$$|4 - 12i + 9i^2 - 1 + 4i|$$
$$|4 - 12i - 9 - 1 + 4i|$$
$$|-6 - 8i|$$

The absolute value of a complex number is its distance from 0 on the complex plane. Use the Pythagorean Theorem (or the 3-4-5 Pythagorean triple and similarity) to find the distance of $-6 - 8i$ from the origin.

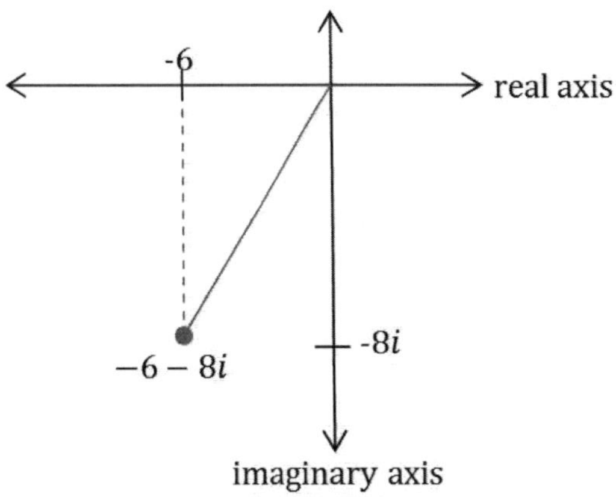

Since the distance from the origin to the point $-6 - 8i$ is 10, $|-6 - 8i| = 10$.

26. B: In order for a set to be a group under operation $*$,

1. The set must be closed under that operation. In other words, when the operation is performed on any two members of the set, the result must also be a member of that set.
2. The set must demonstrate associativity under the operation: $a * (b * c) = (a * b) * c$
3. There must exist an identity element e in the group: $a * e = e * a = a$
4. For every element in the group, there must exist an inverse element in the group: $a * b = b * a = e$

Choice A can easily be eliminated as the correct answer because the set $\{-i, 0, i\}$ does not contain the multiplicative identity 1. Though choices C and D contain the element 1, neither is closed: for example, since $i \cdot i = -1$, -1 must be an element of the group. Choice B is closed, contains the multiplicative identity 1, and the inverse of each element is included in the set as well. Of course, multiplication is an associative operation, so the set $\{-1, 1, i, -i\}$ forms a group under multiplication

×	-1	1	i	$-i$
-1	1	-1	$-i$	i
1	-1	1	i	$-i$
i	$-i$	i	-1	1
$-i$	i	$-i$	1	-1

27. D: The identity element is d since $d\#a = a\#d = a, d\#b = b\#d = b, d\#c = c\#d = c$, and $d\#d = d$. The inverse of element c is c since $c\#c = d$, the identity element. The operation # is commutative because $a\#b = b\#a$, $a\#c = c\#a$, etc. Rather than check that the operation is commutative for each pair of elements, note that elements in the table display symmetry about the diagonal elements; this indicates that the operation is indeed commutative.

#	a	b	c	d
a	c	d	b	a
b	d	c	a	b
c	b	a	d	c
d	a	b	c	d

28. C: "The square of twice the sum of x and three is equal to the product of twenty-four and x" is represented by the equation $[2(x+3)]^2 = 24x$. Solve for x.

$$[2(x+3)]^2 = 24x$$

$$[2x+6]^2 = 24x$$

$$4x^2 + 24x + 36 = 24x$$

$$4x^2 = -36$$

$$x^2 = -9$$

$$x = \pm\sqrt{-9}$$

$$x = \pm 3i$$

So, $-3i$ is a possible value of x.

29. C: If x is a prime number and that the greatest common factor of x and y is greater than 1, the greatest common factor of x and y must be x. The least common multiple of two numbers is equal to the product of those numbers divided by their greatest common factor. So, the least common multiple of x and y is $\frac{xy}{x} = y$. Therefore, the values in the two columns are the same.

30. D: Since a and b are even integers, each can be expressed as the product of 2 and an integer. So, if we write $a = 2x$ and $b = 2y$, $3(2x)^2 + 9(2y)^3 = c$.

$$3(4x^2) + 9(8y^3) = c$$

$$12x^2 + 72y^3 = c$$

$$12(x^2 + 6y^3) = c$$

Since c is the product of 12 and some other integer, 12 must be a factor of c. Incidentally, the numbers 2, 3, and 6 must also be factors of c since each is also a factor of 12.

31. C: Choice C is the equation for the greatest integer function. A function is a relationship in which for every element of the domain (x), there is exactly one element of the range (y). Graphically, a relationship between x and y can be identified as a function if the graph passes the vertical line test.

The first relation is a parabola on its side, which fails the vertical line test for functions. A circle (Choice B) also fails the vertical line test and is therefore not a function. The relation in Choice D pairs two elements of the range with one of the elements of the domain, so it is also not a function.

32. B: The area of a triangle is $A = \frac{1}{2}bh$, where b and h are the lengths of the triangle's base and height, respectively. The base of the given triangle is x, but the height is not given. Since the triangle is a right triangle and the hypotenuse is given, the triangle's height can be found using the Pythagorean Theorem.

$$x^2 + h^2 = 6^2$$
$$h = \sqrt{36 - x^2}$$

To find the area of the triangle in terms of x, substitute $\sqrt{36 - x^2}$ for the height and x for the base of the triangle into the area formula.

$$A = \frac{1}{2}bh$$
$$A(x) = \frac{1}{2}(x)(\sqrt{36 - x^2})$$
$$A(x) = \frac{x\sqrt{36 - x^2}}{2}$$

33. A: $[g \circ f\,]x = g(f(x)) = g(2x + 4) = (2x + 4)^2 - 3(2x + 4) + 2 = 4x^2 + 16x + 16 - 6x - 12 + 2 = 4x^2 + 10x + 6$.

34. C: Use the table of values to first write equations for $f(x)$ and $g(x)$: $f(x) = 2x^2$ and $g(x) = 2x + 5$. Then, use those equations to find $f(g(-4))$. Start by finding $g(-4)$.

$$g(-4) = 2(-4) + 5 = -8 + 5 = -3$$

From here, substitute $g(-4)$ into the function $f(x)$ to find $f(g(-4))$. Since $g(-4) = -3$, plug in -3 anywhere an x is found in $f(x)$.

$$f(-3) = 2(-3)^2 = 2(9) = 18$$

So, $f(g(-4)) = 18$.

35. D: By definition, when $f(x)$ and $g(x)$ are inverse functions, $f(g(x)) = g(f(x)) = x$. So, $f(g(4)) = 4$.

36. B: To find the inverse of an equation, solve for x in terms of y; then, exchange the variables x and y. Or, to determine if two functions $f(x)$ and $g(x)$ are inverses, find $f(g(x))$ and $g(f(x))$; if both results are x, then $f(x)$ and $g(x)$ are inverse functions.

For example, to find the inverse of $y = x + 6$, rewrite the equation $x = y + 6$ and solve for y. Since $y = x - 6$, the two given equations given in Choice A are inverses. Likewise, to find the inverse of $y = \frac{2x+3}{x-1}$, rewrite the equation as $x = \frac{2y+3}{y-1}$ and solve for y:

$$xy - x = 2y + 3$$
$$xy - 2y = x + 3$$
$$y(x - 2) = x + 3$$
$$y = \frac{x + 3}{x - 2}$$

The two equations given in Choice C are inverses.

Here, the second method is used to determine if the two equations given in Choices B and D are inverses: Choice B: $y = 2(2x + 3) - 3 = 4x + 6$. The two given equations are **NOT** inverses. Choice D: $y = \frac{(2x+1)-1}{2} = \frac{2x}{2} = x$ and $y = 2\left(\frac{x-1}{2}\right) + 1 = x - 1 + 1 = x$, so the two given equations are inverses.

37. A: Below is the graph of $g(x)$.

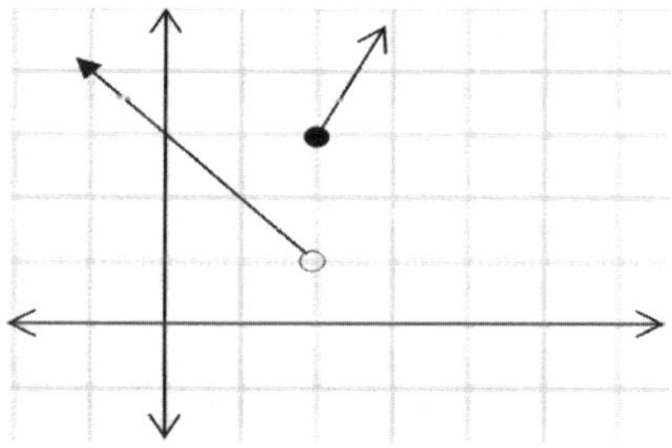

Statement II is true: the graph is indeed discontinuous at $x = 2$. Since $g(3) = 2(3) - 1 = 5$, Statement I is false, and since the range is $y > 1$, Statement III is also false.

38. A: In the range $(-\infty, -1)$, the graph represented is $y = x^2$. In the range $[-1,2)$, the graph is the greatest integer function, $y = [\![x]\!]$. In the range $[-2, \infty)$, the graph is $y = -2x + 6$.

39. B: If $y = a(x + b)(x + c)^2$, the degree of the polynomial is 3. Since the degree of the polynomial is odd and the leading coefficient is positive $(a > 0)$, the end behavior of the graph is below.

Therefore, neither Choice A nor Choice C can be a graph of $y = a(x + b)(x + c)^2$. The maximum number of "bumps" (or critical points) in the graph is at most one less than the degree of the polynomial, so Choice D, which has three bumps, cannot be the graph of the function. Choice B displays the correct end behavior and has two bumps, so it is a possible graph of $y = a(x+b)(x+c)^2$.

40. B: $5n + 3s \geq 300$ when n = number of non-student tickets which must be sold and s = number of student tickets which must be sold. The intercepts of this linear inequality are $n = 60$ and $s = 100$. The solid line through the two intercepts represents the minimum number of each type of ticket which must be sold in order to offset production costs. All points above the line represent sales which result in a profit for the school.

41. D: The vertex form of a quadratic equation is $y = a(x-h)^2 + k$, where $x = h$ is the parabola's axis of symmetry and (h,k) is the parabola's vertex. The vertex of the graph is (-1,3), so the equation can be written as $y = a(x+1)^2 + 3$. The parabola passes through point (1,1), so $1 = a(1+1)^2 + 3$. Solve for a:

$$1 = a(1+1)^2 + 3$$
$$1 = a(2)^2 + 3$$
$$1 = 4a + 3$$
$$-2 = 4a$$
$$-\frac{1}{2} = a$$

So, the vertex form of the parabola is $y = -\frac{1}{2}(x+1)^2 + 3$. Write the equation in the form $y = ax^2 + bx + c$.

$$y = -\frac{1}{2}(x+1)^2 + 3$$
$$y = -\frac{1}{2}(x^2 + 2x + 1) + 3$$
$$y = -\frac{1}{2}x^2 - x - \frac{1}{2} + 3$$
$$y = -\frac{1}{2}x^2 - x + \frac{5}{2}$$

42. D: There are many ways to solve quadratic equations in the form $ax^2 + bx + c = 0$; however, some methods, such as graphing and factoring, may not be useful for some equations, such as those with irrational or complex roots. Solve this equation by completing the square or by using the Quadratic Formula, $x = \frac{-b \pm \sqrt{b^2 - 4ac}}{2a}$.

$$7x^2 + 6x + 2 = 0; a = 7, b = 6, c = 2$$
$$x = \frac{-b \pm \sqrt{b^2 - 4ac}}{2a}$$
$$x = \frac{-6 \pm \sqrt{6^2 - 4(7)(2)}}{2(7)}$$
$$x = \frac{-6 \pm \sqrt{36 - 56}}{14}$$
$$x = \frac{-6 \pm \sqrt{-20}}{14}$$
$$x = \frac{-6 \pm 2i\sqrt{5}}{14}$$

$$x = \frac{-3 \pm i\sqrt{5}}{7}$$

43. C: A system of linear equations can be solved by using matrices or by using the graphing, substitution, or elimination (also called linear combination) method. The elimination method is shown here:

$$3x + 4y = 2$$

$$2x + 6y = -2$$

In order to eliminate x by linear combination, multiply the top equation by 2 and the bottom equation by –3 so that the coefficients of the x-terms will be additive inverses.

$$2(3x + 4y = 2)$$

$$-3(2x + 6y = -2)$$

Then, add the two equations and solve for y.

$$6x + 8y = 4$$

$$\underline{-6x - 18y = 6}$$

$$-10y = 10$$

$$y = -1$$

Substitute -1 for y in either of the given equations and solve for x.

$$3x + 4(-1) = 2$$

$$3x - 4 = 2$$

$$3x = 6$$

$$x = 2$$

The solution to the system of equations is $(2, -1)$.

44. C: The graph below shows that the lines are parallel and that the shaded regions do not overlap. There is no solution to the set of inequalities given in Choice C.

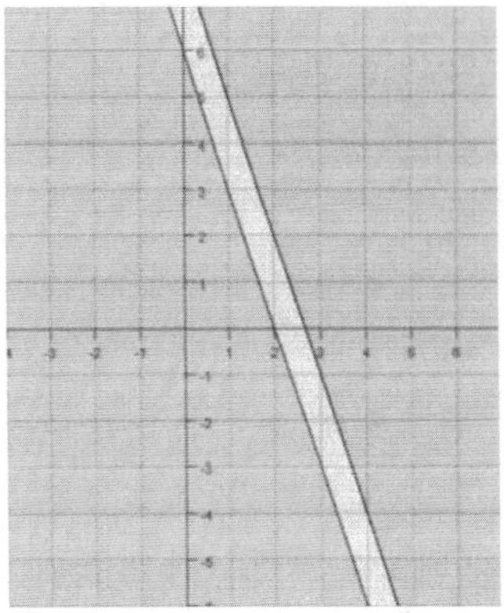

$6x + 2y \leq 12$

$2y \leq -6x + 12$

$y \leq -3x + 6$

$3x \geq 8 - y$

$y \geq -3x + 8$

As in Choice C, the two lines given in Choice A are parallel; however, the shading overlaps between the lines, so that region represents the solution to the system of inequalities.

The shaded regions for the two lines in Choice B do not overlap except at the boundary, but since the boundary is same, the solution to the system of inequalities is the line $y = -2x + 6$.

Choice D contains a set of inequalities which have intersecting shaded regions; the intersection represents the solution to the system of inequalities.

45. A: First, write three equations from the information given in the problem. Since the total number of tickets sold was 810, $\boldsymbol{x + y + z = 810}$. The ticket sales generated \$14,500, so $\boldsymbol{15x + 25y + 20z = 14,500}$. The number of children under ten was the same as twice the number of adults and seniors, so $x = 2(y + z)$, which can be rewritten as $\boldsymbol{x - 2y - 2z = 0}$.

The coefficients of each equation are arranged in the rows of a 3x3 matrix, which, when multiplied by the 3x1 matrix arranging the variables x, y, and z, will give the 3x1 matrix which arranges the constants of the equations.

46. B: There are many ways to solve this system of equations. One is shown below.

1. Multiply the second equation by 2 and combine it with the first equation to eliminate the variable y.

$$\begin{array}{rl} 2x - 4y + z = & 10 \\ \underline{-6x + 4y - 8z =} & \underline{-14} \\ -4x \qquad - 7z = & -4 \end{array}$$

2. Multiply the third equation by –2 and combine it with the original second equation to eliminate y.

$$-3x + 2y - 4z = -7$$

$$\underline{-2x - 2y + 6z = \quad 2}$$

$$-5x \qquad + 2z = -5$$

3. Multiply the equation from step one by 5 and the equation from step two by -4 and combine to eliminate x.

$$-20x - 35z = -20$$

$$\underline{\ 20x - \ 8z = \ 20}$$

$$-43z = 0$$

$$z = 0$$

4. Substitute 0 for z in the equation from step 2 to find x.

$$-5x + 2(0) = -5$$

$$-5x = -5$$

$$x = 1$$

5. Substitute 0 for z and 1 for x into the first original equation to find y.

$$2(1) - 4y + (0) = 10$$

$$2 - 4y = 10$$

$$-4y = 8$$

$$y = -2$$

47. B: One way to solve the equation is to write $x^4 + 64 = 20x^2$ in the quadratic form $(x^2)^2 - 20(x^2) + 64 = 0$. This trinomial can be factored as $(x^2 - 4)(x^2 - 16) = 0$. In each set of parentheses is a difference of squares, which can be factored further: $(x + 2)(x - 2)(x + 4)(x - 4) = 0$. Use the zero product propery to find the solutions to the equation.

$$\begin{array}{cccc} x + 2 = 0 & x - 2 = 0 & x + 4 = 0 & x - 4 = 0 \\ x = -2 & x = 2 & x = -4 & x = 4 \end{array}$$

48. A: First, set the equation equal to zero.

$$3x^3y^2 - 45x^2y = 15x^3y - 9x^2y^2$$

$$3x^3y^2 - 15x^3y + 9x^2y^2 - 45x^2y = 0$$

Then, factor the equation.

$$3x^2y(xy - 5x + 3y - 15) = 0$$

$$3x^2y[x(y - 5) + 3(y - 5)] = 0$$

$$3x^2y[(y-5)(x+3)] = 0$$

Use the zero product property to find the solutions.

$3x^2y = 0$	$y - 5 = 0$	$x + 3 = 0$
$x = 0$	$y = 5$	$x = -3$
$y = 0$		

So, the solutions are $x = \{0, -3\}$ and $y = \{0, 5\}$.

49. D: The degree of $f(x)$ is 1, the degree of $g(x)$ is 2, and the degree of $h(x)$ is 3. The leading coefficient for each function is 2. Functions $f(x)$ and $h(x)$ have exactly one real zero ($x = 1$), while $g(x)$ has two real zeros ($x = \pm 1$):

$f(x)$	$g(x)$	$h(x)$
$0 = 2x - 2$	$0 = 2x^2 - 2$	$0 = 2x^3 - 2$
$-2x = -2$	$-2x^2 = -2$	$-2x^3 = -2$
$x = 1$	$x^2 = 1$	$x^3 = 1$
	$x = 1;\ x = -1$	$x = 1$

50. B: The path of a bullet is a parabola, which is the graph of a quadratic function. The path of a sound wave can be modeled by a sine or cosine function. The distance an object travels over time given a constant rate is a linear relationship, while radioactive decay is modeled by an exponential function.

51. B: First, use the properties of logarithms to solve for y.

$$\begin{aligned} 2\log_4 y + \log_4 16 &= 3 \\ \log_4 y^2 + \log_4 16 &= 3 \\ \log_4 16y^2 &= 3 \\ 16y^2 &= 4^3 \\ 16y^2 &= 64 \\ y^2 &= 4 \\ y &= \pm 2 \end{aligned}$$

Finally, since y is positive, substitute 2 for y in the expression $\log_y 256$ and simplify. $\log_2 256 = 8$ since $2^8 = 256$.

52. B: First, apply the laws of exponents to simplify the expression on the left.

$$\frac{(x^2y)(2xy^{-2})^3}{16x^5y^2} + \frac{3}{xy}$$

$$\frac{(x^2y)(8x^3y^{-6})}{16x^5y^2} + \frac{3}{xy}$$

$$\frac{8x^5y^{-5}}{16x^5y^2} + \frac{3}{xy}$$

$$\frac{1}{2y^7} + \frac{3}{xy}$$

Then, add the two fractions.

$$\frac{1}{2y^7}\cdot\frac{x}{x}+\frac{3}{xy}\cdot\frac{2y^6}{2y^6}$$

$$\frac{x}{2xy^7}+\frac{6y^6}{2xy^7}$$

$$\frac{x+6y^6}{2xy^7}$$

53. C: If $f(x) = 10^x$ and $f(x) = 5$, then $5 = 10^x$. Since $\log_{10}x$ is the inverse of 10^x, $\log_{10}5 = \log_{10}(10^x) = x$. Therefore, $0.7 \approx x$.

54. C: The graph shown is the exponential function $y = 2^x$. Notice that the graph passes through (-2, 0.25), (0,1), (2,4).

	Choice A	**Choice B**	**Choice C**	**Choice D**
x	x^2	$\sqrt{x}$	2^x	$\log_2 x$
-2	4	undefined in $\mathbb{R}$	0.25	undefined
0	0	0	1	undefined
2	4	$\sqrt{2}$	4	1

55. C: The x-intercept is the point at which $f(x) = 0$. When $0 = \log_b x$, $b^0 = x$; since $b^0 = 1$, the x-intercept of $f(x) = \log_b x$ is always 1. If $f(x) = \log_b x$ and $x = b$, then $f(x) = \log_b b$, which is, by definition, 1. ($b^1 = b$.) If $g(x) = b^x$, then $f(x)$ and g(x) are inverse functions and are therefore symmetric with respect to $y = x$. The statement choice C is not necessarily true since $x < 1$ includes numbers less than or equal to zero, the values for which the function is undefined. The statement $f(x) < 0$ is true only for x values between 0 and 1 ($0 < x < 1$).

56. D: Bacterial growth is exponential. Let x be the number of doubling times and a be the number of bacteria in the colony originally transferred into the broth and y be the number of bacteria in the broth after a doubling times.

Time	Number of doubling times (x)	$a(2^x)$	Number of bacteria (y)
0	0	$a(2^0) = a$	1×10^6
20 minutes	1	$a(2^1)$	2×10^6
40 minutes	2	$a(2^2)$	4×10^6
60 minutes	3	$\boldsymbol{a(2^3)}$	$\mathbf{8 \times 10^6}$

Determine how many bacteria were present in the original colony. Either work backwards by halving the number of bacteria (see gray arrows above) or calculate a:

$$a(2^3) = 8 \times 10^6$$

$$8a = 8 \times 10^6$$

$$a = 10^6$$

The equation for determining the number of bacteria is $y = (2^x) \cdot 10^6$. Since the bacteria double every twenty minutes, they go through three doubling times every hour. So, when the bacteria are allowed to grow for eight hours, they will have gone through 24 doubling times. When $x = 24$, $y = (2^{24}) \cdot 10^6 = 16777216 \times 10^6$, which is approximately 1.7×10^{13}.

57. C: Since the pH scale is a base-10 logarithmic scale, a difference in pH of 1 indicates a ratio between strengths of 10. So, an acid with a pH of 3 is 100 times stronger than an acid with a pH of 5.

58. A:

$$\sqrt{\frac{-28x^6}{27y^5}} = \frac{2x^3 i\sqrt{7}}{3y^2\sqrt{3y}} \cdot \frac{\sqrt{3y}}{\sqrt{3y}} = \frac{2x^3 i\sqrt{21y}}{9y^2}$$

59. C:

$-4 \le 2 + 3(x-1) \le 2$ $-6 \le 3(x-1) \le 0$ $-2 \le x - 1 \le 0$ $-1 \le x \le 1$	$-2x^2 + 2 \ge x^2 - 1$ $-3x^2 \ge -3$ $x^2 \le 1$ $-1 \le x \le 1$	$\frac{11 - \lvert 3x \rvert}{7} \ge 2$ $11 - \lvert 3x \rvert \ge 14$ $-\lvert 3x \rvert \ge 3$ $\lvert 3x \rvert \le -1$ No solution	$3\lvert 2x \rvert + 4 \le 10$ $3\lvert 2x \rvert \le 6$ $\lvert 2x \rvert \le 2$ $-2 \le 2x \le 2$ $-1 \le x \le 1$

60. D: To solve this equation, start by squaring both sides, then isolate the variable.

$$2 - \sqrt{x} = \sqrt{x - 20}$$
$$\left(2 - \sqrt{x}\right)^2 = \left(\sqrt{x - 20}\right)^2$$
$$\left(2 - \sqrt{x}\right)\left(2 - \sqrt{x}\right) = x - 20$$
$$4 - 4\sqrt{x} + x = x - 20$$
$$-4\sqrt{x} = -24$$
$$\sqrt{x} = 6$$
$$x = 36$$

When solving radical equations, check for extraneous solutions by substituting the found value into the original equation.

$$2 - \sqrt{x} = \sqrt{x - 20}$$

$$2 - \sqrt{36} = \sqrt{36 - 20}$$
$$2 - 6 = \sqrt{16}$$
$$-4 \neq 4$$

Since the solution results in an untrue statement, there is no solution. Alternatively, consider the graphs of the left and right side of the given equation. Notice the graphs $y = 2 - \sqrt{x}$ and $y = \sqrt{x - 20}$ do not intersect, which confirms there is no solution.

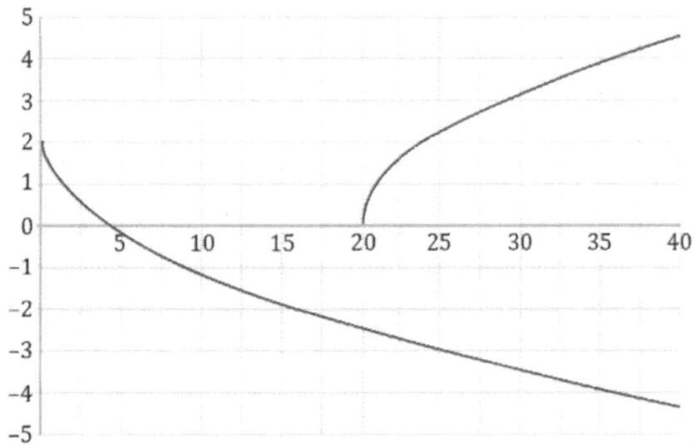

61. B: Notice that choice C cannot be correct since $x \neq 1$. ($x = 1$ results in a zero in the denominator.)

$$\frac{x-2}{x-1} = \frac{x-1}{x+1} + \frac{2}{x-1}$$

$$(x-1)(x+1)\left(\frac{x-2}{x-1} = \frac{x-1}{x+1} + \frac{2}{x-1}\right)$$

$$(x+1)(x-2) = (x-1)^2 + 2(x+1)$$

$$x^2 - x - 2 = x^2 - 2x + 1 + 2x + 2$$

$$x^2 - x - 2 = x^2 + 3$$

$$-x = 5$$

$$x = -5$$

62. A: The denominator of a fraction cannot equal zero. Therefore, for choices A and B,.

$$x^2 - x - 2 \neq 0$$

$$(x+1)(x-2) \neq 0$$

$$x + 1 \neq 0 \quad x - 2 \neq 0$$

$$x \neq -1 \quad x \neq 2.$$

Since choice A is in its simplest form, there are vertical asymptotes at $x = -1$ and $x = 2$. However, for choice B,

$$\frac{3x+3}{x^2-x-2} = \frac{3(x+1)}{(x+1)(x-2)} = \frac{3}{x-2}.$$

So, at $x = -2$ there is an asymptote, while at $x = -1$, there is simply a hole in the graph. So, choice B does not match the given graph. For choice C, there are asymptotes at $x = -1$ and $x = 2$; however, notice that it is possible for the graph of choice C to intersect the x-axis since it is possible that $y = 0$ (when $x = 0.5$). Since the given graph does not have an x-intercept, choice C is incorrect. For choice A, it is not possible that y=0, so it is a possible answer. Check a few points on the graph to make sure they satisfy the equation.

x	y
-2	$\frac{3}{4}$
0	$-\frac{3}{2}$
$\frac{1}{2}$	$-\frac{4}{3}$
1	$-\frac{3}{2}$
3	$\frac{3}{4}$

The points $\left(-2,\frac{3}{4}\right)$, $\left(0,-\frac{3}{2}\right)$, $\left(\frac{1}{2},-\frac{4}{3}\right)$, $\left(1,-\frac{3}{2}\right)$, and $(3,\frac{3}{4})$ are indeed points on the graph.

63. A: An easy way to determine which is the graph of $f(x) = -2|-x+4| - 1$ is to find $f(x)$ for a few values of x. For example, $f(x) = -2|0+4| - 1 = -9$. Graphs A and B pass through (0, -9), but graphs C and D do not. $f(4) = -2|-4+4| - 1 = -1$. Graphs A and D pass through (4, -1), but graphs B and C do not. Graph A is the correct graph. $f(x) = -2|-x+4| - 1$ shifts the graph of $y = |x|$ to the left four units, reflects it across the y-axis, inverts it, makes it narrower, and shifts it down one unit.

64. C: The first function shifts the graph of $y = \frac{1}{x}$ to the right one unit and up one unit. The domain and range of $y = \frac{1}{x}$ are $\{x: x \neq 0\}$ and $\{y: y \neq 0\}$, so the domain and range of $y = \frac{1}{x-1} + 1$ are $\{x: x \neq 1\}$ and $\{y: y \neq 1\}$. The element 1 is not in its domain.

The second function inverts the graph of $y = \sqrt{x}$ and shifts it to the left two units and down one unit. The domain and range of $y = \sqrt{x}$ are $\{x: x \geq 0\}$ and $\{y: y \geq 0\}$, so the domain and range of $y = -\sqrt{x+2} - 1$ are $\{x: x \geq -2\}$ and $\{y: y \leq -1\}$. The range does not contain the element 2.

The third function shifts the graph of $y = |x|$ to the right one unit and up three units. The domain of $y = |x|$ the set of all real numbers and range is $\{y: y \geq 0\}$, so the domain of $y = |x+2| - 3$ is the set of all real numbers and the range is $\{y: y \geq -3\}$. The domain contains the element 1 and the range contains the element 2.

This is the graph of the fourth function. The domain of this piece-wise function is the set of all real numbers, and the range is $\{y: y < -1\}$. The range does not contain the element 2.

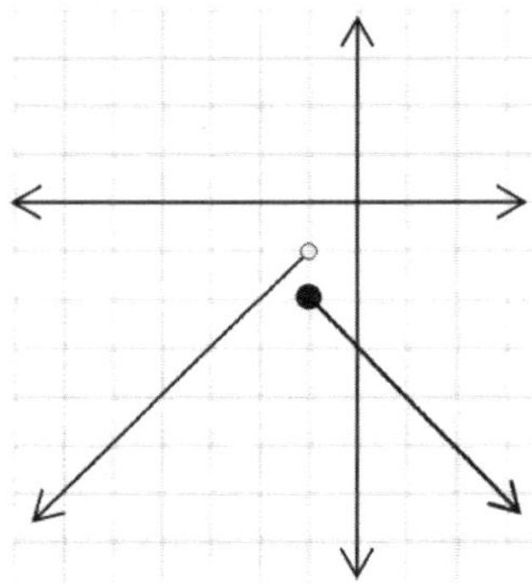

65. B: First, state the exclusions of the domain.

$$x^3 + 2x^2 - x - 2 \neq 0$$

$$(x + 2)(x - 1)(x + 1) \neq 0$$

$$x + 2 \neq 0 \quad x - 1 \neq 0 \quad x + 1 \neq 0$$

$$x \neq -2 \quad x \neq 1 \quad x \neq -1$$

To determine whether there are asymptotes or holes at these values of x, simplify the expression $\frac{x^2-x-6}{x^3+2x^2-x-2}$.

$$\frac{(x-3)(x+2)}{(x+2)(x-1)(x+1)} = \frac{x-3}{(x-1)(x+1)}$$

There are asymptotes at $x = 1$ and at $x = -1$ and a hole at $x = 2$. Statement I is false.

To find the x-intercept of $f(x)$, solve $f(x) = 0$. $f(x) = 0$ when the numerator is equal to zero. The numerator equals zero when $x = 2$ and $x = 3$; however, 2 is excluded from the domain of $f(x)$, so the x-intercept is 3. To find the y-intercept of $f(x)$, find $f(0)$. $\frac{0^2-0-6}{0^3+2(0)^2-0-2} = \frac{-6}{-2} = 3$. The y-intercept is 3. Statement II is true.

66. C: The period of the pendulum is a function of the square root of the length of its string, and is independent of the mass of the pendulum or the angle from which it is released. If the period of Pendulum 2's swing is four times the period of Pendulum 1's swing, then the length of Pendulum 1's string must be 16 times the length of Pendulum 2's swing since all other values besides L in the expression $2\pi\sqrt{\frac{L}{g}}$ remain the same.

67. D: There are many ways Josephine may have applied her knowledge to determine how to approximately measure her medicine using her plastic spoon. The only choice which correctly uses dimensional analysis is choice D: the dosage $\approx 25 \text{ cc} \cdot \frac{1 \text{ ml}}{1 \text{ cc}} \cdot \frac{1\text{L}}{1000\text{ml}} \cdot \frac{0.5 \text{ gal}}{2\text{L}} \cdot \frac{16\text{c}}{1 \text{ gal}} \cdot \frac{48\text{t}}{1\text{c}} \cdot \frac{1 \text{ spoonful}}{1\text{t}}$ $\rightarrow \frac{25}{1000} \cdot \frac{1}{4} \cdot 16 \cdot 48 \approx 5.$

68. C: Start by setting up a proportion to solve by cross multiplication: $\frac{1\text{ inch}}{60\text{ feet}} = \frac{10\text{ inches}}{x\text{ feet}}$. When the numbers are cross multiplied, you get $x = 600$ feet. Now we need to convert 600 feet to yards. There are 3 feet in 1 yard, so divide 600 by 3 to find the number of yards between the two points: $600 \div 3 = 200$. Therefore, the two points are 200 yards apart.

69. D: If the distance between the two houses is 10 cm on the map, then the actual distance between the houses is 100 m.

To find x, use the Pythagorean Theorem:

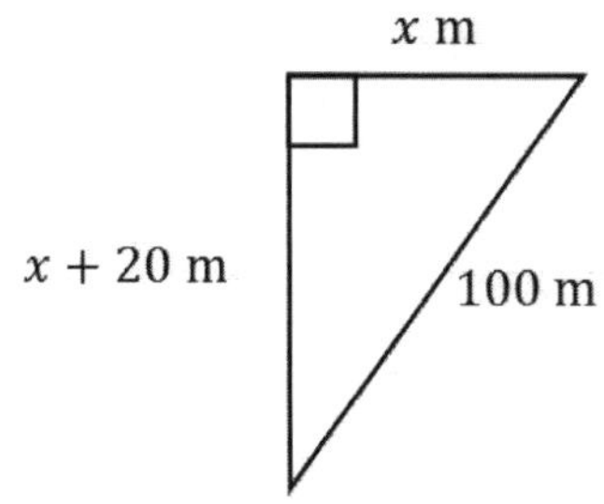

$x^2 + (x + 20)^2 = (100)^2$

$x^2 + x^2 + 40x + 400 = 10000$

$2x^2 + 40x - 9600 = 0$

$2(x^2 + 20x - 4800) = 0$

$2(x - 60)(x + 80) = 0$

$x = 60 \quad x = -80$

Since x represents a distance, it cannot equal –80. Since $x = 60$, $x + 20 = 80$. Roxana walks a total of 140 m to get to her friend's house.

70. D: ΔABC is similar to the smaller triangle with which it shares vertex A. $AB = (2x - 1) + (x + 7) = 3x + 6$. $AC = 4 + 8 = 12$. Set up a proportion and solve for x:

$$\frac{3x + 6}{12} = \frac{2x - 1}{4}$$

$$12x + 24 = 24x - 12$$

$$36 = 12x$$

$$3 = x$$

So, $AB = 3x + 6 = 3(3) + 6 = 15$.

71. B: Percent error $= \frac{|\text{actual value} - \text{measured value}|}{\text{actual value}} \times 100\%$, and the average percent error is the sum of the percent errors for each trial divided by the number of trials.

	% error Trial 1	% error Trial 2	% error Trial 3	% error Trial 4	Average percent error
Scale 1	0.1%	0.2%	0.2%	0.1%	0.15%
Scale 2	2.06%	2.09%	2.10%	2.08%	2.08%

The percent error for Scale 1 is less than the percent error for Scale 2, so it is more accurate. The more precise scale is Scale 2 because its range of values, 10.210 g − 10.206 g = 0.004 g, is smaller than the Scale 2's range of values, 10.02 g − 9.98 g = 0.04 g.

72. C: If l and w represent the length and width of the enclosed area, its perimeter is equal to $2l + 2w$; since the fence is positioned x feet from the lot's edges on each side, the perimeter of the lot is $2(l + 2x) + 2(w + 2x)$. Since the amount of money saved by fencing the smaller are is \$432, and since the fencing material costs \$12 per linear foot, 36 fewer feet of material are used to fence around the playground than would have been used to fence around the lot. This can be expressed as the equation $2(l + 2x) + 2(w + 2x) - (2l + 2w) = 36$.

$$2(l + 2x) + 2(w + 2x) - (2l + 2w) = 36$$

$$2l + 4x + 2w + 4x - 2l - 2w = 36$$

$$8x = 36$$

$$x = 4.5 \text{ ft}$$

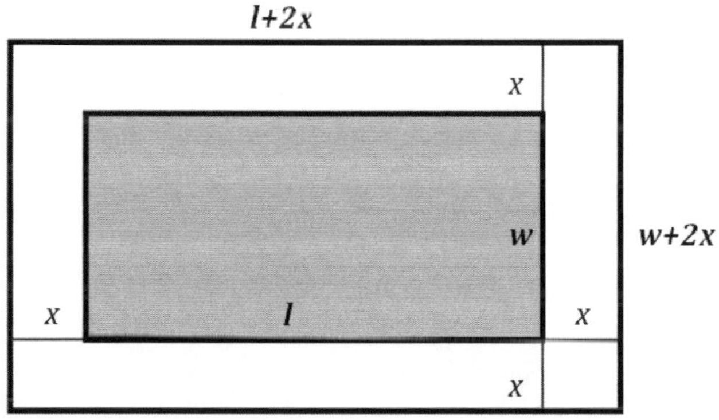

The difference in the area of the lot and the enclosed space is 141 yd^2, which is the same as 1269 ft^2. So, $(l + 2x)(w + 2x) - lw = 1269$. Substituting 4.5 for x,

$$(l + 9)(w + 9) - lw = 1269$$

$$lw + 9l + 9w + 81 - lw = 1269$$

$$9l + 9w = 1188$$

$$9(l + w) = 1188$$

$$l + w = 132 \text{ ft}$$

Therefore, the perimeter of the enclosed space, $2(l+w)$, is $2(132) = 264$ ft. The cost of 264 ft of fencing is $264 \cdot \$12 = \$3{,}168$.

73. B: The volume of a square pyramid can be calculated using the formula $V = \frac{Bh}{3}$, where B is the area of the base and h is the height of the pyramid. Therefore, the volume of Natasha's tent is $\frac{x^2h}{3}$. If she were to increase by 1 ft the length of each side of the square base, the tent's volume can be calculated by substituting $x+1$ for x in the original tent volume formula.

$$\frac{(x+1)^2h}{3} = \frac{(x^2+2x+1)(h)}{3} = \frac{x^2h+2xh+h}{3} = \frac{x^2h}{3} + \frac{2xh+h}{3}$$

Notice this is the volume of Natasha's tent, $\frac{x^2h}{3}$, increased by $\frac{2xh+h}{3}$, or $\frac{h(2x+1)}{3}$. This is how much more interior space the tent would have.

74. A: The area of a circle is πr^2, so the area of a semicircle is $\frac{\pi r^2}{2}$. Illustrated below is a method which can be used to find the area of the shaded region.

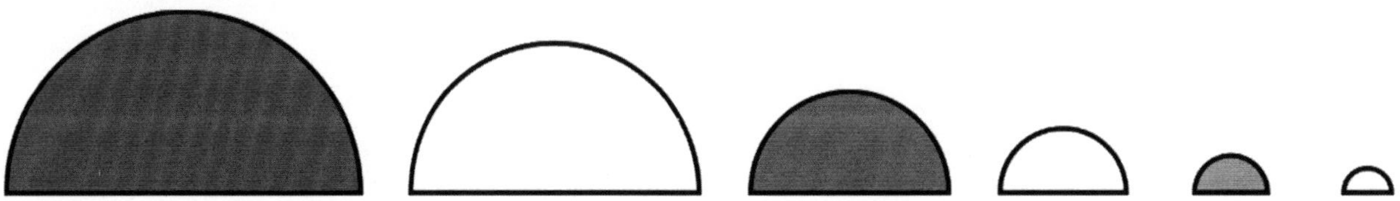

$r = 6x$ $r = 5x$ $r = 4x$ $r = 3x$ $r = 2x$ $r = x$

$$A = \frac{36\pi x^2}{2} - \frac{25\pi x^2}{2} + \frac{16\pi x^2}{2} - \frac{9\pi x^2}{2} + \frac{4\pi x^2}{2} - \frac{1\pi x^2}{2}$$
$$A = \frac{(36-25+16-9+4-1)\pi x^2}{2}$$
$$A = \frac{21\pi x^2}{2}$$

75. B. Euclidean geometry is based on the flat plane. One of Euclid's five axioms, from which all Euclidean geometric theorems are derived, is the parallel postulate, which states that in a plane, for any line l and point A not on l, exactly one line which passes through A does not intersect l.

Non-Euclidean geometry considers lines on surfaces which are not flat. For instance, on the Earth's surface, if point A represents the North Pole and line l represents the equator (which does not pass through A), all lines of longitude pass through point A and intersect line l. In elliptical geometry, there are infinitely many lines which pass though A and intersect l, and there is no line which passes through A which does not also intersect l. In hyperbolic geometry, the opposite is true. When A is not on l, all lines which pass through A diverge from l, so none of the lines through A intersect l.

76. B: When four congruent isosceles trapezoids are arranged in an arch, the bases of the trapezoid come together to form regular octagons, the smaller of which is shown to the right. The measure of each angle of a regular octagon is 135°. $\left(\frac{(8-2)(180°)}{8} = 135°.\right)$ From the relationship of two of the trapezoid's base angles with one of the octagon's interior angles, write and solve an equation:

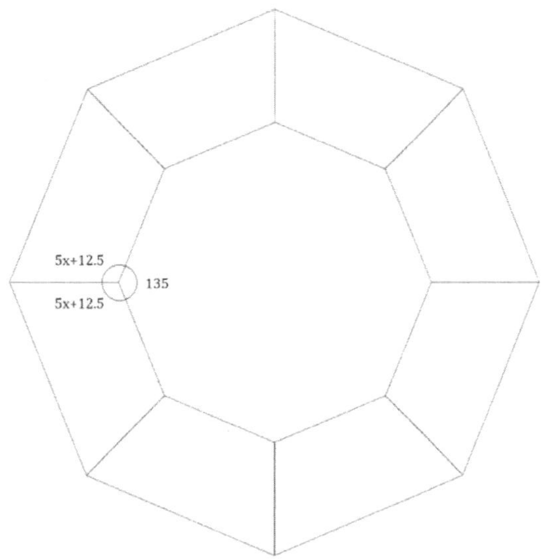

$(5x + 12.5) + (5x + 12.5) + 135 = 360$

$10x + 160 = 360$

$10x = 200$

$x = 20$

77. C: Sketch a diagram (this one is not to scale) and label the known segments. Use the property that two segments are congruent when they originate from the same point outside of a circle and are tangent to the circle.

The point of tangency of $\overline{CB}$ divides the segment into two pieces measuring 4 and 6; the point of tangency of $\overline{BA}$ divides the segment into two pieces measuring 6 and 8; the point of tangency of $\overline{AD}$ divides the segment into two pieces measuring 8 and 4. Therefore $AD = 8 + 4 = 12$.

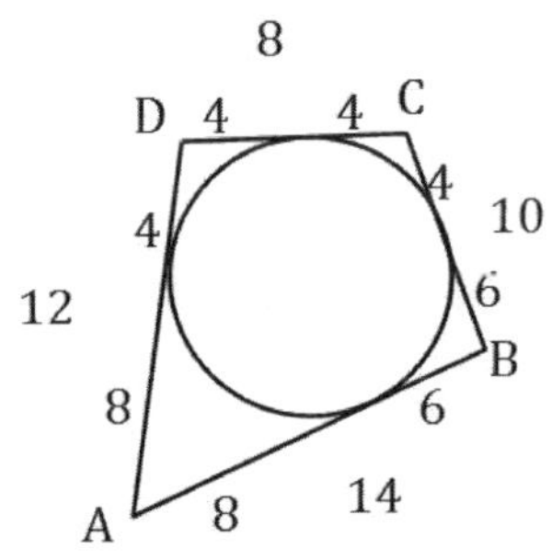

78. D: Let b represent the base of the triangle. The height h of the triangle is the altitude drawn from the vertex opposite of b to side b.

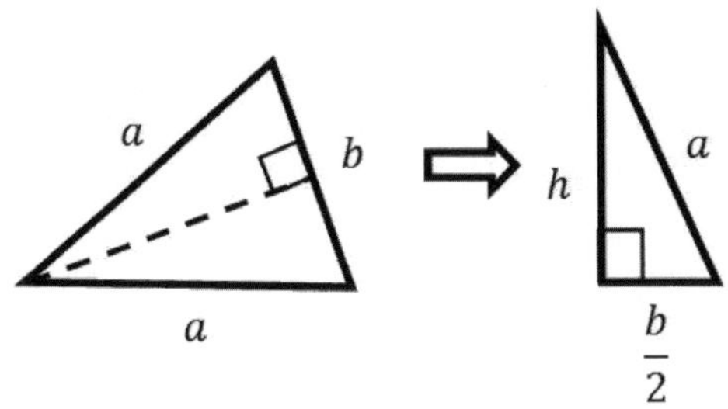

The height of the triangle can be found in terms of a and b by using the Pythagorean theorem:

$$h^2 + \left(\frac{b}{2}\right)^2 = a^2$$

$$h = \sqrt{a^2 - \frac{b^2}{4}} = \sqrt{\frac{4a^2 - b^2}{4}} = \frac{\sqrt{4a^2 - b^2}}{2}$$

The area of a triangle is $A = \frac{1}{2}bh, so\ A = \frac{1}{2}b\left(\frac{\sqrt{4a^2-b^2}}{2}\right) = \frac{b\sqrt{4a^2-b^2}}{4}$.

79. B: Since $\angle ADC$ is a right triangle with legs measuring 5 and 12, its hypotenuse measures 13. (5-12-13 is a Pythagorean triple.)

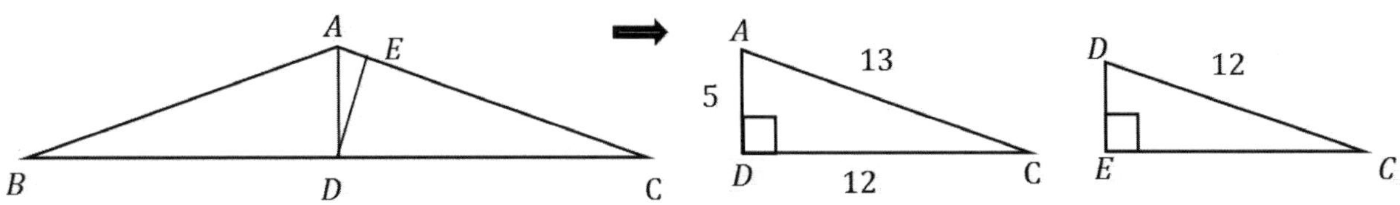

$\angle ADC$ and $\angle DEC$ are both right triangles which share vertex C. By the AA similarity theorem $\angle ADC \sim \angle DEC$. Therefore, a proportion can be written and solved to find DE.

$$\frac{5}{DE} = \frac{13}{12}$$

$$DE = 4.6$$

80. C: The center of the sphere is shared by the center of the cube, and each of the corners of the cube touches the surface of the sphere. Therefore, the diameter of the sphere is the line which passes through the center of the cube and connects one corner of the cube to the opposite corner on the opposite face. Notice in the illustration below that the diameter d of the sphere can be represented as the hypotenuse of a right triangle with a short leg measuring 4 units. (Since the volume of the cube is 64 cubic units, each of its sides measures $\sqrt[3]{64} = 4$ units.) The long leg of the triangle is the diagonal of the base of the cube. Its length can be found using the Pythagorean theorem: $4^2 + 4^2 = x^2; x = \sqrt{32} = 4\sqrt{2}$.

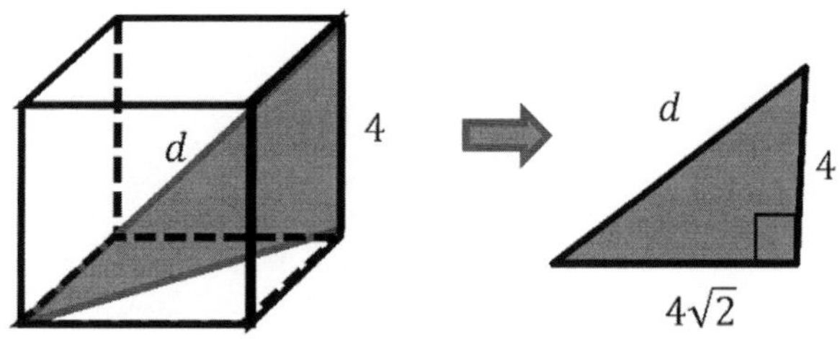

Use the Pythagorean theorem again to find d, the diameter of the sphere: $d^2 = \left(4\sqrt{2}\right)^2 + 4^2$; $d = \sqrt{48} = 4\sqrt{3}$. To find the volume of the sphere, use the formula $V = \frac{4}{3}\pi r^3$. Since the radius r of the sphere is half the diameter, $r = 2\sqrt{3}$, and $V = \frac{4}{3}\pi(2\sqrt{3})^3 = \frac{4}{3}\pi\left(24\sqrt{3}\right) = 32\pi\sqrt{3}$ cubic units.

81. D. Since it is given that $\overline{FD} \cong \overline{BC}$ and $\overline{AB} \cong \overline{DE}$, step 2 needs to establish either that $\overline{AC} \cong \overline{EF}$ or that $\Delta ABC \cong \Delta FDE$ in order for step 5 to show that $\Delta ABC \cong \Delta EDF$. The statement $\overline{AC} \cong \overline{EF}$ cannot be shown directly from the given information. On the other hand, $\Delta ABC \cong \Delta FDE$ can be determined: when two parallel lines ($\overline{BC} \| \overline{FG}$) are cut by a transversal ($\overline{AE}$), alternate exterior angles (ΔABC, ΔFDE) are congruent. Therefore, $\Delta ABC \cong \Delta EDF$ by the side-angle-side (SAS) theorem.

82. A: Step 5 established that $\Delta ABC \cong \Delta EDF$. Because corresponding parts of congruent triangles are congruent (CPCTC), $\angle BAC \cong \angle DEF$. This is useful to establish when trying to prove $\overline{FE} \| \overline{AG}$: when two lines ($\overline{FE}$ and $\overline{AG}$) are cut by a transversal ($\overline{AE}$) and alternate interior angles ($\angle BAC$, $\angle DEF$) are congruent, then the lines are parallel. The completed proof is shown immediately following.

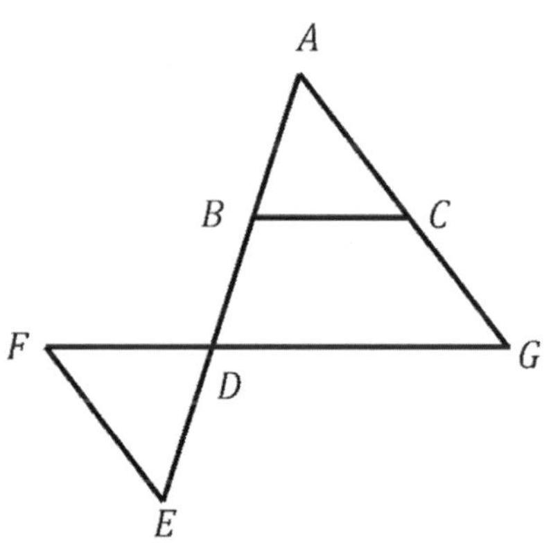

Statement	Reason
1. $\overline{BC} \| \overline{FG}$	Given
2. $\angle ABC \cong \angle FDE$	Alt. ext. ∠s of ‖ lines ≅
3. $\overline{FD} \cong \overline{BC}$	Given
4. $\overline{AB} \cong \overline{DE}$	Given
5. $\Delta ABC \cong \Delta EDF$	SAS
6. $\angle BAC \cong \angle DEF$	CPCTC
7. $\overline{FE} \| \overline{AG}$	Alt. int. ∠s ≅ → ‖ lines

Given: $\overline{BC} \| \overline{FG}$; $\overline{FD} \cong \overline{BC}$; $\overline{AB} \cong \overline{DE}$
Prove: $\overline{FE} \| \overline{AG}$

83. B: A cube has six square faces. The arrangement of these faces in a two-dimensional figure is a net of a cube if the figure can be folded to form a cube. If this is folded, the bottom square in the second column will overlap the fourth square in the top row, so the figure does not represent a net of a cube. The other figures represent three of the eleven possible nets of a cube.

84. D: The cross-section is a hexagon.

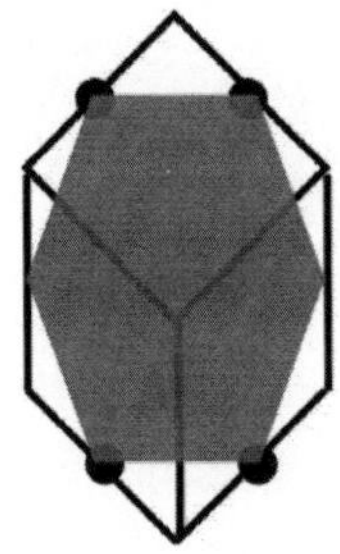

85. A: Use the formula for the volume of a sphere to find the radius of the sphere:

$$V = \frac{4}{3}\pi r^3$$

$$36\pi = \frac{4}{3}\pi r^3$$

$$36 = \frac{4}{3}r^3$$

$$36 = \frac{4}{3}r^3$$

$$27 = r^3$$

$$3 = r$$

Then, substitute the point $(h, k, l) = (1, 0, -2)$ and the radius $r = 3$ into the equation of a sphere:

$$(x-h)^2 + (y-k)^2 + (z-l)^2 = r^2$$

$$(x-1)^2 + y^2 + (z+2)^2 = 3^2$$

$$(x-1)^2 + y^2 + (z+2)^2 = 9$$

$$x^2 - 2x + 1 + y^2 + z^2 + 4z + 4 = 9$$

$$x^2 + y^2 + z^2 - 2x + 4z = 4$$

86. B: The triangle is a right triangle with legs 3 and 4 units long.

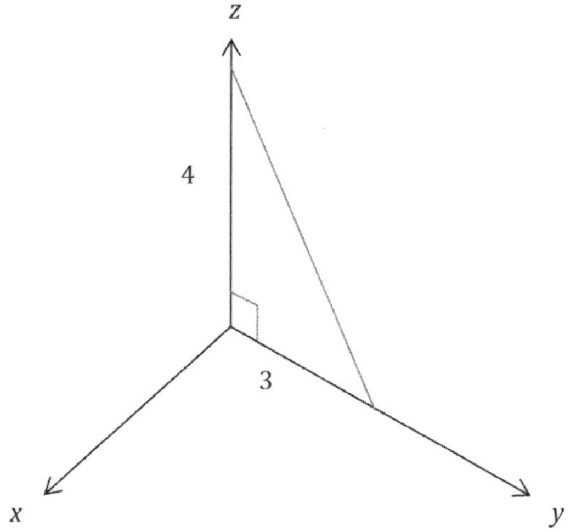

If the triangle is rotated about the z-axis, the solid formed is a cone with a height of 4 and a radius of 3; this cone has volume $V = \frac{1}{3}\pi r^2 h = \frac{1}{3}\pi 3^2 4 = 12\pi$ cubic units. If the triangle is rotated about the y-axis, the solid formed is a cone with a height of 3 and a radius of 4. This cone has volume $V = \frac{1}{3}\pi r^2 h = \frac{1}{3}\pi 4^2 3 = 16\pi$ cubic units. The difference in the volumes of the two cones is $16\pi - 12\pi = 4\pi$ cubic units.

87. D: The point $(5, -5)$ lies on the line segment that has a slope of -2 and passes through $(3, -1)$. If $(5, -5)$ is one of the endpoints of the line segment, then the other would be $(1,3)$.

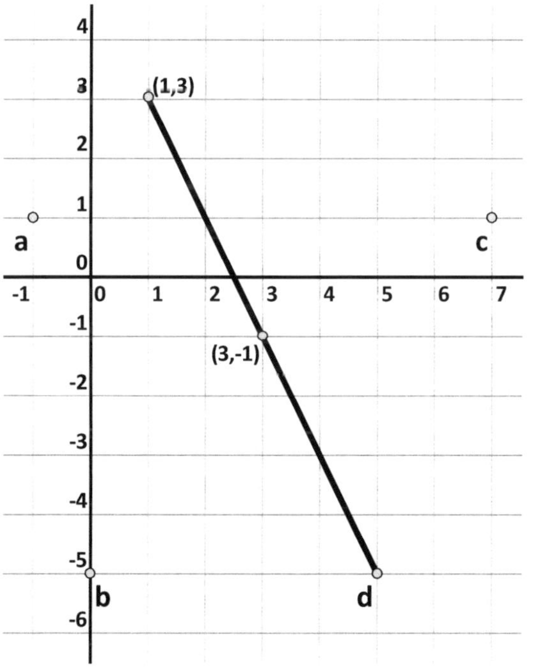

88. D: Since all of the answer choices are parallelograms, determine whether the parallelogram is also a rhombus, a rectangle, or both. One way to do this is by examining the parallelogram's diagonals. If the parallelogram's diagonals are perpendicular, then the parallelogram is a rhombus. If the parallelogram's diagonals are congruent, then the parallelogram is a rectangle. If a parallelogram is both a rhombus and a rectangle, then it is a square.

To determine whether the diagonals are perpendicular, find the slopes of the diagonals of the quadrilateral:

Diagonal 1: $\frac{6-2}{-5-3} = \frac{4}{-8} = -\frac{1}{2}$

Diagonal 2: $\frac{0-8}{-3-1} = -\frac{8}{-4} = 2$

The diagonals have opposite inverse slopes and are therefore perpendicular. Thus, the parallelogram is a rhombus.

To determine whether the diagonals are congruent, find the lengths of the diagonals of the quadrilateral:

Diagonal 1: $\sqrt{(6-2)^2 + (-5-3)^2} = \sqrt{(4)^2 + (-8)^2} = \sqrt{16+64} = \sqrt{80} = 4\sqrt{5}$

Diagonal 2: $\sqrt{(0-8)^2 + (-3-1)\text{^}2} = \sqrt{(-8)^2 + (-4)\text{^}2} = \sqrt{64+16} = \sqrt{80} = 4\sqrt{5}$

The diagonals are congruent, so the parallelogram is a rectangle.

Since the polygon is a rhombus and a rectangle, it is also a square.

89. A: The equation of the circle is given in general form. When the equation is written in the standard form $(x-h)^2 + (y-k)^2 = r^2$, where (h, k) is the center of the circle and r is the radius of the circle, the radius is easy to determine. Putting the equation into standard form requires completing the square for x and y:

$$x^2 - 10x + y^2 + 8y = -29$$

$$(x^2 - 10x + 25) + (y^2 + 8y + 16) = -29 + 25 + 16$$

$$(x-5)^2 + (y+4)^2 = 12$$

Since $r^2 = 12$, and since r must be a positive number, $r = \sqrt{12} = 2\sqrt{3}.$

90. D: One way to determine whether the equation represents an ellipse, a circle, a parabola, or a hyperbola is to find the discriminant $b^2 - 4ac$ of the general equation form of a conic section, $ax^2 + bxy + cy^2 + dx + ey + f = 0$, where a, b, c, d, e, and f are constants. Given that the conic section is non-degenerate, if the discriminant is positive, then the equation is a hyperbola; if the discriminant is negative, then the equation is a circle (when $a = c$ and $b = 0$) or an ellipse; and if the discriminant is zero, then the equation is a parabola. For $2x^2 - 3y^2 - 12x + 6y - 15 = 0, a = 2,$ $b = 0,\ c = -3,\ d = -12,\ e = 6,$ and $f = -15$. The discriminant $b^2 - 4ac$ is equal to $0^2 - 4(2)(-3) = 24$. Since the discriminant is positive, the graph is hyperbolic.

Another way to determine the shape of the graph is to look at the coefficients for the x^2 and y^2 terms in the given equation. If one of the coefficients is zero (in other words, if there is either an x^2 or a y^2 term in the equation but not both), then the equation is a parabola; if the coefficients have the same sign, then the graph is an ellipse or circle; and if the coefficients have opposite signs, then the graph is a hyperbola. Since the coefficient of x^2 is 2 and the coefficient of y^2 is -3, the graph is a hyperbola. That the equation can be written in the standard form for a hyperbola, $\frac{(x-h)^2}{a^2} - \frac{(y-k)^2}{b^2} = 1$, confirms the conclusion.

$$2x^2 - 3y^2 - 12x + 6y - 15 = 0$$

$$2x^2 - 12x - 3y^2 + 6y = 15$$

$$2(x^2 - 6x) - 3(y^2 - 2y) = 15$$

$$2(x^2 - 6x + 9) - 3(y^2 - 2y + 1) = 15 + 2(9) - 3(1)$$

$$2(x-3)^2 - 3(y-1)^2 = 30$$

$$\frac{(x-3)^2}{15} - \frac{(y-1)^2}{10} = 1$$

91. B: The graph of $f(x)$ is a parabola with a focus of (a, b) and a directrix of $y = -b$. The axis of symmetry of a parabola passes through the focus and vertex and is perpendicular to the directrix. Since the directrix is a horizontal line, the axis of symmetry is $x = a$; therefore, the x-coordinate of the parabola's vertex must be a. The distance between a point on the parabola and the directrix is equal to the distance between that point and the focus, so the y-coordinate of the vertex must be $y = \frac{-b+b}{2} = 0$. So, the vertex of the parabola given by $f(x)$ is $(a, 0)$.

If $g(x)$ were a translation of $f(x)$, as is the case for choices B, C, and D, the vertices of $f(x)$ and $g(x)$ would differ. Since the vertex of the graph of $g(x)$ is $(a, 0)$, none of those choices represent the correct response. However, if $g(x) = -(x)$, the vertices of the graphs of both functions would be the same; therefore, this represents a possible relation between the two functions.

92. C: When a figure is reflected twice over non-parallel lines, the resulting transformation is a rotation about the point of intersection of the two lines of reflection. The two lines of reflection $y = x + 2$ and $x = 0$ intersect at (0,2). So, $\Delta A''B''C''$ represents a rotation of ΔABC about the point (0,2). The angle of rotation is equal to twice the angle between the two lines of reflection when measured in a clockwise direction from the first to the second line of reflection. Since the angle between the lines or reflection measures 135°, the angle of rotation which is the composition of the two reflections measures 270°. All of these properties can be visualized by drawing ΔABC, $\Delta A'B'C'$, and $\Delta A''B''C''$.

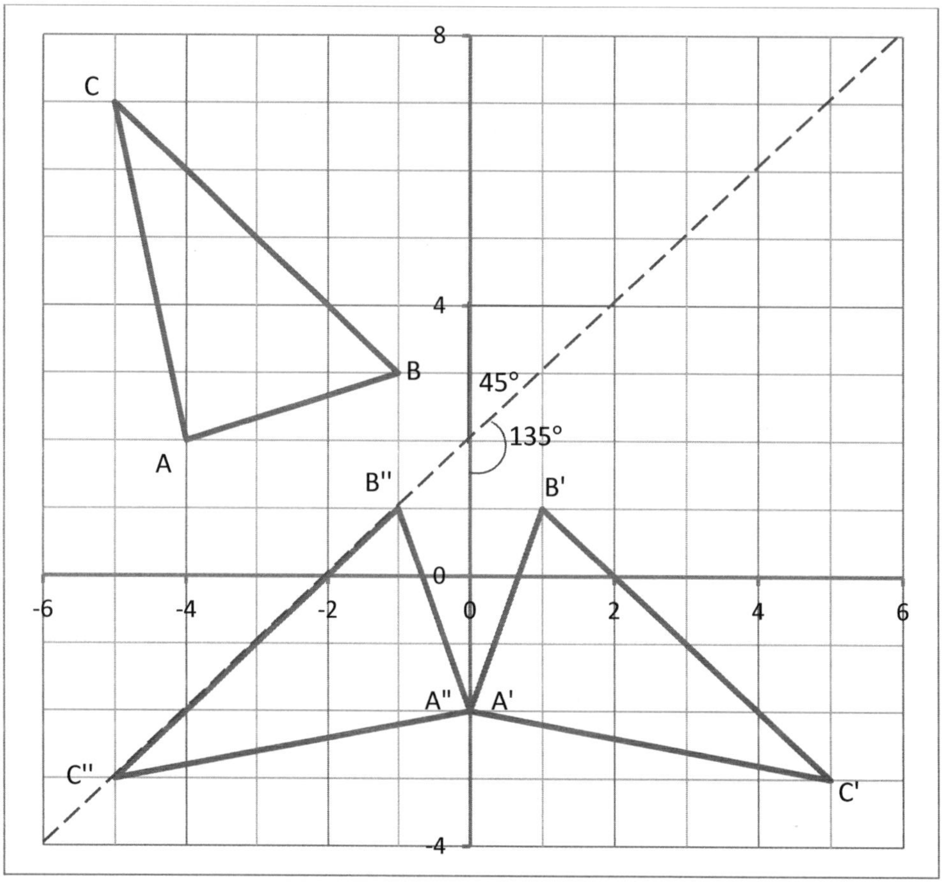

93. B: All regular polygons have rotational symmetry. The angle of rotation is the smallest angle by which the polygon can be rotated such that it maps onto itself; any multiple of this angle will also map the polygon onto itself. The angle of rotation for a regular polygon is the angle formed between two lines drawn from consecutives vertices to the center of the polygon. Since the vertices of a regular polygon lie on a circle, for a regular polygon with n sides, the angle of rotation measures $\frac{360°}{n}$.

Number of sides of regular polygon	Angle of rotation	Angles $\leq 360°$ which map the polygon onto itself
4	$\frac{360}{4} = 90°$	$90°, 180°, 270°, 360°$
6	$\frac{360}{6} = 60°$	$60°, 120°, 180°, 240°, 300°, 360°$
8	$\frac{360}{8} = 45°$	$45°, 90°, 135°, 180°, 225°, 270°, 315°, 360°$
10	$\frac{360}{10} = 36°$	$36°, 72°, 108°, 144°, 180°, 216°, 252°, 288°, 324°, 360°$

94. A: Since the y-coordinates of points P and Q are the same, line segment $\overline{PQ}$ is a horizontal line segment whose length is the difference in the x-coordinates a and c. Because the length of a line cannot be negative, and because it is unknown whether $a > c$ or $a < c$, $PQ = |a - c|$ or $|c - a|$. Since the x-coordinates of Q and Q' are the same, line segment $\overline{P'Q}$ is a vertical line segment whose length is $|d - b|$or $|b - d|$. The quadrilateral formed by the transformation of $\overline{PQ}$ to $\overline{P'Q'}$ is a parallelogram. If the base of the parallelogram is $\overline{PQ}$, then the height is $\overline{P'Q}$ since $\overline{PQ} \perp \overline{P'Q}$. For a parallelogram, $A = bh$, so $A = |a - c| \cdot |b - d|$.

95. B: Since $\tan B = \frac{opposite}{adjacent} = \frac{b}{a'}$ choice A is incorrect.

$\cos B = \frac{adjacent}{hypotenuse}$. The hypotenuse of a right triangle is equal to the square root of the sum of the squares of the legs, so $\cos B = \frac{adjacent}{hypotenuse} = \frac{a}{\sqrt{a^2+b^2}}$. Rationalize the denominator: $\frac{a}{\sqrt{a^2+b^2}} \cdot \frac{\sqrt{a^2+b^2}}{\sqrt{a^2+b^2}} = \frac{a\sqrt{a^2+b^2}}{a^2+b^2}$. Choice B is correct.

$\sec B = \frac{hypotenuse}{adjacent} = \frac{\sqrt{a^2+b^2}}{a}$, and $\csc B = \frac{\sqrt{a^2+b^2}}{b}$, so choices C and D are incorrect.

96. C: Find the missing angle measures in the diagram by using angle and triangle properties. Then, use the law of sines to find the distance y between the window and the wife's car: $\frac{60}{\sin 15°} = \frac{y}{\sin 45°}$, so $y = \frac{60 \sin 45°}{\sin 15} \approx 163.9$ ft. Use this number in a sine or cosine function to find x: $\sin 30° \approx \frac{x}{163.9}$, so $x \approx 163.9 \sin 30° \approx 82$. Therefore, the man's wife is parked approximately 82 feet from the building.

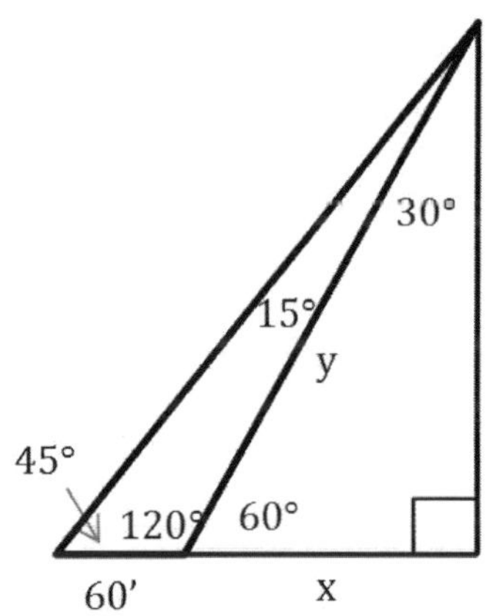

Alternatively, notice that when the man is looking down at a 45 degree angle, the triangle that is formed is an isosceles triangle, meaning that the height of his office is the same as the distance from the office to his car, or $x + 60$ feet. With this knowledge, the problem can be modeled with a single equation:

$$\frac{x + 60}{x} = \tan 60° \quad or \quad x = \frac{60}{\tan 60° - 1}$$

97. A: The reference angle for $-\frac{2\pi}{3}$ is $2\pi - \frac{2\pi}{3} = \frac{4\pi}{3}$, so $\tan(-\frac{2\pi}{3}) = \tan\left(\frac{4\pi}{3}\right) = \frac{\sin\left(\frac{4\pi}{3}\right)}{\cos\left(\frac{4\pi}{3}\right)}$. From the unit circle, the values of $\sin\left(\frac{4\pi}{3}\right)$ and $\cos\left(\frac{4\pi}{3}\right)$ are $-\frac{\sqrt{3}}{2}$ and $-\frac{1}{2'}$ respectively. Therefore, $\tan(-\frac{2\pi}{3}) = \frac{-\frac{\sqrt{3}}{2}}{-\frac{1}{2}} = \sqrt{3}$.

98. D: On the unit circle, $\sin\theta = \frac{1}{2}$ when $\theta = \frac{\pi}{6}$ and when $\theta = \frac{5\pi}{6}$. Since only $\frac{5\pi}{6}$ is in the given range of $\frac{\pi}{2} < \theta < \pi, \theta = \frac{5\pi}{6}$.

99. C: Use trigonometric equalities and identities to simplify. $\cos\theta\cot\theta = \cos\theta \cdot \frac{\cos\theta}{\sin\theta} = \frac{\cos^2\theta}{\sin\theta} = \frac{1-\sin^2\theta}{\sin\theta} = \frac{1}{\sin\theta} - \sin\theta = \csc\theta - \sin\theta$.

100. B: The trigonometric identity $\sec^2\theta = \tan^2\theta + 1$ can be used to rewrite the equation $\sec^2\theta = 2\tan\theta$ as $\tan^2\theta + 1 = 2\tan\theta$, which can then be rearranged into the form $\tan^2\theta - 2\tan\theta + 1 = 0$. Solve by factoring and using the zero product property:

$$\tan^2\theta - 2\tan\theta + 1 = 0$$

$$(\tan\theta - 1)^2 = 0$$

$$\tan\theta - 1 = 0$$

$$\tan\theta = 1.$$

Since $\tan\theta = 1$ when $\sin\theta = \cos\theta$, for $0 < \theta \leq 2\pi$, $\theta = \frac{\pi}{4}$ or $\frac{5\pi}{4}$.

101. A: Since the graph shows a maximum height of 28 inches above the ground, and since the maximum distance from the road the pebble reaches is when it is at the top of the tire, the diameter of the tire is 28 inches. Therefore, its radius is 14 inches. From the graph, it can be observed that the tire makes 7.5 rotations in 0.5 seconds. Thus, the tire rotates 15 times in 1 second, or $15 \cdot 60 = 900$ times per minute.

102. C: The dashed line represents the sine function (x), and the solid line represents a cosine function $g(x)$. The amplitude of $f(x)$ is 4, and the amplitude of $g(x)$ is 2. The function $y = \sin x$ has a period of 2π, while the graph of function $f(x) = a_1\sin(b_1x)$ has a period of 4π; therefore, $b_1 = \frac{2\pi}{4\pi} = 0.5$, which is between 0 and 1. The graph of $g(x) = a_2\cos(b_2x)$ has a period of π, so $b_2 = \frac{2\pi}{\pi} = 2$.

103. B: The graph of $f(x)$ is stretched vertically by a factor of 4 with respect to $y = \sin x$, so $a_1 = 4$. The graph of $g(x)$ is stretched vertically by a factor of two and is inverted with respect to the graph of $y = \cos x$, so $a_2 = -2$. Therefore, the statement $a_2 < 0 < a_1$ is true.

104. A: The graph to the right shows the height h in inches of the weight on the spring above the table as a function of time t in seconds. Notice that the height is 3 in above the table at time 0 since the weight was pulled down two inches from its starting position 5 inches above the table. The spring fluctuates 2 inches above and below its equilibrium point, so its maximum height is 7 inches above the table. The graph represents a cosine curve which has been inverted, stretched vertically by a factor of 2, and shifted up five units; also, the graph has been compressed horizontally, with a period of 1 rather than 2π. So, the height of the weight on the spring as a function of time is $h = -2\cos(2\pi t) + 5$.

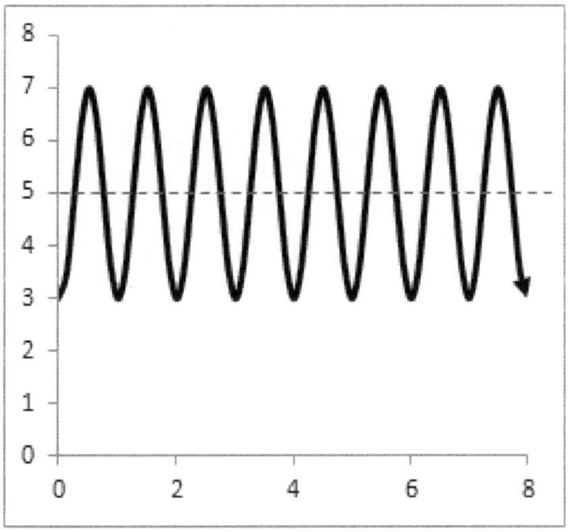

105. C: Since evaluating $\frac{x^3+3x^2-x-3}{x^2-9}$ at $x = -3$ produces a fraction with a zero denominator, simplify the polynomial expression before evaluating the limit:

$$\frac{x^3 + 3x^2 - x - 3}{x^2 - 9} = \frac{x^2(x + 3) - 1(x + 3)}{(x + 3)(x - 3)} = \frac{(x + 3)(x^2 - 1)}{(x + 3)(x - 3)} = \frac{(x + 1)(x - 1)}{x - 3}$$

$$\lim_{x \to -3} \frac{(x + 1)(x - 1)}{x - 3} = \frac{(-3 + 1)(-3 - 1)}{-3 - 3} = -\frac{8}{-6} = -\frac{4}{3}.$$

106. B: To evaluate the limit, divide the numerator and denominator by x^2 and use these properties of limits: $\lim_{x \to \infty} \frac{1}{x} = 0$; the limit of a sum of terms is the sum of the limits of the terms; and the limit of a product of terms is the product of the limits of the terms.

$$\lim_{x \to \infty} \frac{x^2 + 2x - 3}{2x^2 + 1} = \lim_{x \to \infty} \frac{\frac{x^2}{x^2} + \frac{2x}{x^2} - \frac{3}{x^2}}{\frac{2x^2}{x^2} + \frac{1}{x^2}} = \lim_{x \to \infty} \frac{1 + \frac{2}{x} - \frac{3}{x^2}}{2 + \frac{1}{x^2}} = \frac{1 + 0 - 0}{2 + 0} = \frac{1}{2}.$$

107. B: Evaluating $\frac{|x-3|}{3-x}$ when $x = 3$ produces a fraction with a zero denominator. To find the limit as x approaches 3 from the right, sketch a graph or make a table of values.

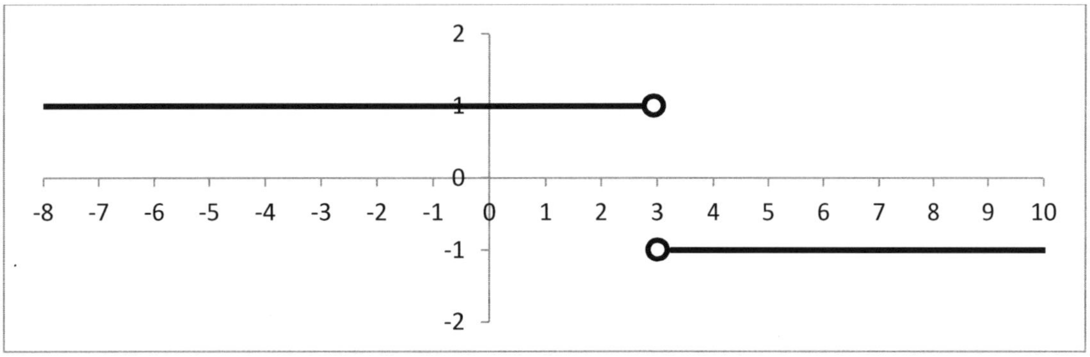

The value of the function approaches -1 as x approaches three from the right, so $\lim_{x \to 3^+} \frac{|x-3|}{3-x} = -1$.

108. C: The slope of the line tangent to the graph of a function f at $x = a$ is $f'(a)$. Since $f(x) = \frac{1}{4}x^2 - 3$, $f'(x) = 2\left(\frac{1}{4}\right)x^{(2-1)} - 0 = \frac{1}{2}x$. So, the slope at $x = 2$ is $f'(2) = \frac{1}{2}(2) = 1$.

109. D: The definition of the derivative of f at 2, or $f'(2)$, is the limit of the difference quotient $\lim_{h\to 0}\frac{f(2+h)-f(2)}{h}$. Rather than find the limit, simply evaluate the derivative of the function at $x = 2$:

$$f(x) = 2x^3 - 3x^2 + 4$$

$$f'(x) = 6x^2 - 6x$$

$$f'(2) = 6(2)^2 - 6(2)$$

$$f'(2) = 12$$

110. D: To find the derivative of $y = e^{3x^2-1}$, use the Chain Rule. Let $u = 3x^2 - 1$. Thus, $y = e^u$, and $\frac{dy}{du} = e^u$. Since $\frac{dy}{dx} = \frac{dy}{du}\cdot\frac{du}{dx}$, and since $\frac{du}{dx} = 6x$, $\frac{dy}{dx} = e^{3x^2-1}\cdot 6x = 6x\, e^{3x^2-1}$.

111. C: To find the derivative of $y = \ln(2x + 1)$, use the Chain Rule. Let $u = 2x + 1$. Thus, $y = \ln u$, and $\frac{dy}{du} = \frac{1}{u}$. Since $\frac{dy}{dx} = \frac{dy}{du}\cdot\frac{du}{dx}$, and since $\frac{du}{dx} = 2$, $\frac{dy}{dx} = \left(\frac{1}{2x+1}\right)(2) = \frac{2}{2x+1}$.

112. A: If $\lim_{x\to a^+} f(x) = \lim_{x\to a^-} f(x)$, then $\lim_{x\to a^+} f(x) = \lim_{x\to a^-} f(x) = \lim_{x\to a} f(x)$. Otherwise, $\lim_{x\to a} f(x)$ does not exist. If $\lim_{x\to a} f(x)$ exists, and if $\lim_{x\to a} f(x) = f(a)$, then the function is continuous at a. Otherwise, f is discontinuous at a.

113. A: To find the second derivative of the function, take the derivative of the first derivative of the function:

$$f(x) = 2x^4 - 4x^3 + 2x^2 - x + 1$$

$$f'(x) = 8x^3 - 12x^2 + 4x - 1$$

$$f''(x) = 24x^2 - 24x + 4.$$

114. A: The critical points of the graph occur when $f'(x) = 0$.

$$f(x) = 4x^3 - x^2 - 4x + 2$$

$$f'(x) = 12x^2 - 2x - 4$$

$$= 2(6x^2 - x - 2)$$

$$= 2(3x - 2)(2x + 1)$$

$$0 = 2(3x - 2)(2x + 1)$$

$$3x - 2 = 0 \quad 2x + 1 = 0$$

$$x = \frac{2}{3} \quad x = -\frac{1}{2}$$

If $f''(x) > 0$ for all x in an interval, the graph of the function is concave upward on that interval, and if $f''(x) < 0$ for all x in an interval, the graph of the function is concave downward on that interval. Find the second derivative of the function and determine the intervals in which $f''(x)$ is less than zero and greater than zero:

$$f''(x) = 24x - 2$$

$$24x - 2 < 0 \quad 24x - 2 > 0$$

$$x < \frac{1}{12} \quad x > \frac{1}{12}$$

The graph of f is concave downward on the interval $\left(-\infty, -\frac{1}{12}\right)$ and concave upward on the interval $\left(-\frac{1}{12}, \infty\right)$. The inflection point of the graph is $\left(\frac{1}{12}, f\left(\frac{1}{12}\right)\right) = \left(\frac{1}{12}, \frac{359}{216}\right)$. The point $\left(\frac{2}{3}, f\left(\frac{2}{3}\right)\right) = \left(\frac{2}{3}, \frac{2}{27}\right)$ is a relative minimum and the point $\left(-\frac{1}{2}, f\left(-\frac{1}{2}\right)\right) = \left(-\frac{1}{2}, 3\frac{1}{4}\right)$ is a relative maximum.

115. D: The velocity v of the ball at any time t is the slope of the line tangent to the graph of h at time t. The slope of a line tangent to the curve $h = -16t^2 + 50t + 3$ is h'.

$$h' = v = -32t + 50$$

When $t = 2$, the velocity of the ball is $-32(2) + 50 = -14$. The velocity is negative because the slope of the tangent line at $t = 2$ is negative; velocity has both magnitude and direction, so a velocity of -14 means that the velocity is 14 ft/s downward.

116. B: The manufacturer wishes to minimize the surface area A of the can while keeping its volume V fixed at 0.5 L = 500 mL = 500 cm^3. The formula for the surface area of a cylinder is $A = 2\pi rh + 2\pi r^2$, and the formula for volume is $V = \pi r^2 h$. To combine the two formulas into one, solve the volume formula for r or h and substitute the resulting expression into the surface area formula for r or h. The volume of the cylinder is 500 cm^3, so $500 = \pi r^2 h \rightarrow h = \frac{500}{\pi r^2}$. Therefore, $A = 2\pi rh + 2\pi r^2 \rightarrow 2\pi r\left(\frac{500}{\pi r^2}\right) + 2\pi r^2 = \frac{1000}{r} + 2\pi r^2$. Find the critical point(s) by setting the first derivative equal to zero and solving for r. Note that r represents the radius of the can and must therefore be a positive number.

$$A = 1000r^{-1} + 2\pi r^2$$

$$A' = -1000r^{-2} + 4\pi r$$

$$0 = -\frac{1000}{r^2} + 4\pi r$$

$$\frac{1000}{r^2} = 4\pi r$$

$$1000 = 4\pi r^3$$

$$\sqrt[3]{\frac{1000}{4\pi}} = r$$

So, when r≈4.3 cm, the minimum surface area is obtained. When the radius of the can is 4.30 cm, its height is $h \approx \frac{500}{\pi(4.30)^2} \approx 8.6$ cm, and the surface area is approximately $\frac{1000}{4.3} + 2\pi(4.3)^2 \approx 348.73 \text{ cm}^2$. Confirm that the surface area is greater when the radius is slightly smaller or larger than 4.3 cm. For instance, when r=4 cm, the surface area is approximately 350.5 cm^2, and when r=4.5 cm, the surface area is approximately 349.5 cm^2.

117. C: Partitioned into rectangles with length of 1, the left Riemann sum is 20+25+28+30+29+26+22+16+12+10+10+13=241 square units, and the right Riemann sum is 25+28+30+29+26+22+16+12+10+10+13+17=238 square units.

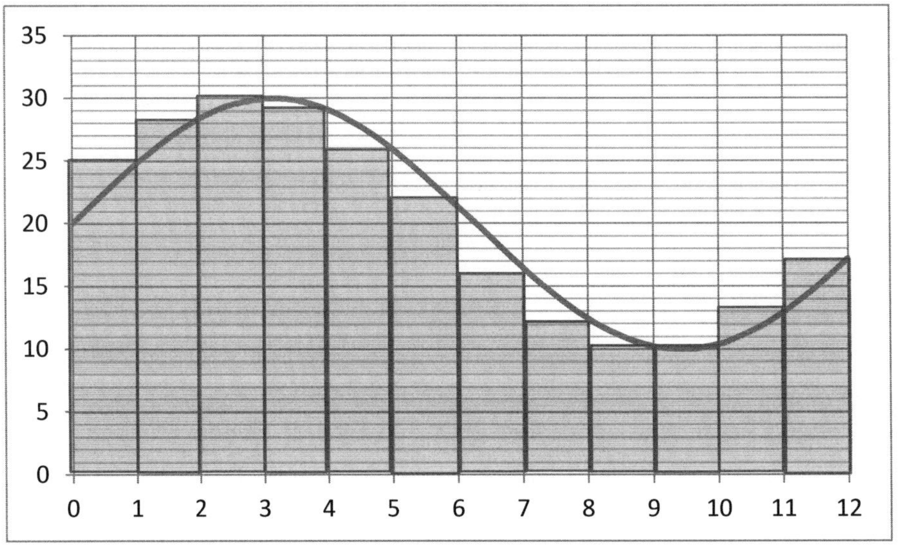

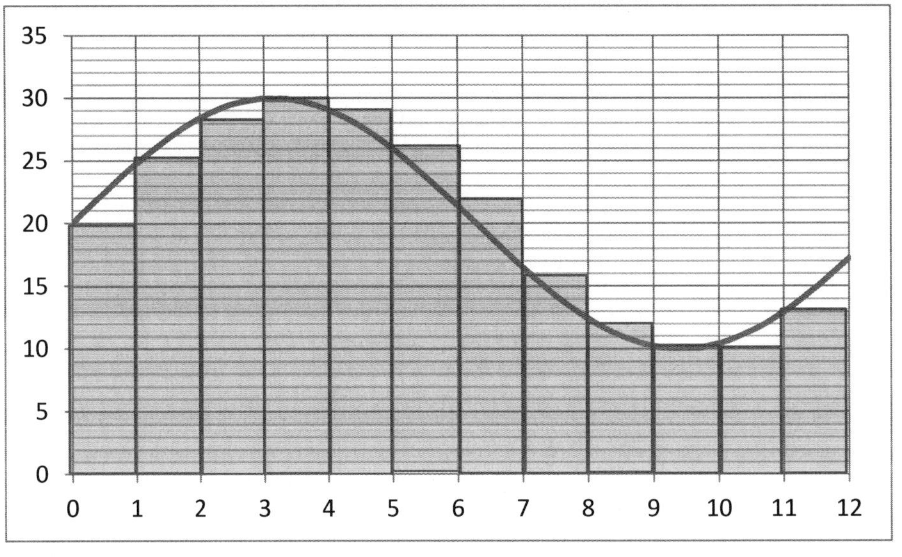

118. B: The area under curve $f(x)$ is $\int_1^2 \frac{1}{x} = [\ln(2)] - [\ln(1)] \approx 0.69$.

119. A: $\int 3x^2 + 2x - 1 = \frac{3}{2+1}x^{2+1} + \frac{2}{1+1}x^{1+1} - x + c = x^3 + x^2 - x + c$.

120. B: To calculate $\int 3x^2 e^{x^3}\,dx$, let $u = x^3$. Since $du = 3x^2dx$, $\int 3x^2 e^{x^3}\,dx = \int e^u\,du \to e^u + c \to e^{x^3} + c$.

121. B: Find the points of intersection of the two graphs:

$$x^2 - 4 = -x + 2$$

$$x^2 + x - 6 = 0$$

$$(x + 3)(x - 2) = 0$$

$$x = -3 \quad x = 2$$

The finite region is bound at the top by the line $y = -x + 2$ and at the bottom by $y = x^2 - 4$, so the area is between the graphs on [-3,2], and the height of the region at point x is defined by $[(-x + 2) - (x^2 - 4)]$. Thus, the area of the region is

$$A = \int_{-3}^{2} [(-x + 2) - (x^2 - 4)]dx$$

$$= \int_{-3}^{2} (-\mathrm{x}^2 - \mathrm{x} + 6\,)\,dx$$

$$= \left[-\frac{1}{3}(2)^3 - \frac{1}{2}(2)^2 + 6(2)\right] - \left[-\frac{1}{3}(-3)^3 - \frac{1}{2}(-3)^2 + 6(-3)\right]$$

$$= \left[-\frac{8}{3} - 2 + 12\right] - \left[9 - \frac{9}{2} - 18\right] = \frac{22}{3} - \left(-\frac{27}{2}\right) = \frac{125}{6}$$

122. C: The acceleration a of an object at time t is the derivative of the velocity v of the object at time t, which is the derivative of the position x of the object at time t. So, given the velocity of an object at time t, $x(t)$ can be found by taking the integral of the $v(t)$, and $a(t)$ can be found by taking the derivative of $v(t)$.

$x(t) = \int v(t)dt = \int(12t - t^2)dt = 6t^2 - \frac{1}{3}t^3 + c$. Since the position of the car at time 0 is 0, $v(0) = 0 = 6(0)^2 - \frac{1}{3}(0)^3 + c \rightarrow 0 = 0 - 0 + c \rightarrow c = 0$. Therefore, $x(t) = 6t^2 - \frac{1}{3}t^3$.

$a(t) = v'(t) = 12 - 2t$.

Find the time at which the acceleration is equal to 0: $0 = 12 - 2t \rightarrow t = 6$. Then, find $x(6)$ to find the position of the car when the velocity is 0: $6(6)^2 - \frac{1}{3}(6)^3 = 216 - 72 = 144$.

123. D: To draw a box-and-whisker plot from the data, find the median, quartiles, and upper and lower limits.

3	6 799	
4	2|3889	Key
5	0|11157|	2|123 = 21, 22, 23
6	0 0123	

The median is $\frac{50+51}{2} = 50.5$, the lower quartile is $\frac{42+43}{2} = 42.5$, and the upper quartile is $\frac{57+60}{2} = 58.5$. The box of the box-and-whisker plot goes through the quartiles, and a line through the box represents the median of the data. The whiskers extend from the box to the lower and upper limits, unless there are any outliers in the set. In this case, there are no outliers, so the box-and-whisker plot in choice A correctly represents the data set.

To draw a pie chart, find the percentage of data contained in each of the ranges shown. There are four out of twenty numbers between 30 and 39, inclusive, so the percentage shown in the pie chart for that range of data is $\frac{4}{20} \times 100\% = 20\%$; there are five values between 40 to 49, inclusive, so the percentage of data for that sector is $\frac{5}{20} \times 100\% = 25\%$; $\frac{6}{20} \times 100\% = 30\%$ of the data is within the range of 50-59, and $\frac{5}{20} \times 100\% = 25\%$ is within the range of 60-69. The pie chart shows the correct percentage of data in each category.

To draw a cumulative frequency histogram, find the cumulative frequency of the data.

Range	Frequency	Cumulative frequency
30-39	4	4
40-49	5	9
50-59	6	15
60-69	5	20

The histogram shows the correct cumulative frequencies. Therefore, all of the graphs represent the data set.

124. B: A line graph is often used to show change over time. A Venn diagram shows the relationships among sets. A box and whisker plot shows displays how numeric data are distributed throughout the range. A pie chart shows the relationship of parts to a whole.

125. B: In choice A, the teacher surveys all the members of the population in which he is interested. However, since the response is voluntary, the survey is biased: the participants are self-selected rather than randomly selected. It may be that students who have a strong opinion are more likely to respond than those who are more neutral, and this would give the teacher a skewed perspective of student opinions. In choice B, students are randomly selected, so the sampling technique is not biased. In choice C, the student uses convenience sampling, which is a biased technique. For example, perhaps the student is in an honors class; his sampling method would not be representative of the entire class of eleventh graders, which includes both students who take and who do not take honors classes. Choice D also represents convenience sampling; only the opinions of parents in the PTA are examined, and these parents' opinions may not reflect the opinions of all parents of students at the school.

126. A: Nominal data are data that are collected which have no intrinsic quantity or order. For instance, a survey might ask the respondent to identify his or her gender. While it is possible to compare the relative frequency of each response (for example, "most of the respondents are women"), it is not possible to calculate the mean, which requires data to be numeric, or median, which requires data to be ordered. Interval data are both numeric and ordered, so mean and median can be determined, as can the mode, the interval within which there are the most data. Ordinal data has an inherent order, but there is not a set interval between two points. For example, a survey might ask the respondents whether they were very dissatisfied, dissatisfied, neutral, satisfied, or very satisfied with the customer service received. Since the data are not numeric, the mean cannot be calculated, but since ordering the data is possible, the median has context.

127. A: The average number of male students in the 11th and 12th grades is 125 $\left(\text{calculated as } \frac{131 + 119}{2}\right)$. The number of Hispanic students at the school is 10% of 1219, which is 122 students (rounded up from 121.9). The difference in the number of male and female students at the school is $630 - 589 = 41$, and the difference in the number of 9th and 12th grade students at the school is 354 - 255 = 99.

128. C: 52% of the student population is white. There are 630 female students at the school out of 1219 students, so the percentage of female students is $\frac{630}{1219} \cdot 100\% \approx 52\%$. The percentages rounded to the nearest whole number are the same.

129. D: 131 of 283 eleventh graders are male. Given that an 11th grader is chosen to attend the conference, the probability that a male is chosen is $\frac{\text{number of males}}{\text{number of 11th graders}} = \frac{131}{283} \approx 0.46$. Note that this is **NOT** the same question as one which asks for the probability of selecting at random from the school a male student who is in eleventh grade, which has a probability of $\frac{131}{1219} \approx 0.11$.

130. A: The range is the spread of the data. It can be calculated for each class by subtracting the lowest test score from the highest, or it can be determined visually from the graph. The difference between the highest and lowest test scores in class A is 98-23=75 points. The range for each of the other classes is much smaller.

131. D: 75% of the data in a set is above the first quartile. Since the first quartile for this set is 73, there is a 75% chance that a student chosen at random from class 2 scored above a 73.

132. C: The line through the center of the box represents the median. The median test score for classes 1 and 2 is 82.

Note that for class 1, the median is a better representation of the data than the mean. There are two outliers (points which lie outside of two standard deviations from the mean) which bring down the average test score. In cases such as this, the mean is not the best measure of central tendency.

133. D: Since there are 100 homes' market times represented in each set, the median time a home spends on the market is between 50th and 51st data point in each set. The 50th and 51st data points for Zip Code 1 are six months and seven months, respectively, so the median time a house in Zip Code 1 spends on the market is between six and seven months (6.5 months), which by the realtor's definition of market time is a seven-month market time. The 50th and 51st data points for Zip Code 2 are both thirteen months, so the median time a house in Zip Code 2 spends on the market is thirteen months.

To find the mean market time for 100 houses, find the sum of the market times and divide by 100. If the frequency of a one month market time is 9, the number 1 is added nine times (1·9), if frequency of a two month market time is 10, the number 2 is added ten times (2·10), and so on. So, to find the average market time, divide by 100 the sum of the products of each market time and its corresponding frequency. For Zip Code 1, the mean market time is 7.38 months, which by the realtor's definition of market time is an eight month market time. For Zip Code 2, the mean market time is 12.74, which by the realtor's definition of market time is a thirteen month market time.

The mode market time is the market time for which the frequency is the highest. For Zip Code 1, the mode market time is three months, and for Zip Code 2, the mode market time is eleven months.

The statement given in choice D is true. The median time a house spends on the market in Zip Code 1 is less than the mean time a house spends on the market in Zip Code 1.

Time on market	Frequency for Zip Code 1	Frequency for Zip Code 2	Time·Frequency for Zip Code 1	Time·Frequency for Zip Code 1
1	9	6	9	6
2	10	4	20	8
3	12	3	36	9
4	8	4	32	16
5	6	3	30	15
6	5	5	30	30
7	8	2	56	14
8	8	1	64	8
9	6	3	54	27
10	3	5	30	50
11	5	7	55	77
12	4	6	48	72
13	2	6	26	78
14	3	5	42	70
15	1	3	15	45
16	2	2	32	32
17	2	3	34	51
18	1	5	18	90
19	0	6	0	114
20	2	4	40	80
21	1	5	21	105
22	1	4	22	88
23	0	3	0	69
24	1	5	24	120
SUM	100	100	738	1274

134. C: The probability of an event is the number of possible occurrences of that event divided by the number of all possible outcomes. A camper who is at least eight years old can be eight, nine, or ten years old, so the probability of randomly selecting a camper at least eight years old is $\frac{\text{number of eight-, nine-, and ten-year old campers}}{\text{total number of campers}} = \frac{14+12+10}{12+15+14+12+10} = \frac{36}{63} = \frac{4}{7}$.

135. B: There are three ways in which two women from the same department can be selected: two women can be selected from the first department, or two women can be selected from the second department, or two women can be selected from the third department.

The probability that two women are selected from Department 1 is $\frac{12}{103} \times \frac{11}{102} = \frac{132}{10506}$, the probability that two women are selected from Department 2 is $\frac{28}{103} \times \frac{27}{102} = \frac{756}{10506}$, and the probability that two women are selected from Department 3 is $\frac{16}{103} \times \frac{15}{102} = \frac{240}{10506}$. Since any of these is a discrete possible outcome, the probability that two women will be selected from the same department is the sum of these outcomes: $\frac{132}{10506} + \frac{756}{10506} + \frac{240}{10506} \approx 0.107$, or **10.7%.**

	Department 1	Department 2	Department 3	Total
Women	12	28	16	56
Men	18	14	15	47
Total	30	42	31	103

136. B: The number of students who like broccoli is equal to the number of students who like all three vegetables plus the number of students who like broccoli and carrots but not cauliflower plus the number of students who like broccoli and cauliflower but not carrots plus the number of students who like broccoli but no other vegetable: $3 + 15 + 4 + 10 = 32$. These students plus the numbers of students who like just cauliflower, just carrots, cauliflower and carrots, or none of the vegetables represents the entire set of students sampled: $32 + 2 + 27 + 6 + 23 = 90$. So, the probability that a randomly chosen student likes broccoli is $\frac{32}{90} \approx 0.356$.

The number of students who like carrots and at least one other vegetable is $15 + 6 + 3 = 24$. The number of students who like carrots is $24 + 27 = 51$. So, the probability that a student who likes carrots will also like at least one other vegetable is $\frac{24}{51} \approx 0.471$. The number of students who like cauliflower and broccoli is $4 + 3 = 7$. The number of students who like all three vegetables is 3. So, the probability that a student who likes cauliflower and broccoli will also like carrots is $\frac{3}{7} \approx 0.429$.

The number of students who do not like carrots, broccoli, or cauliflower is 23. The total number of students surveyed is 90. So, the probability that a student does not like any of the three vegetables is $23/90 \approx 0.256$.

137. C: Since each coin toss is an independent event, the probability of the compound event of flipping the coin three times is equal to the product of the probabilities of the individual events. For example, $P(HHH) = P(H) \cdot P(H) \cdot P(H)$, $P(HHT) = P(H) \cdot P(H) \cdot P(T)$, etc. When a coin is flipped three times, all of the possible outcomes are HHH, HHT, HTH, HTT, THH, THT, TTH, and TTT. Since the only way to obtain three heads is by the coin landing on heads three times,

$$P(three\ heads) = P(HHH) = P(H)P(H)P(H).$$

Likewise,

$$P(no\ heads) = P(T)P(T)P(T).$$

Since there are three ways to get one head,

$$P(one\ head) = P(HTT) + P(THT) + P(TTH) = P(H)P(T)P(T) + P(T)P(H)P(T) + P(T)P(T)P(H) \\ = P(H)[(3P(T)^2],$$

And since there are three ways to get two heads,

$$P(two\ heads) = P(HHT) + P(HTH) + P(THH) \\ = P(H)P(H)P(T) + P(H)P(T)P(H) + P(T)P(H)P(H) = P(H)^2[3P(T)]$$

Use these properties to calculate the experimental probability P(H):

30 out of 100 coin tosses resulted in three heads, and $P(three\ heads) = P(H)P(H)P(H) = P(H)^3$. So, experimental P(H) can be calculated by taking the cube root of $\frac{30}{100}$. $\sqrt[3]{0.3} \approx 0.67$.

Similarly, $P(no\ heads) = P(T)P(T)P(T) = \frac{4}{100}$. $P(T) = \sqrt[3]{0.04} \approx 0.34$. $P(H) + P(T) = 1$, $P(T) = 1 - P(H)$. Thus, $P(H) = 1 - P(T) \approx 0.66$.

Notice that these calculated values of P(H) re approximately the same, Since 100 is a fairly large sample size for this kind of experiment, the approximation for $P(H)$ ought to consistent for the compiled data set. Rather than calculating $P(H)$ using the data for one head and two heads, use the average calculated probability to confirm that the number of expected outcomes of one head and two head matches the number of actual outcomes.

The number of expected outcomes of getting one head in three coin flips out of 100 trials $100\{0.665[3(1 - 0.665)^2]\} \approx 22$, and the expected outcome getting of two heads in three coin flips out of 100 trials three flips is $100\{0.665^2[3(1 - 0.665)]\} \approx 44$. Since 22 and 44 are, in fact, the data obtained, 0.665 is indeed a good approximation for P(H) when the coin used in this experiment is tossed.

138. D: A fair coin has a symmetrical binomial distribution which peaks in its center. Since choice B shows a skewed distribution for the fair coin, it cannot be the correct answer. From the frequency histogram given for the misshapen coin, it is evident that the misshapen coin is more likely to land on heads. Therefore, it is more likely that ten coin flips would result in fewer tails than ten coin flips of a fair coin; consequently, the probability distribution for the misshapen coin would be higher than the fair coin's distribution towards the left of the graph since the misshapen coin is less likely to land on tails. Choice A shows a probability distribution which peaks at a value of 5 and which is symmetrical with respect to the peak, which verifies that it cannot be correct. (Furthermore, in choice A, the sum of the probabilities shown for each number of tails for the misshapen coin is not equal to 1.) The distribution for the misshapen coin in choice C is skewed in the wrong direction, favoring tails instead of heads, and must therefore also be incorrect. Choice D shows the correct binomial distribution for the fair coin and the appropriate shift for the misshapen coin.

Another way to approach this question is to use the answer from the previous problem to determine the probability of obtaining particular events, such as no tails and no heads, and then compare those probabilities to the graphs. For example, for the misshapen coin, P(0 tails)=P(10 heads) $\approx (0.67)^{10}$, or 0.018, and the P(10 tails) $\approx (0.33)^{10}$, which is 0.000015. For a fair coin, P(0 tails)=$(0.5)^{10}$=P(0 heads). To find values other than these, it is helpful to use the binomial distribution formula $({}_nC_r)p^r q^{n-r}$, where n is the number of trials, r is the number of successes, p is the probability of success, and q is the probability of failure. For this problem, obtaining tails is a success, and the probability of obtaining tails is $p = 0.33$ for the misshapen coin and $p = 0.5$ for the fair coin; so, $q = 0.67$ for the misshapen coin and $q = 0.5$ for the fair coin. To find the probability of, say, getting three tails for ten flips of the misshapen coin, find $({}_nC_r)p^r q^{n-r}$=$({}_{10}C_3)(0.33)^3(0.67)^7$=$\frac{10!}{3!7!}(0.33)^3(0.67)^7 \approx 0.261$. The calculated probabilities match those shown in choice C.

139. C: When rolling two dice, there is only one way to roll a sum of two (rolling a 1 on each die) and twelve (rolling 6 on each die). In contrast, there are two ways to obtain a sum of three (rolling a 2 and 1 or a 1 and 2) and eleven (rolling a 5 and 6 or a 6 and 5), three ways to obtain a sum of four (1 and 3; 2 and 2; 3 and 1) or ten (4 and 6; 5 and 5; 6 and 4), and so on. Since the probability of obtaining each sum is inconsistent, choice C is not an appropriate simulation. Choice A is acceptable since the probability of picking A, 1, 2, 3, 4, 5, 6, 7, 8, 9, or J from the modified deck cards of cards is equally likely, each with a probability of $\frac{4}{52-8} = \frac{4}{44} = \frac{1}{11}$. Choice B is also acceptable since the computer randomly generates one number from eleven possible numbers, so the probability of generating any of the numbers is $\frac{1}{11}$.

140. C: The number 00 represents the genotype aa. The numbers 11, 12, 21, and 22 represent the genotype bb.

```
28 93 97 37 92 00 27 21 87 13 62 63 10 31 55 09 47 07 54 88 38 88 10
98 34 01 45 14 34 46 38 61 93 22 37 39 57 03 93 50 53 16 28 65 81 60
21 12 13 10 19 91 04 18 49 01 99 30 11 16 00 48 04 63 59 24 02 42 23
06 32 52 19 18 94 94 46 63 87 41 79 39 85 20 43 20 15 03 39 33 77 45
66 77 70 92 25 27 68 71 89 35 98 55 85 47 60 97 12 92 53 44 45 41 51
22 09 23 81 33 04 35 43 48 32 80 36 95 64 56 34 74 55 37 64 84 51 50
25 99 51 94 19 46 10 44 17 25 75 52 47 35 70 65 08 50 98 09 02 24 30
59 00 03 21 40 30 86 16 53 91 28 17 97 58 75 76 73 83 54 40 54 13 38
36 67 74 80 63 12 41 27 96 61 66 05 60 69 96 15 56 82 57 31 83 26 24
78 42 76 49 56 06 57 78 67 02 96 40 82 29 14 07 29 62 90 31 08 26 71
61 18 22 84 23 33 49 29 90 07 08 05 14 59 72 86 44 69 68 99 06 11 95
43 72 58 28 93 97 37 92 00 27 21 87 13 62 61 15 31 55 09 47 07 54 88
38 88 10 98 34 01 45 14 34 46 38 61 93 22 37 39 57 03 93 50 53 16 28
65 81 60 21 12 13 10 19 91 04 18 49 01 99 30 11 16 00 48 04 63 59 24
02 42 23 06 32 52 19 18 94 94 46 63 87 41 79 39 85 20 43 20 15 03 39
33 77 45 66 77 70 92 25 27 68 71 89 35 98 55 85 47 60 97 12 92 53 44
45 41 51 22 09 23 81 33 04 35 43 48 32 80 36 95 64 56 34 74 55 37 64
84 51 50 25 99 51 94 19 46 10 44 17 25 75 52 47 35 70 65 08 50 98 09
02 24 30 59 00 03 21 40 30 86 16 53 91 28 17 97 58 75 76 73 83 54 40
54 13 38 36 67 74 80 63 12 41 27 96 61 66 05 60 69 96 15 56 82 57 31
83 26 24 78 42 76 49 56 06 57 78 67 02 96 40 82 29 14 07 29 62 90 31
08 26 71 61 18 22 84 23 33 49 29 90 07 08 05 14 59
```

There are six occurrences of 00, so the experimental probability of getting genotype aa is 6/500 = 0.012. There are 21 occurrences of 11, 12, 21, and 22, so the experimental probability of getting genotype bb is 21/500=0.042. The experimental probability of either getting genotype aa or bb is 0.012+0.042=0.054. Multiply this experimental probability by 100,000 to find the number of individuals expected to be homozygous for either allele in a population of 100,000. $0.054 \cdot 100{,}000 = 5{,}400$. Notice that this is higher than the expected number based on the theoretical probability. Since the allele frequencies are in a ratio of 1:2:7, the theoretical probability of getting either aa or bb is $\frac{1}{10} \cdot \frac{1}{10} + \frac{2}{10} \cdot \frac{2}{10} = \frac{5}{100} = 0.05$. Based on the theoretical probability, one would expect 5,000 members of a population of 100,000 to be homozygous for a or b.

141. D: A score of 85 is one standard deviation below the mean. Since approximately 68% of the data is within one standard deviation of the mean, about 32% (100%-68%) of the data is outside of one standard deviation within the mean. Normally distributed data is symmetric about the mean, which means that about 16% of the data lies below one standard deviation below the mean and about 16% of data lies above one standard deviation above the mean. Therefore, approximately 16% of individuals have IQs less than 85, while approximately 84% of the population has an IQ of at least 85. Since 84% of 300 is 252, about 252 people from the selected group have IQs of at least 85.

142. C: There are nine ways to assign the first digit since it can be any of the numbers 1-9. There are nine ways to assign the second digit since it can be any digit 0-9 EXCEPT for the digit assigned in place 1. There are eight ways to assign the third number since there are ten digits, two of which have already been assigned. There are seven ways to assign the fourth number, six ways to assign the fifth, five ways to assign the sixth, and four ways to assign the seventh. So, the number of combinations is $9 \cdot 9 \cdot 8 \cdot 7 \cdot 6 \cdot 5 \cdot 4 = 544{,}320$.

Another way to approach the problem is to notice that the arrangement of nine digits in the last six places is a sequence without reputation, or a permutation. (Note: this may be called a partial permutation since all of the elements of the set need not be used.) The number of possible sequences of a fixed length r of elements taken from a given set of size n is permutation ${}_nP_r = \frac{n!}{(n-r)!}$. So, the number of ways to arrange the last six digits is ${}_9P_6 = \frac{9!}{(9-6)!} = \frac{9!}{3!} = 60{,}480$. Multiply this number by nine since there are nine possibilities for the first digit of the phone number. $9 \cdot {}_9P_6 = 544{,}320$.

143. B: If each of the four groups in the class of twenty will contain three boys and two girls, there must be twelve boys and eight girls in the class. The number of ways the teacher can select three boys from a group of twelve boys is ${}_{12}C_3 = \frac{12!}{3!(12-3)!} = \frac{12!}{3!9!} = \frac{12 \cdot 11 \cdot 10 \cdot 9!}{3!9!} = \frac{12 \cdot 11 \cdot 10}{3 \cdot 2 \cdot 1} = 220$. The number of ways she can select two girls from a group of eight girls is ${}_8C_2 = \frac{8!}{2!(8-2)!} = \frac{8!}{2!6!} = \frac{8 \cdot 7 \cdot 6!}{2!6!} = \frac{8 \cdot 7}{2 \cdot 1} = 28$. Since each combination of boys can be paired with each combination of girls, the number of group combinations is $220 \cdot 28 = 6{,}160$.

144. B: One way to approach this problem is to first consider the number of arrangements of the five members of the family if Tasha (T) and Mac (M) must sit together. Treat them as a unit seated in a fixed location at the table; then arrange the other three family members (A, B, and C):

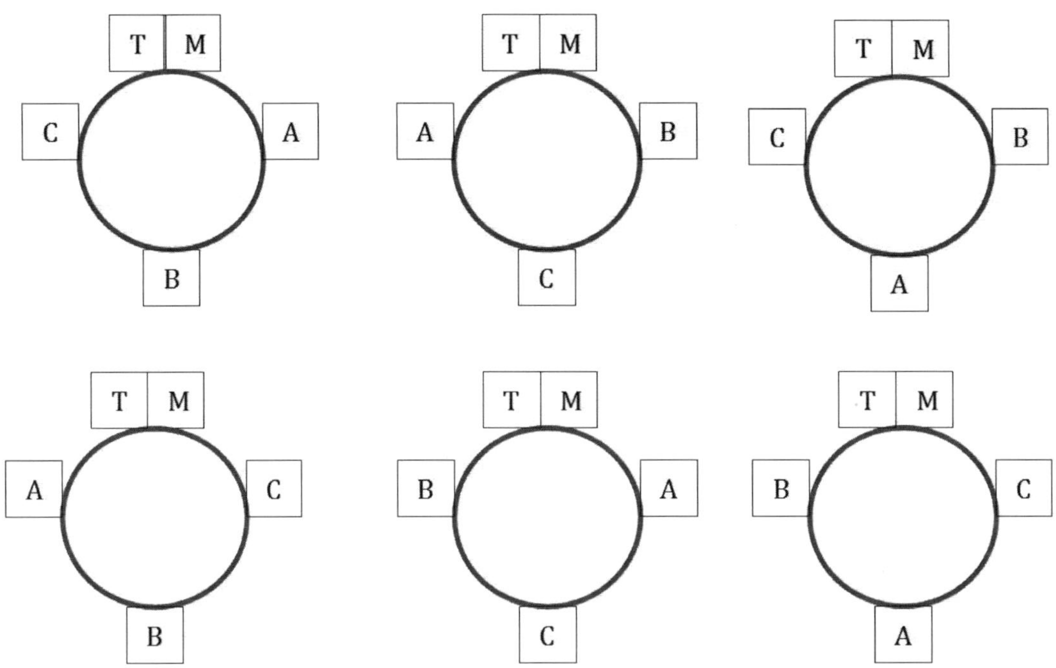

There are six ways to arrange four units around a circle as shown. (Any other arrangement would be a rotation in which the elements in the same order and would therefore not be a unique arrangement.) Note that there are $(n-1)!$ ways to arrange n units around a circle for $n > 1$.

Of course, Mac and Tasha are not actually a single unit. They would still be sitting beside each other if they were to trade seats, so there are twelve arrangements in which the two are seated next to one another. In all other arrangements of the five family members, they are separated. Therefore, to find the number of arrangements in which Tasha and Mac are not sitting together, subtract twelve from the possible arrangement of five units around a circle: $(5-1)! - 12 = 12$.

145. A: The recursive definition of the sequence gives the first term of the series, $a_1 = -1$. The definition also defines each term in the series as the sum of the previous term and 2. Therefore, the second term in the series is $-1 + 2 = 1$, the third term in the series is $1 + 2 = 3$, and so on.

n	a_n
1	-1
2	1
3	3

The relationship between n and a_n is linear, so the equation of the sequence can be found in the same way as the equation of a line. The value of a_n increases by two each time the value of n increases by 1.

n	$2n$	a_n
1	2	-1
2	4	1
3	6	3

Since the difference in $2n$ and a_n is 3, $a_n = 2n - 3$.

n	$2n-3$	a_n
1	2-3	-1
2	4-3	1
3	6-3	3

146. B: The series is an infinite geometric series, the sum of which can be found by using the formula $\sum_{n=0}^{\infty} ar^n = \frac{a}{1-r}, |r| < 1$, where a is the first term in the series and r is the ratio between successive terms. In the series 200+100+50+25+ ..., $a = 200$ and $r = \frac{1}{2}$. So, the sum of the series is $\frac{200}{1-\frac{1}{2}} = \frac{200}{\frac{1}{2}} = 400$.

147. A: The sum of two vectors is equal to the sum of their components. Using component-wise addition, $\boldsymbol{v} + \boldsymbol{w} = (4 + (-3), 3 + 4) = (1,7)$. To multiply a vector by a scalar, multiply each component by that scalar. Using component-wise scalar multiplication, $2(1,7) = (2 \cdot 1, 2 \cdot 7) = (2,14)$.

148. A: First, subtract the two column matrices in parentheses by subtracting corresponding terms.

$$[2 \quad 0 \quad -5]\left(\begin{bmatrix} 4-3 \\ 2-5 \\ -1-(-5) \end{bmatrix}\right) = [2 \quad 0 \quad -5]\begin{bmatrix} 1 \\ -3 \\ 4 \end{bmatrix}$$

Then, multiply the matrices. The product of a 1×3 matrix and a 3×1 matrix is a 1×1 matrix.

$$\begin{bmatrix} 2 & 0 & -5 \end{bmatrix} \begin{bmatrix} 1 \\ -3 \\ 4 \end{bmatrix} = [(2)(1) + (0)(-3) + (-5)(4)] = [-18]$$

Note that matrix multiplication is NOT commutative. The product of the 3x1 matrix $\begin{bmatrix} 1 \\ -3 \\ 4 \end{bmatrix}$ and the 1x3 matrix $\begin{bmatrix} 2 & 0 & -5 \end{bmatrix}$ is the 3x3 matrix $\begin{bmatrix} 2 & 0 & -5 \\ -6 & 0 & 15 \\ 8 & 0 & -20 \end{bmatrix}$.

149. B: The table below shows the intersections of each set with each of the other sets.

Set	{2,4,6,8,10,12,...}	{1,2,3,4,6,12}	{1,2,4,9}
{2,4,6,8,10,12,... }	{2,4,6,8,10,12,...}	{2,4,6,12}	{2,4}
{1,2,3,4,6,12}	{2,4,6,12}	{1,2,3,4,6,12}	{1,2,4}
{1,2,4,9}	{2,4}	{1,2,4}	{1,2,4,9}

Notice that {2,4} is a subset of {2,4,6,12} and {1,2,4}. So, the intersection of {1,2,4,9} and the even integers is a subset of the intersection of the even integers and the factors of twelve, and the intersection of the set of even integers and {1,2,4,9} is a subset of the intersection of {1,2,4,9} and the factors of twelve. So, while it is not possible to determine which set is A and which is B, set C must be the set of factors of twelve: {1,2,3,4,6,12}.

150. D: Use a Venn diagram to help organize the given information. Start by filling in the space where the three circles intersect: Jenny tutored three students in all three areas. Use that information to fill in the spaces where two circles intersect: for example, she tutored four students in chemistry and for the ACT, and three of those were students she tutored in all three areas, so one student was tutored in chemistry and for the ACT but not for math. Once the diagram is completed, add the number of students who were tutored in all areas to the number of students tutored in only two of the three areas to the number of students tutored in only one area. The total number of students tutored was 3+2+2+1+3+2+1=14.

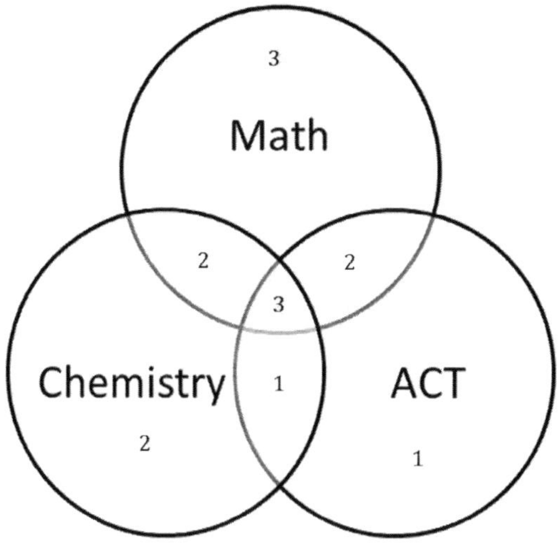

How to Overcome Test Anxiety

Just the thought of taking a test is enough to make most people a little nervous. A test is an important event that can have a long-term impact on your future, so it's important to take it seriously and it's natural to feel anxious about performing well. But just because anxiety is normal, that doesn't mean that it's helpful in test taking, or that you should simply accept it as part of your life. Anxiety can have a variety of effects. These effects can be mild, like making you feel slightly nervous, or severe, like blocking your ability to focus or remember even a simple detail.

If you experience test anxiety—whether severe or mild—it's important to know how to beat it. To discover this, first you need to understand what causes test anxiety.

Causes of Test Anxiety

While we often think of anxiety as an uncontrollable emotional state, it can actually be caused by simple, practical things. One of the most common causes of test anxiety is that a person does not feel adequately prepared for their test. This feeling can be the result of many different issues such as poor study habits or lack of organization, but the most common culprit is time management. Starting to study too late, failing to organize your study time to cover all of the material, or being distracted while you study will mean that you're not well prepared for the test. This may lead to cramming the night before, which will cause you to be physically and mentally exhausted for the test. Poor time management also contributes to feelings of stress, fear, and hopelessness as you realize you are not well prepared but don't know what to do about it.

Other times, test anxiety is not related to your preparation for the test but comes from unresolved fear. This may be a past failure on a test, or poor performance on tests in general. It may come from comparing yourself to others who seem to be performing better or from the stress of living up to expectations. Anxiety may be driven by fears of the future—how failure on this test would affect your educational and career goals. These fears are often completely irrational, but they can still negatively impact your test performance.

Elements of Test Anxiety

As mentioned earlier, test anxiety is considered to be an emotional state, but it has physical and mental components as well. Sometimes you may not even realize that you are suffering from test anxiety until you notice the physical symptoms. These can include trembling hands, rapid heartbeat, sweating, nausea, and tense muscles. Extreme anxiety may lead to fainting or vomiting. Obviously, any of these symptoms can have a negative impact on testing. It is important to recognize them as soon as they begin to occur so that you can address the problem before it damages your performance.

The mental components of test anxiety include trouble focusing and inability to remember learned information. During a test, your mind is on high alert, which can help you recall information and stay focused for an extended period of time. However, anxiety interferes with your mind's natural processes, causing you to blank out, even on the questions you know well. The strain of testing during anxiety makes it difficult to stay focused, especially on a test that may take several hours. Extreme anxiety can take a huge mental toll, making it difficult not only to recall test information but even to understand the test questions or pull your thoughts together.

Effects of Test Anxiety

Test anxiety is like a disease—if left untreated, it will get progressively worse. Anxiety leads to poor performance, and this reinforces the feelings of fear and failure, which in turn lead to poor performances on subsequent tests. It can grow from a mild nervousness to a crippling condition. If allowed to progress, test anxiety can have a big impact on your schooling, and consequently on your future.

Test anxiety can spread to other parts of your life. Anxiety on tests can become anxiety in any stressful situation, and blanking on a test can turn into panicking in a job situation. But fortunately, you don't have to let anxiety rule your testing and determine your grades. There are a number of relatively simple steps you can take to move past anxiety and function normally on a test and in the rest of life.

Physical Steps for Beating Test Anxiety

While test anxiety is a serious problem, the good news is that it can be overcome. It doesn't have to control your ability to think and remember information. While it may take time, you can begin taking steps today to beat anxiety.

Just as your first hint that you may be struggling with anxiety comes from the physical symptoms, the first step to treating it is also physical. Rest is crucial for having a clear, strong mind. If you are tired, it is much easier to give in to anxiety. But if you establish good sleep habits, your body and mind will be ready to perform optimally, without the strain of exhaustion. Additionally, sleeping well helps you to retain information better, so you're more likely to recall the answers when you see the test questions.

Getting good sleep means more than going to bed on time. It's important to allow your brain time to relax. Take study breaks from time to time so it doesn't get overworked, and don't study right before bed. Take time to rest your mind before trying to rest your body, or you may find it difficult to fall asleep.

Along with sleep, other aspects of physical health are important in preparing for a test. Good nutrition is vital for good brain function. Sugary foods and drinks may give a burst of energy but this burst is followed by a crash, both physically and emotionally. Instead, fuel your body with protein and vitamin-rich foods.

Also, drink plenty of water. Dehydration can lead to headaches and exhaustion, especially if your brain is already under stress from the rigors of the test. Particularly if your test is a long one, drink water during the breaks. And if possible, take an energy-boosting snack to eat between sections.

Along with sleep and diet, a third important part of physical health is exercise. Maintaining a steady workout schedule is helpful, but even taking 5-minute study breaks to walk can help get your blood pumping faster and clear your head. Exercise also releases endorphins, which contribute to a positive feeling and can help combat test anxiety.

When you nurture your physical health, you are also contributing to your mental health. If your body is healthy, your mind is much more likely to be healthy as well. So take time to rest, nourish your body with healthy food and water, and get moving as much as possible. Taking these physical steps will make you stronger and more able to take the mental steps necessary to overcome test anxiety.

Mental Steps for Beating Test Anxiety

Working on the mental side of test anxiety can be more challenging, but as with the physical side, there are clear steps you can take to overcome it. As mentioned earlier, test anxiety often stems from lack of preparation, so the obvious solution is to prepare for the test. Effective studying may be the most important weapon you have for beating test anxiety, but you can and should employ several other mental tools to combat fear.

First, boost your confidence by reminding yourself of past success—tests or projects that you aced. If you're putting as much effort into preparing for this test as you did for those, there's no reason you should expect to fail here. Work hard to prepare; then trust your preparation.

Second, surround yourself with encouraging people. It can be helpful to find a study group, but be sure that the people you're around will encourage a positive attitude. If you spend time with others who are anxious or cynical, this will only contribute to your own anxiety. Look for others who are motivated to study hard from a desire to succeed, not from a fear of failure.

Third, reward yourself. A test is physically and mentally tiring, even without anxiety, and it can be helpful to have something to look forward to. Plan an activity following the test, regardless of the outcome, such as going to a movie or getting ice cream.

When you are taking the test, if you find yourself beginning to feel anxious, remind yourself that you know the material. Visualize successfully completing the test. Then take a few deep, relaxing breaths and return to it. Work through the questions carefully but with confidence, knowing that you are capable of succeeding.

Developing a healthy mental approach to test taking will also aid in other areas of life. Test anxiety affects more than just the actual test—it can be damaging to your mental health and even contribute to depression. It's important to beat test anxiety before it becomes a problem for more than testing.

Study Strategy

Being prepared for the test is necessary to combat anxiety, but what does being prepared look like? You may study for hours on end and still not feel prepared. What you need is a strategy for test prep. The next few pages outline our recommended steps to help you plan out and conquer the challenge of preparation.

Step 1: Scope Out the Test

Learn everything you can about the format (multiple choice, essay, etc.) and what will be on the test. Gather any study materials, course outlines, or sample exams that may be available. Not only will this help you to prepare, but knowing what to expect can help to alleviate test anxiety.

Step 2: Map Out the Material

Look through the textbook or study guide and make note of how many chapters or sections it has. Then divide these over the time you have. For example, if a book has 15 chapters and you have five days to study, you need to cover three chapters each day. Even better, if you have the time, leave an extra day at the end for overall review after you have gone through the material in depth.

If time is limited, you may need to prioritize the material. Look through it and make note of which sections you think you already have a good grasp on, and which need review. While you are studying, skim quickly through the familiar sections and take more time on the challenging parts.

Write out your plan so you don't get lost as you go. Having a written plan also helps you feel more in control of the study, so anxiety is less likely to arise from feeling overwhelmed at the amount to cover.

Step 3: Gather Your Tools

Decide what study method works best for you. Do you prefer to highlight in the book as you study and then go back over the highlighted portions? Or do you type out notes of the important information? Or is it helpful to make flashcards that you can carry with you? Assemble the pens, index cards, highlighters, post-it notes, and any other materials you may need so you won't be distracted by getting up to find things while you study.

If you're having a hard time retaining the information or organizing your notes, experiment with different methods. For example, try color-coding by subject with colored pens, highlighters, or post-it notes. If you learn better by hearing, try recording yourself reading your notes so you can listen while in the car, working out, or simply sitting at your desk. Ask a friend to quiz you from your flashcards, or try teaching someone the material to solidify it in your mind.

Step 4: Create Your Environment

It's important to avoid distractions while you study. This includes both the obvious distractions like visitors and the subtle distractions like an uncomfortable chair (or a too-comfortable couch that makes you want to fall asleep). Set up the best study environment possible: good lighting and a comfortable work area. If background music helps you focus, you may want to turn it on, but otherwise keep the room quiet. If you are using a computer to take notes, be sure you don't have any other windows open, especially applications like social media, games, or anything else that could distract you. Silence your phone and turn off notifications. Be sure to keep water close by so you stay hydrated while you study (but avoid unhealthy drinks and snacks).

Also, take into account the best time of day to study. Are you freshest first thing in the morning? Try to set aside some time then to work through the material. Is your mind clearer in the afternoon or evening? Schedule your study session then. Another method is to study at the same time of day that you will take the test, so that your brain gets used to working on the material at that time and will be ready to focus at test time.

Step 5: Study!

Once you have done all the study preparation, it's time to settle into the actual studying. Sit down, take a few moments to settle your mind so you can focus, and begin to follow your study plan. Don't give in to distractions or let yourself procrastinate. This is your time to prepare so you'll be ready to fearlessly approach the test. Make the most of the time and stay focused.

Of course, you don't want to burn out. If you study too long you may find that you're not retaining the information very well. Take regular study breaks. For example, taking five minutes out of every hour to walk briskly, breathing deeply and swinging your arms, can help your mind stay fresh.

As you get to the end of each chapter or section, it's a good idea to do a quick review. Remind yourself of what you learned and work on any difficult parts. When you feel that you've mastered the material, move on to the next part. At the end of your study session, briefly skim through your notes again.

But while review is helpful, cramming last minute is NOT. If at all possible, work ahead so that you won't need to fit all your study into the last day. Cramming overloads your brain with more information than it can process and retain, and your tired mind may struggle to recall even previously learned information when it is overwhelmed with last-minute study. Also, the urgent nature of cramming and the stress placed on your brain contribute to anxiety. You'll be more likely to go to the test feeling unprepared and having trouble thinking clearly.

So don't cram, and don't stay up late before the test, even just to review your notes at a leisurely pace. Your brain needs rest more than it needs to go over the information again. In fact, plan to finish your studies by noon or early afternoon the day before the test. Give your brain the rest of the day to relax or focus on other things, and get a good night's sleep. Then you will be fresh for the test and better able to recall what you've studied.

Step 6: Take a Practice Test

Many courses offer sample tests, either online or in the study materials. This is an excellent resource to check whether you have mastered the material, as well as to prepare for the test format and environment.

Check the test format ahead of time: the number of questions, the type (multiple choice, free response, etc.), and the time limit. Then create a plan for working through them. For example, if you have 30 minutes to take a 60-question test, your limit is 30 seconds per question. Spend less time on the questions you know well so that you can take more time on the difficult ones.

If you have time to take several practice tests, take the first one open book, with no time limit. Work through the questions at your own pace and make sure you fully understand them. Gradually work up to taking a test under test conditions: sit at a desk with all study materials put away and set a timer. Pace yourself to make sure you finish the test with time to spare and go back to check your answers if you have time.

After each test, check your answers. On the questions you missed, be sure you understand why you missed them. Did you misread the question (tests can use tricky wording)? Did you forget the information? Or was it something you hadn't learned? Go back and study any shaky areas that the practice tests reveal.

Taking these tests not only helps with your grade, but also aids in combating test anxiety. If you're already used to the test conditions, you're less likely to worry about it, and working through tests until you're scoring well gives you a confidence boost. Go through the practice tests until you feel comfortable, and then you can go into the test knowing that you're ready for it.

Test Tips

On test day, you should be confident, knowing that you've prepared well and are ready to answer the questions. But aside from preparation, there are several test day strategies you can employ to maximize your performance.

First, as stated before, get a good night's sleep the night before the test (and for several nights before that, if possible). Go into the test with a fresh, alert mind rather than staying up late to study.

Try not to change too much about your normal routine on the day of the test. It's important to eat a nutritious breakfast, but if you normally don't eat breakfast at all, consider eating just a protein bar. If you're a coffee drinker, go ahead and have your normal coffee. Just make sure you time it so that the caffeine doesn't wear off right in the middle of your test. Avoid sugary beverages, and drink enough water to stay hydrated but not so much that you need a restroom break 10 minutes into the test. If your test isn't first thing in the morning, consider going for a walk or doing a light workout before the test to get your blood flowing.

Allow yourself enough time to get ready, and leave for the test with plenty of time to spare so you won't have the anxiety of scrambling to arrive in time. Another reason to be early is to select a good seat. It's helpful to sit away from doors and windows, which can be distracting. Find a good seat, get out your supplies, and settle your mind before the test begins.

When the test begins, start by going over the instructions carefully, even if you already know what to expect. Make sure you avoid any careless mistakes by following the directions.

Then begin working through the questions, pacing yourself as you've practiced. If you're not sure on an answer, don't spend too much time on it, and don't let it shake your confidence. Either skip it and come back later, or eliminate as many wrong answers as possible and guess among the remaining ones. Don't dwell on these questions as you continue—put them out of your mind and focus on what lies ahead.

Be sure to read all of the answer choices, even if you're sure the first one is the right answer. Sometimes you'll find a better one if you keep reading. But don't second-guess yourself if you do immediately know the answer. Your gut instinct is usually right. Don't let test anxiety rob you of the information you know.

If you have time at the end of the test (and if the test format allows), go back and review your answers. Be cautious about changing any, since your first instinct tends to be correct, but make sure you didn't misread any of the questions or accidentally mark the wrong answer choice. Look over any you skipped and make an educated guess.

At the end, leave the test feeling confident. You've done your best, so don't waste time worrying about your performance or wishing you could change anything. Instead, celebrate the successful completion of this test. And finally, use this test to learn how to deal with anxiety even better next time.

Review Video: Test Anxiety
Visit mometrix.com/academy and enter code: 100340

Important Qualification

Not all anxiety is created equal. If your test anxiety is causing major issues in your life beyond the classroom or testing center, or if you are experiencing troubling physical symptoms related to your anxiety, it may be a sign of a serious physiological or psychological condition. If this sounds like your situation, we strongly encourage you to seek professional help.

Online Resources

Due to our efforts to try to keep this book to a manageable length, we've created a link that will give you access to all of your online resources:

mometrix.com/resources719/dsstbusmath

It's Your Moment, Let's Celebrate It!

Share your story @mometrixtestpreparation